MUDDY RIVER RUNNING

I0555348

by
Catherine Howard

Copyright © 2025 *Catherine Howard*

All rights reserved. No part of this book may be reproduced in any manner whatsoever without written permission except in the case of brief quotations embodied in critical articles and reviews.

First Printing, 2025

TABLE OF CONTENT

A WORD FROM THE AUTHOR

Captured by the story about the Sultana (America's most tragic maritime disaster in history), Catherine began to imagine the lives affected by that tragic event and the many untold stories that led up to it.

Catherine, through the wide-open eyes of Laureen, walks you through the unstable and unpredictable time of the post–civil war era. Although Laureen's journey includes the rocky terrain of despair sprinkled, she walks boldly as a prisoner of hope.

CHAPTER 1

The argument with Florence had left Laureen angry and drained. Laureen was not at all fond of her sister-in-law, but the two women rarely let tempers fly the way they did that morning. She stood looking out of the second story window of her bedroom, her face flushed with anger, trying to get control of her emotions. The mid-April day was soft with warm air gently stirring the long Spanish Moss in Live Oak trees growing in a small cluster a short distance from the plantation house. At least those were still there. The once beautiful grounds surrounding the white columned house were weed-choked with neglect. The lush array of flowers that once graced the yard next to the edge of the wide front veranda no longer grew there. Everywhere she looked, there were only reminders of what had been, and so very recently. If only she could wake up from this terrible nightmare in which she found herself living these days and things would be the way they were.

As she held the sheer lace curtains aside with one hand, she watched the aging servant, Willard, hoeing that meager garden of theirs. He looked so shabby in his worn and patched pants and shirt. She sighed, knowing there was no help for it. There was no money for new clothes for anyone at Three Willows. What little money still remaining in the household must be carefully hoarded.

There were so few seeds to plant this spring, so what the garden would produce in the coming summer would barely be sufficient to feed the family, let alone share it with the few servants who remained at Three Willows. But, it was certainly not her fault the Yankees came and nearly burned the house down. It was not her fault the South had lost the war and that this once thriving plantation was reduced to abstract poverty. It was not her fault her brother died fighting for a lost cause, leaving behind a widow with three children to bring up in harshly reduced circumstances.

What did Florence expect of her, anyway? It was only a silly quarrel in the first place. What difference did it make which one of them had planned that garden party just before the war started? How could they have actually argued over such a trivial matter?

At age 27, Laureen still retained her striking good looks. She had grown unaccountably tall, considering that both her parents were of rather small stature. She was fashionably slender, and carried herself with a regal bearing that would have made her stand out in any crowd even if she had lacked the much-envied beauty she possessed. Her long, dark blonde hair was thick and shiny, which she wore pinned high on her head in a rather intricate fashion.

She learned how to do that in her early teens, and began wearing her hair up at an age much younger than most girls of her generation, much to her father's chagrin. It was only because of her mother's intervention that she was able to retain such a grown-up appearance.

Her fair, porcelain smooth skin and gray-green eyes that fairly flashed when she was excited or angry, as well as her well-proportioned figure, made her an attractive addition to any setting, that is, from the men's point of view. But her very appearance managed to arouse a strong feeling of jealousy in the women when she was in mixed company and, for that reason, she never had much opportunity to enjoy the close friendship of any of the women in her social circle.

As the years went by and Laureen grew up, she had long felt that she was also merely tolerated by her sister-in-law, rather than being included in the household as a beloved member of the family. From time to time Florence suggested that it was time for Laureen find someone to marry, but Laureen was not inclined to favor the attentions of the few men who showed interest in her. Since Laureen would not inherit any property, she was not looked upon as a good "catch" by the parents of the young men in their social circle, and was passed over by them in spite of her beauty. Now, it seemed unlikely that Laureen would ever marry and she was more and more feeling the need to find a way to become independent of her sister-in-law. A kind of bitterness and resentment at life in general had been growing deep within her for a number of years, and the South's losing the war between the states only served to solidify those feelings.

As she continued to wrestle with her emotions over this quarrel with Florence, she saw the young darkie, Tolly, start to pass by the garden. She wondered where he might be going. Tolly was an especially good looking young man and with every movement he made he seemed very much aware of it. He was taller than average, muscular, had very light skin and straight black hair. He lacked the Negroid facial features common to most slaves, a certain give-away that his father must have been a white man. He came to the plantation, along with his mother, as a very small boy.

Laureen was quite young when her father bought those two slaves. One evening shortly after their arrival, Laureen as usual joined her parents in the living room. She busied herself with a new book they had bought for her and their easy conversation across the room made her feel very comfortable and secure. They talked quietly about various plantation matters as Laureen's mother busied herself darning socks and her father occupied himself filling, lighting and smoking his favorite pipe. As time passed, Laureen grew sleepy and lay down on the braided rug in front of the still bright fire in the fireplace. As she drifted off to sleep, she felt her father push a pillow under her head and spread a light blanket over her.

This was such a familiar ritual during cold weather. She would fall asleep in front of the fireplace then wake up in her own bed the following morning. Sometimes she woke up just enough to realize her father was carrying her up the stairs, then he would ever so gently put her into her bed, even though she had almost outgrown this custom.

On this particular night, as the evening wore on, the conversation between Laureen's parents turned to their most recent slave purchase, they apparently having forgotten all about the sleeping Laureen. Laureen was awakened by their soft, almost whispered, voices and quickly realized she might learn something if she kept still and quiet. She continued to lie where she was, even keeping her eyes closed as though she were still sleeping.

Sure enough, she learned there was a special reason why the young mother and her small son were brought to Three Willows. The owner of a plantation at Baton Rouge, a friend of Laureen's father, owned the pair and had put the word out he wanted to sell them. His wife had decided the young Negress, the mother of Tolly, meant more to her husband than she was comfortable with and insisted he get both of them off their plantation.

Plantation wives were accustomed to their husbands' dallying with the female slaves. Most of the wives did not complain about such things. In fact, in many cases, they felt it relieved them to some extent of what they often thought of as the 'burdens' of marriage. But experience had shown that when the husbands let their emotions get involved with the slave women, problems invariably followed. So, in the interests of peace in the household, the husband decided it was best to remove the source of the problem while emotions were still manageable, rather than wait until he grew to care overly much for the slave woman. When Laureen's father learned this mother and son twosome were for sale, he decided they would suit him very nicely at

4

Three Willows.

Laureen never spoke to anyone about what she heard on that long-ago evening.

Now, as she watched this very grown up young man move across the yard, she could not help admiring Tolly's lithe and strong body, the ease and grace with which he carried himself. If the war had not come, the Wallaces would have been on the lookout to find a suitable wife for him, even if it meant buying one from a slave market or another plantation. But, as it was, that was no longer a possibility for them. The thought did not even occur to them.

Still watching Tolly, Laureen could not resist allowing her thoughts to wander into areas that long held custom and circumstance made forbidden territory. She admired his muscular bare arms and chest glistening with perspiration from the heat of the morning sun and the exertion of the work he had been doing. All the white men Laureen had ever seen were always wearing shirts and she wondered if they, too, had muscles that rippled as they moved about in the same way Tolly's did.

Suddenly an idea took shape in Laureen's mind and she hurried downstairs and out onto the back porch.

"Tolly, Tolly, come here."

The 22 year old Negro man had almost reached the barn when he heard her calling and turned, somewhat insolently and slowly, and started walking toward the back of the house. As he approached her he made no pretense at hiding his long gaze as his eyes ran slowly from her face to her feet and back again.

Laureen flushed but said nothing, waiting for him to answer her. Finally, he spoke. "Yes'm, Miz Laureen. Does ya wan' sump'in'?"

"Yes, Tolly, I do want something," she said, "I want you to hitch up the mule and take me into town to the river dock. I want to see if there's any mail for us. The *Sultana* is due in from up north today and I need to get out of the house for a little while. Go, right now. And put a shirt on." Laureen mentally scolded herself for trying to explain her actions to Tolly. One did not explain oneself to a slave, after all. Even though the slaves had been freed Laureen still thought of them as such.

"Yes'm, Miz Laureen It tek jes' a few minutes." He turned toward the stables, which held their remaining one old mule and a rather rickety wagon. It was only because the Yankee soldiers thought those weren't worth taking that they were left behind.

Laureen went back into the house. Florence was helping their aging housemaid, Pansy, in the kitchen with preparations for their noon meal. The aroma of boiling collard greens and baking cornbread seemed to fill the whole kitchen. There was nothing else to eat that day, but there was enough of it for all in the household to be satisfied. Normally, Laureen would have savored the whole scene as the simple food pleased her well enough, but there was still too much tension between herself and Florence, dulling any appetite she might have had. "I'm going into town to see if there's any mail for us, Flo. I'm sure you can get along without my help until I can get back," she said, cooly.

"What help?" was the sarcastic reply. Clearly, Florence was not ready to end the quarrel.

"Florence, I don't know what's gotten into you lately, but you need to remember that I'm not the enemy here. I didn't make this war. I didn't make us poor...."

Florence interrupted. "You haven't done much to keep us from being poor, either, have you?"

6

"What do you mean? What do you expect me to do?"

"Well, you might have gotten married, and then there would be one less mouth here to feed."

So, that was it. "Florence, I've told you this before, but I'm going to say it once again. You know I don't inherit any of this property. It all went to Gerald and now that he's dead it all goes to you and to your children. But I was living here long before you came into the family and this is my home, too. Most of the men I might have been interested in looked elsewhere for a better match, and most of the men who have shown an interest in me were very poor or were not the kind of men who would make good husbands. And I think you know that. But it seems you would have me marry one of them anyway, just to get me away from here. Well you can forget about that because I won't do it. The man I marry is going to be better than anything I've seen so far." Then she looked at her sister-in-law and added, "Oh, what's the use. I'm going into town. I'll see you when I get back. Tolly's going to drive me." Laureen turned on her heels and was out the back door before Florence could say any more.

In the wagon, Laureen's spirits began to return. She sat on the rough wagon seat next to Tolly and was keenly aware this was a grown man sitting beside her. She felt he was just as keenly aware of her presence too, even though the silence between them had not been broken since he helped her into the wagon and they started down the driveway of Three Willows. The mid-morning sun was making Laureen uncomfortably warm and she held above her head the one remaining parasol she owned, attempting to protect herself from the burning rays. The sky was intensely blue with big puffy clouds floating here and there like giant pieces of popcorn across the vast sky, making it seem all the more blue with the sharp contrast in color. A pesky horsefly was tormenting the poor old mule, making him keep his tail switching constantly in a futile effort to rid himself of it.

Finally Tolly broke the silence by saying, "Miz Laureen, wha' meks ya t'ink dey's goin' be mail fer ya on dat boat?"

"Look here, Tolly. I don't account to you for what I do. You'd better watch yourself."

"Oh, Ah'se watchin' m'se'f, Miz Laureen. Ah'se watchin' m'self jes' fine."

"See that you do!" she shot back at him.

"It's jes' tha' when dey's mail, somebody bring it out ta ya' and ya' don' go gits it. Ah wuz jes' wond'rin' why ya' wuz spectin' sump'in' dis time.

"Tolly, what is it that you want? You don't care whether I'm looking for mail or not. So, what are you getting at?" Laureen was getting exasperated. Tolly was very close to the truth and it was making her much more uncomfortable than she cared to admit.

"Wal, Ah knows dat ya 'n' Miz Wallace is mad at each odder. Ah wuz t'inkin' dat maybe ya gots it in ya haid to git on dat boat and runs 'way. And, if da's it, I wuz t'inkin' ya might wan' sum he'p. Look at me, Miz Laureen. Ah could he'p ya, if'n ya wan's me ta."

"Tolly! What are you saying? You want me to help you 'pass?' You must be out of your mind! Why, the first time you opened your mouth you'd be exposed!" she exclaimed.

"No'm, Miz Laureen. Ah jes' said Ah'se willin' to he'p ya if'n ya wan's ta run 'way. An' dat odder t'in', if'n Ah had haf' a chance, Ah could learn how ta ta'k lak' white fo'ks." He looked directly into her eyes and said in as cultivated a voice as she had ever heard, very slowly as if translating each word, "Miss Wallace, you're looking rather shocked. Have I said something that offended you?" He looked at Laureen with such amusement as well as obvious desire in his eyes, that she turned away in horror.

But she immediately faced him again. "Tolly, where did you learn to speak like that? I've never heard you talk that way before. I don't understand!" Her voice was angry, but there was a tinge of respect in it, too.

He answered her in his usual voice, "Miz Laureen, Ah been 'round white fo'ks all mah life. But no slave's s'posed to ta'k lak dem. White fo'ks don' lak it. But, as ya kin see, we kin ta'k good as ya when we wan's to. 'Cou'se, it don' cum nat'raly right now. But it could if'n Ah practiced a while."

"Well, Tolly, talk any way you like. It makes no difference to me."

"Yes'm, Miz Laureen." Again, that unmistakable expression was on his face. This simply would not do. And, yet, as she thought about it, there was a certain delicious temptation, to actually allow herself to do something so firmly forbidden. This was a very desirable looking young man. He was certainly strong enough to protect her in almost any situation, and he was offering his services to her. He certainly was right about being able to learn how to speak properly. As intelligent as he was it would be a cinch to have him speaking like a white man in no time at all. It was like he said all he needed was a little practice. A wicked thought emerged on her consciousness. Just what would those services he was offering include? She turned her head so he could not see the blush that slowly spread across her face.

Fortunately, from her point of view, they were getting close to town. The road had turned muddy and was badly rutted. Tolly did not need to hold the old mule back as he walked in only one speed these days. Slow. Tolly tried to make the ride as easy for his passenger as he could, but the mud holes and deep ruts in the road made that difficult to do. As unpleasant as the ride was becoming, however, Laureen did not complain. In fact by this time, she was so caught up in the turmoil of her thoughts that she scarcely noticed the bumpy ride and she had long since ceased to notice the unpleasant odor coming from that smelly old mule.

CHAPTER 2

The streets in Natchez were unusually muddy from the swollen river. Heavy rains farther north had made it swell out of its banks in many places, so being in town under those circumstances was not a pleasant experience. Still it was better to be away from Three Willows for the time being.

By the time the pair neared the river front Laureen had completely pushed her quarrel with Florence to the back of her mind. Her conversation with Tolly had driven all such thoughts far into the background. When she was deciding to go into town there was no conscious thought of leaving Three Willows, but she knew it had been turning somewhere in her subconscious thoughts for quite some time. Her exchange with Tolly simply brought it to the forefront. She knew if she left to try to make her own way, it should not be to go farther south and by meeting the *Sultana,* she could learn when it would be expected back on its next trip north. By that time she could have worked out her plan to leave and be ready to go. She had only that morning told Florence she was not going to leave Three Willows, but Laureen was a realist. She knew she could not go on indefinitely the way she had been living. In fact, none of them could. Something must change. And, Laureen was beginning to realize she could not afford to wait and see what change might chance to come her way. It was time for her to take charge of her life and make the change herself.

By the time they reached the river The *Sultana* had been at the dock only a matter of several minutes, and it was plain to see there was much excitement among the passengers leaving the boat as well as those there to meet it. Tolly found a shady spot for the wagon under a huge Magnolia tree and stopped there. A few of the blossoms were beginning to open, and the fragrance perfumed the air all around the tree. Laureen breathed deeply suddenly realizing what a contrast in that smell and what she had been enduring most of the way into town.

"I think I'd like to sit here and wait while you go check on the mail, Tolly. I didn't think about how muddy everything would be here. And judging from the excited looks on the faces of those people, I would say something is going on at the boat. See if you can find out what it is." There was another reason for Laureen's not wanting to go to the boat dock herself. She was feeling somewhat self-conscious about her appearance, totally unconscious of the fact that she would turn the heads of all she met regardless of how shabby her clothes were. She wore the customary long dress with three petticoats but had not put on a hoop skirt. House dresses were not made long enough to accommodate the extra width a hoop skirt called for. Not only that, but she had only one, which she tried to save for special occasions. Then too, she had felt it would be too much in the way in the old wagon."

"Yes'm, Miz' Laureen. Ah be's back quick as Ah kin. Anyt'in' else ya wan's me ta do?" answered Tolly.

"Yes, there is. If you can see the captain of the boat, try to find out when he expects to be here on the trip back north. And," she added with an extra firmness in her voice, "don't try to read anything into that. I'm just curious."

"Yes'm, Ah knowd ya is. Ah won' t'ink not'in' of it."

As he got within hearing distance of the crowd Tolly had confirmed to him Laureen's presumption there was something exciting going on. President Lincoln had just a few days before been shot and killed. At least that was what the *Sultana* captain was telling everyone within earshot. At first Tolly stood back and listened. He was stunned. This was lot to take in all at once.

He had refused to run away with most of the other slaves at Three Willows after President Lincoln decreed emancipation for all the slaves in most southern states. He had no intention of making his situation worse than what it already was. He was a thinking young man and wanted to know where he would land before leaping.

Many slaves stayed with their masters, being fearful of change. But that did not protect them from those feared changes. The South had seceded from the Union, declaring itself to be a separate country from the rest of the United States so the Emancipation Proclamation was given no validity there. However, the invading Union armies looted and burned and even killed. Devastation permeated the South. Now that the South had lost the war, Tolly was not at all certain what that would mean for him and the three other slaves who also chose not to run away and who were still living at Three Willows. And now this news about President Lincoln could make an even greater difference.

He waited impatiently until some of the crowd moved away. He was in a hurry to get back to the wagon and Laureen with the news. This news was of such significance that he almost forgot his primary mission of checking to see if there was any mail. However, as he started back toward the wagon he remembered, turned on his heel, and approached the boat. Sure enough, there was a letter for Mrs. Wallace. Tolly looked at the writing on the envelope but he could not read, therefore the words held no meaning for him, including the return address. And with all the excitement about the assassination, he almost forgot to ask the river boat captain when he expected to be back at Natchez. He had accepted the letter and already turned back toward the wagon a second time when he remembered his secondary errand.

"Scuz' me, Cap'n," he said as he respectfully stood at the captain's side, head lowered. "Would ya tell me when de *Sultana* be back in

Natchez? ."

"Why would you want to know that, Boy? You planning on going somewhere? Well, it won't be on my boat, so forget it."

"Ma mistress, she dun' tol' me ta find out."

As the captain looked him over slowly, Tolly pointed to the wagon waiting in the distance under the magnolia tree where Laureen sat absently watching two mischievous little boys making faces at passersby. "Nah, Sir. Not me. It ma lady. She wan' ta know."

The captain looked at her for a long moment, then seemed satisfied with Tolly's answer. "We should be back, let's see,........." The captain mumbled to himself a moment, calculating how long it would take to go from Natchez to New Orleans and back, then continued, "O.K. I figure four days. You tell your mistress that we should be back here about Sunday. But, I don't know what time. You just tell her that if she wants to get on this boat to be here when we get back, 'cause I won't wait for her. We'll dock just long enough to let off any passengers who want to get off here and take on any new ones. I've got to be in Vicksburg on schedule so I can't wait for her."

"Yessir, Cap'n. Ah tells her." Still holding the letter in his hand, he hurried back to the waiting wagon and Laureen.

"Well, Tolly," she remarked, "I see there is a letter after all. Maybe it's good news. Give it to me. And did you remember to ask when the *Sultana* will be back?"

As he leaped up onto the rough seat, he handed her the letter, not even hearing her question. "Miz' Laureen, dey's big news. Mr. Lincoln dun' got hisself killed!"

"Tolly, what in the world are you talking about. What do you mean 'Mr. Lincoln's gotten himself killed?'" exclaimed Laureen as she

14

absently put the letter into her dress pocket without looking at it, then promptly forgetting about it.

"De *Sultana* cap'n wuz sayin dat Mr. Lincoln wuz in a t'eater and sum man jes' cum in dere and shot 'im an' he daid. Das' all Ah knows."

As he took the reins in his hands and positioned himself next to her on the rough seat, he said, "C'mon, Mule, Gidup. I'se in a pow'ful hurry. Gidup, Mule!"

But the old mule was in no hurry at all so the ride of three miles back to the plantation went no faster than the one into town.

As soon as the wagon reached the yard of the big house, Tolly leaped off the wagon, letting the reins lie on the floor even forgetting to help Laureen out of the wagon in his excitement. The mule was used to standing and would not go anywhere. As he ran toward the back porch Tolly started to call out, "Miz Wallace! Miz Wallace!"

Florence was still in the kitchen, helping Pansy clean up after the meal she and the children had just finished eating, so heard him right away. She stepped out onto the porch and answered, "Tolly, what in the world are you making so much noise about? Did the *Sultana* bring any mail for us?"

"Oh, yes'm, but ya needs ta know wha's done happened? Mr. Lincoln dun' got 'isself killed!"

"What did you say, Tolly?" asked Florence. "You must be mistaken. Things like that don't happen!"

"It true, Miz Wallace. Mr. Lincoln daid. Ah heerd da cap'n tellin' fo'ks all 'bout it. Sum man in a t'eater shot 'im, an' 'e daid."

"Oh, Good God!" exclaimed the shocked Florence as she absently

15

reached her hand up to smooth back a lock of hair that had strayed from its customary tight bun at the back of her head. The worry lines deepened on her brow as she continued, "First I lost my husband to this war, then the South is lost to this war, and now you say Mr. Lincoln is dead. What next?" She leaned against one of the porch pillars to steady herself but after a moment recovered and demanded, "The mail, Tolly. Give me the mail."

"Miz Laureen got dat. Ah dun' give it ta 'er right 'way."

While that exchange was going on between Florence and Tolly, Laureen got down off the wagon by herself and followed Tolly to the back porch. As she reached into her dress pocket to retrieve the almost forgotten letter, she sensed Florence had regained her composure and the anger toward her was subsided at least for the time being. She absently handed the letter to Florence, not even caring who the letter was addressed to, and said to the young Negro, "All right, Tolly. You've delivered your message. Now go take care of the mule and wagon. I'll call you if I need you for anything else."

As Tolly made his way back to the mule and wagon, Florence moved to a nearby rocking chair and sat down heavily. She was only 34 and still had her slender figure and dark beauty, in spite of the few strands of silver beginning to show in her almost black, wavy hair. But she was so tired. Tired of the hard work she had to do, tired of having to make do with so few resources, tired of being too poor to rebuild the burned out wing of the house that the "Yankees" had set fire to and seeing the gradual decline of the house as a result. But on that count, she was just grateful it had not been worse.

It would have been so much worse if the soldiers were not in such a hurry to get on the road that terrible morning. Otherwise, they would have seen to it that the whole house burned. As it was, as soon as the soldiers were out of sight, the slaves who remained on the plantation came out of their hiding places, formed a bucket line, and were able to confine the damage to the south wing of the house. It was a good thing it had happened then and not later. Within a week after the fire most of the remaining slaves ran away from the plantation. Actually there were only four left at present.

Florence looked at the envelope Laureen gave her and saw that it was from her sister who had lived in southeastern Missouri for the last ten years. As she pulled the single page from its envelope, she read, "My Dear Florence, I regret I didn't write this letter much sooner because we have heard Natchez was under siege by the Yankees and suffered some damage. We don't know how badly you and Three Willows were affected but it would seem likely you did not get by unscathed. If you are in need, John and I would like to invite you to move your family here to our farm to live until you can get on your feet again. I know you love Three Willows and want to pass it on to Gerald. But Gerald is only a boy still, 14, I believe. He is a long way from being ready to take on the responsibility of running a plantation, assuming there is still a plantation to run.

"Our house is not as large as yours at Three Willows, but we can manage to find a place for you and the children as well as Laureen, if she would care to come with you. You could also bring a few of the darkies if you like. We might have to fix up a little space in the shed for them, but that would be all right. Do think about it and let us know. Come if you can, and soon.

From your loving sister, Zinnia."

Just as Florence was folding the page to put it back in its envelope, Laureen, who was standing near the edge of the porch, asked, "Aren't you going to tell me who the letter is from. I realize it's not for me, since you kept it, but we don't get letters every day. May I know who it's from?"

Florence sighed. "It's from my sister, Zinnia, in Missouri. She has written to invite all of us, including you, to go to Missouri to live with her."

Florence sat quietly in her chair for several seconds, apparently contemplating the contents of the letter, then asked, "What do you think, Laureen? Do you think we should? It would be a huge job to pack up this family and move." By this time, the quarrel of the morning was nearly forgotten. Other, more important matters were crowding in.

Without waiting for a reply, Florence went on talking, as if to herself. "It's just that I don't really know what we'd do when we got there? They don't have slaves in Missouri. I've never lived without slaves."

Laureen interrupted, "In case you don't remember, we don't have slaves in Mississippi any more, either. We lost them when we lost the war. Or have you completely forgotten that?"

"Well, we have at least a few of ours still here or hadn't you noticed that?" She emphasized the word *that*, letting the sarcasm in her voice pierce the space between them, the familiar antagonism beginning to resurface.

Laureen chose to ignore it. "I know," she responded , " but things will be different from now on. They know they aren't really slaves any more. They're servants now. They know they can leave if they want to. We're going to have to pay them something to keep them here. And we don't have enough money for that any more." She paused for a moment, then got a very bitter tone in her voice as she added, " If we

18

could find some Yankees, maybe we could kill a few and take their money. I hear most of them are rich."

"Oh, stop it Laureen. That kind of talk won't get us anywhere. Our situation is serious. This letter, coming just when it did, means I have to make a decision, and make it now. And you're not being any help at all." She dropped her head down, and appeared about to cry.

Laureen was only slightly sympathetic, hardly feeling close enough to Florence to offer her much comfort. The two women were being polite to one another now, but the memory of the quarrel of the morning had returned to near the surface of both women's memory.

In reality they had never been able to form a close friendship. Their personalities were much too different. Florence was cool and distant with most people, and Laureen had wondered many times what had made her brother want to marry Florence. Perhaps it was she who was the one person able to comfort him most when their parents died in a freak accident some fifteen years before and Gerald inherited the plantation. It was only two months after that tragedy when he brought the radiant Florence home as his bride, much to Laureen's surprise and chagrin.

Florence proved to be a capable wife, frugal with money, with good organizational skills, and easily took her place as mistress of Three Willows. Laureen resented her for that, plus the fact that Laureen was rarely included in any decisions relating to the plantation, even though she had been only 12 when Florence came into the house as a 19 year old bride.

Children soon followed the marriage. Gerald, Jr. was born the following year, then four years later Dora was came along. Another seven years went by and then little Adele arrived to join the family and complete it.

But this was 1865 and the family were in rather dire circumstances. Florence raised her head and drew in a deep breath. "Oh Laurie, I just don't know what to do. I have three children to raise and I don't know if I can do it here, by myself. Things seemed bad enough, and now this dreadful news of Mr. Lincoln's death....."

Laureen interrupted. "And, what makes you think that's so dreadful?" she drawled. "After all, it's his fault that we don't have our slaves any more. And probably his fault that our house got burned. Maybe he got just what he deserved!"

"Laureen! How can you say such a thing! No one deserves to be shot and killed."

"No, maybe not. But Gerald is dead and he didn't deserve to be killed, either. I wouldn't care if all the Yankees were dead. In fact, I wish they were!"

"Well, they're not. So, now we have to deal with things the way they are. And I have to decide whether to move this family to Missouri. If we go there and live with John and Zinnia, that would give us a good roof over our heads. And I just thought of something. Zinnia would be there to look after the children and I might be able to get a job as a teacher. I was trained to teach, you know, before Gerald and I were married."

"Well, Flo, I'd be glad of a chance to get away from here. We don't have the money to fix this house and it's just going to get worse. Eventually it's all going to fall down around our heads and then where will we live? I say if we can have a solid house to go to then we should go. When do we have to let your sister know?"

"She said we could come anytime. I was even thinking that perhaps we should be ready to go when the *Sultana* gets back from

New Orleans. That wouldn't give us time to let Zinnia know we're coming, but we can probably find someone to take us out to their farm from Cairo. Or we might be able to find someone to put us up until we could get word to them to come get us. Oh, Laurie, do you really think we should? It's such a major decision. I haven't ever had to make such an important one without Gerald. I just don't know."

"Oh for heavens sake, Flo. All you have to do is think about what our future will be here, and what it could be there. We don't have anything left here to keep us. These few darkies we have left can't work this plantation. And pretty soon we won't even have enough money left to pay the taxes. At least if we go north, you might be able to earn enough money to keep title to the property until things get better and young Gerald grows up."

"I suppose you're right," Florence sighed, but then her face brightened. "Well if we're going to do this, then we must get started packing. I wonder when the *Sultana* will come back here on its way north."

Without thinking, Laureen, replied, "It's due back next Sunday."

"Now, how would you know that?" Florence asked, giving her a quizzical look.

"Oh, Tolly mentioned it," she said, trying to think fast. "He said he heard the captain tell someone." Laureen saw no reason to disclose to Florence she had already been thinking about leaving Three Willows when the *Sultana* returned, and certainly not that Tolly had offered to go with her.

"I see," said Florence. Her face betrayed that she was still wondering about the reason Laureen had that bit of information, but she said nothing more. Instead, she continued with the matter at

21

hand. "That won't give us much time, but I suppose it's enough. We'll have to leave most of our things behind and they probably won't be here very long. Looters, you know. In no time at all word will get out that we've left. But, there's no help for that." Now the decision to go was made, the proficient facet of Florence's personality was beginning to take over. Laureen learned long ago that once Florence made a decision, she did not bother to look back and try to second guess herself. Typically, it was time to move forward.

She stood up smoothed out her faded and much mended skirt, very purposefully walked inside and called, "Bessie, Bessie, come here."

The 19 year old Negro girl was scrubbing the dining room floor on her hands and knees and appeared grateful to have a reason to stand up. The April day was warm and there was almost no breeze to relieve the heaviness in the air. "Bessie," Florence continued, "forget cleaning the floor. Get it dry as quickly as you can, then I want you to go up into the attic and bring down all the trunks. We're going to leave Three Willows and go live with my sister in Missouri. We have only a few days to get ready, so hurry!"

Bessie had taken directions from Florence for most of her life so did not question her now. She reached for a dry rag and moved it around on the floor with her bare foot to absorb as much of the moisture as she could, then the tall, slightly rounded young woman made her way to the attic. There were five large trunks there and a few more smaller ones. One at a time, she brought them all down and placed them in the upstairs hall, lined up against the wall.

CHAPTER 3

Still in the kitchen, putting away the last of the cooking utensils, Pansy heard what Florence said to Bessie so when Florence returned to the kitchen Pansy questioned her. "Is it so dat de fam'ly goin' ta Missouri, Miz. Wallace? I heerd what ya wuz sayin' ta Bessie."

"Yes, Pansy, you heard correctly. And you're going with us. You and Willard and Bessie and Tolly. All of us are going."

"Do Willard know 'bout dis, Miz Wallace?"

"No not yet. As soon as he finishes what he's doing in the garden I'll tell him."

"Ah don' t'ink he go'n like dat, Miz Wallace."

"Why not, Pansy?"

"Well he dun got ol' and don' tek to change much. Da's why."

"Pansy, things **have** changed. Haven't you noticed. Nothing's the same any more. Just look at this house. The burned-out wing will grow more and more rotten, so in time the whole house will be so rotten we can't live here. Don't you see that?"

"Yes.m, Miz Wallace. Ah sees da't. But us slaves don' sleep in de big house. An' our cabins all still standin'. Fo' us, t'in's is pretty much de same as befo' de fire!" An' Ah don' t'ink Willard gon' wan' leave heah."

"Well, we'll see about that," snapped Florence. "I'm still mistress around here and I'll not have my decisions questioned."

Laureen waited until Bessie had time to get the trunks down out of the attic then went upstairs. She pulled one of the smaller trunks into her room to get her packing started. As she thought about what she needed to pack, she looked about the room she was about to leave, perhaps never to return to it. It was smaller than the one she lived in before the fire and it had only one window, as opposed to the two double windows her corner room in the south wing boasted. But the fire had damaged that room badly. Also she lost most of her clothes and personal possessions in that fire and there was no money to replace them, so there were very few things left for her to pack. If Florence had not shared some of her clothes, Laureen would have had little more than the clothes she was wearing the morning of the fire. Even so all their clothes, in spite of the good quality that they had been at first, were looking worn and shabby.

Actually, as she thought about it, Laureen felt delighted they were going to be leaving this place. No one would have to wait on her when it came time to leave. "I'm going to be the first one on that boat and the first one off," she thought. "And, I'm going to find some way to get some money and make a life for myself. I don't know how or when but I know I will. And it's not going to be on anybody's farm! I'm done with that kind of life!" There was no doubt at all in her mind that she would find a way to do exactly that.

Willard came onto the back porch of the house a short time later, looking and acting old and tired. But he was soon listening to Florence in wide-eyed dismay as she explained to him about President Lincoln's death. Willard was a wiry, graying, thin old man, somewhat stooped from his years of hard work. Even so, he was used to things in his life moving along in a very measured pace. But ever since the Yankee soldiers had come to Natchez, his world had been turned upside down. This latest news was almost more than he could assimilate. Yet there was more to come, the most upsetting development yet.

Florence was saying, "We're all going to leave Three Willows and move to Missouri, Willard. I hope someday we'll be able to come back here and repair the house. But for now, we can't even afford to live here, let alone make any repairs. And, if it doesn't get repaired before very much longer, there won't be enough of it left to bother with. We have to do something, so this is what we've decided."

"But, Miz Wallace. Ah don' wan's ta go ta Missouri. Ah don' eben know whar dat is. Ah's 62 y'ars old an' Ah ain't niver lived nowhere's else. Ah wan's ta stay heah."

"Nonsense, Willard. You'll do just fine in Missouri. At least there, on my sister's farm, we'll have plenty to eat."

"No'm, Miz Wallace. Ah'se stayin' heah. Ah ain't goin' ta Missouri." As Willard spoke, he straightened himself to his full height and his lined and sagging face began to take on a defiant look, a look Florence had never seen on his face before.

She said, "So this is what we're going to have to deal with now. You slaves are free and you think that makes you independent, doesn't it?" She paused for several seconds, then continued, "All right, Willard. But you need to ask yourself how you will support yourself. There's no money any more. You'll be completely on your own if you stay here."

"Ah gits along jes' fine, Miz Wallace. Ah'se got de ga'den an' a place ta sleep. Ah don' needs no money."

Pansy, standing off to one side and unnoticed, was listening to this conversation and joined in. "Miz Wallace, Ah been t'inkin' jes' lek Willard. Ah'se too ol' ta go movin' off to sum place might be terrible ta live in. Ah t'ink Ah wan's ta stay heah, too."

"So, we have a conspiracy going here," Florence said acidly. "Very well. If the two of you want to stay here, then do so. In fact it's better this way. All of you can stay. We won't need you up there, anyway. But remember, I can't give you any money and I won't be able to send any to you unless it's to pay the taxes on this place. You'll just have to do what you can to survive. If you think you can make it that way, then stay here. I just don't care."

Laureen came back downstairs just in time to hear that last exchange. She said to Florence, "I should think you'd be relieved not to have to take the darkies with us. That means you won't have to pay the fares for them on the boat, and you won't have to be responsible for them once we get to Missouri. And if there's someone living at Three Willows, don't you think it will be less likely looters will be so quick to steal the things we have to leave here? I really think it's better this way."

Florence sighed. "Perhaps you're right. In any case, we don't seem to have much choice in the matter."

The four days before the *Sultana* was due back at Natchez were filled with all sorts of activity relating to the move from Three Willows. Bessie and Tolly were obviously disappointed they would not be going with the family to Missouri. So they were less than enthusiastic in helping the family prepare for their journey.

Each day the trunks got a little fuller. The two women often disagreed on what to take and what to leave behind. Laureen had some sentimental attachment to only a few of her mothers' things, so she chose to take all of them along. Florence had brought little from her own mother into the house, so was able to be more objective about what was practical to take along. Both women agreed the silverware should go with them. Dishes and cookware would take up too much room and were too heavy to pack, so they were to be left in the house. No furniture could be taken. Most of the linens were packed, though.

Each of the children was given a small trunk and allowed to decide how to fill it. Florence would have chosen differently in many cases for each of them, but she felt it was important to give them the freedom to make their own choices. After all, they were being uprooted from the only home they had ever known, and she had the wisdom to realize that when a plant must be transplanted, it will fare much better in its new place if a measure of the old dirt can be kept clinging to its roots. What the children chose to take was like the soil clinging to the roots of the plant. She only hoped it would be enough.

Of the three children, ten year old Dora had most outspokenly objected to the move. "Mama, do we truly have to go?" she asked again and again.

Finally, her mother asked "Do you think I would go to all this trouble and leave 'most everything I own behind if I didn't feel we truly have to go, Dora? There's not a person here who wants to make this move except Bessie and Tolly, and they can't go.

"I'd trade places with them if you'd let me," responded the almost defiant child.

"Oh Dora, why do you even say things like that. You know you can't be left behind when the rest of us go. Oh Child, I wouldn't do this if there were any other way, but I just don't know of any."

"Why do you say that, Mama? You know that grown-ups can do anything they want to. I think you're being mean to do this to us. Gerald doesn't want to go, either. If you'd give us any choice we'd stay here!"

"I see," said her mother. "And what about Adelle? Is she in on this conspiracy, too?"

"Oh, Adelle's too little to even know what she wants. As long as she's fed and warm, she doesn't care where she is."

"I see. Well Dora, let's just see what you would do if you were in my place. I think a girl of ten should learn how to make decisions."

"I don't understand."

"No, you don't. That's where the problem lies. You have no idea what's behind the necessity to make this decision. But I'm going to share the problem with you and then you tell me how to solve it if we stay on here."

Florence explained about the burned-out wing of the house, the lack of money to repair it, the fact that there was no more money coming into the household since there was no farming being done. And that there was so little left of what money they already had. Clothes were wearing out. So much wood was needed for heating and cooking Who would be able to do that before another winter arrived? There were too few slaves left to farm the plantation, aside from the fact they weren't even slaves any more. There was no equipment left to farm it even if they had the slaves to do it. And there was no money to buy the seeds to plant, even if those other things were all right. As she finished with all the explanations, she asked, "So, Missy, how do we continue to live here and solve all those problems? I'd like to know just what you'd do if it were up to you to make the decisions!"

Dora was silent for a long time, head bowed with hands folded in her lap. Finally she looked up and said, "Oh, Mama. I didn't know! I never realized things were so bad for us. We really are poor people now, aren't we?"

"I'm afraid so, Dora. It's my hope that if we go to Missouri, we can recover our finances and someday may be able to come back here. Then again, maybe not. I just don't know. But I would truly appreciate it if you children would work with me more instead of pulling against me with every move I make."

"We will, Mama," replied the much-chastened Dora. "I'll talk to Gerald and tell him what you've told me. We'll be good from now on, Mama."

She was as good as her word. For the remaining days left for packing, both children basically cooperated with what their mother asked of them. They even went out of their way to occupy little Adelle's time so their mother could work unhindered.

For the first time in quite a while, real peace seemed to settle over the household. Even Florence and Laureen became more comfortable in each others' company. Now that the time to actually leave was at hand, they had begun to work in cooperation with one another. Each woman was feeling the enormity of the decision they made. Neither one had actually anticipated the reality of the move when they decided to do it. But as the trunks were filled and they actually came to grips with how little they could take with them, both of them were feeling very subdued. It was much like a death in the family, with the accompanying grief over leaving behind so much of what they loved.

Laureen saw little of Tolly after the day he drove her into Natchez and to the river dock. She was much too busy with the complexities of helping to get the family ready to go to give it any thought. Besides that day was merely a passing fancy, born of her need to let off steam from the quarrel with Florence. Neither woman had discussed the planned move with him. It never even occurred to either of them that they would. After all, he was a slave, or at least a former slave. He had no standing with them. It was never the custom of the family to discuss their plans with slaves, except when the slaves were directly involved, and only then after decisions were made. Then the slaves were given instructions. So Tolly learned from Willard the family would move to Missouri and they intended to leave all the servants behind.

CHAPTER 4

Tolly said nothing when he learned of the planned move, but inside he was seething. He had allowed himself to think he had touched a nerve with Laureen. He let himself dare to hope he might use her to escape his lowly station in life. Also he had seen in her the willingness to use him to help her to leave when she thought she would be leaving by herself. He knew he had not misread the expression on her face, as well as her body language. He wondered how all that could have changed so quickly.

Now he just wanted to get away from that awful place, Three Willows, and he was resentful of being left behind when they had come so close to taking him with them. He resented Willard for refusing to go, knowing he was the reason all of the servants were not to make the trip. Tolly felt life had never treated him fairly and this new development was the worst cruelty yet.

For the rest of the time the Wallaces occupied Three Willows, Tolly did no more work than he actually had to. He was aware that Florence and Laureen were so busy they barely noticed what he did or did not do. He knew they were about to leave and then there would be no reason for him to do anything he did not want to do.

As the hours went by, a plan began to form in his mind. He would not be left at Three Willows to starve, while the white folks went north. He would get on that boat too, whether they liked it or not. He spent the remaining time before the sailing working out the details in his mind. He had no money to buy a ticket for his passage, but that did not deter him. There must be a way to do it and he promised himself he would find it. And if he had to take unfair advantage of any and all of them, then so be it. He would be on that boat.

Gradually his plan took shape. He would need better clothes than any he had. He could not let his clothes give him away as a slave. He remembered that his former master, Mister Gerald, was close to his size. His clothes must still be in the big house. But Tolly never went into the big house. And since the bedrooms were on the second floor, it would be next to impossible for him to get to them without being caught. But Bessie was in the house most of the time. She could get the clothes for him. He just had to make her want to do it. And for a young man of Tolly's charm and intelligence, that should be an easy task.

Tolly watched the house, waiting for an opportunity to talk to Bessie alone. Toward evening of the next day after he learned of the planned move, he was rewarded for his patience. He saw her slip out the kitchen door and sit on the steps leading down from the back porch. He sauntered over to her and stood looking down at her with an air of complete indifference for several seconds before he said, "It go'n be good when all de white fo'ks gone. Good nobody tellin' us wha' ta do. I gits plenty tired o' dat'."

"Yeah, I duz, too. But, I ain' nevah had it no otha' way?"

"Wha' ya t'ink ya gonna lak bes'?"

Bessie hesitated. Then she answered emphatically., "No mo' scrubbin' flo's."

Tolly laughed softly. "Cum 'way frum de hous' a minute," he said.

"Why? Wha' chu got in min'?"

"I jes' wanna ta'k ta ya 'bout sum'in'."

Tolly reached for her hand and gently tugged as she got to her feet. Keeping hold of her hand, he led her a little distance away from the house and out of sight of the back porch. "Ya lak me a little bit, don'

32

ya, Bessie?"

Bessie jerked her hand away from his. Her face took on an expression of surprise, shock, and just a little fear. "Wha' ya ta'kin' 'bout, Tolly? I'se a house slave and youse a fiel' han'. I'se hardly evah see'd ya."

"But wi' all de white fo'ks leavin', tha's go'n' change. Wha' ya thin's go'n' happen ta us? Ya' t'ink we go'n' mek' it on our own?"

"Ah don' know. I been t'inkin' 'bout dat, too."

"Is ya scared?"

"Ah guess so. We ain' nevah had to 'cide t'in's afore."

"Ah'm scared, too. Da's why Ah been mekin' plans. But, ya hafta he'p me."

"How'm Ah gon' do dat?"

"Does ya wan's to sta' heah or leave wi'd de white fo'ks?"

"When Ah thou't we wuz goin', Ah was glad."

"Well, Ah t'ink I figured a way ta go. But Ah needs yo' he'p"

"Ain't nothin' Ah kin do fo' ya."

"Yeah, da' is. Ah needs ya ta git sum o' Mista' Gerald's clothes fo' me."

"Why wud Ah wanna do dat? Wha' good's dem ta ya?"

"Ah'm gonna git on dat boat when dem white fo'ks do. But, I can' look lak' no slave. Ah'm gonna' haf ta slip on when dey ain't nobody lookin, and iffen sombody sees me latah, Ah haf' ta look lak Ah's s'pos' be dere."

33

Bessie looked skeptical. "An iffen Ah do dat fo' ya', how dat s'posed he'p me? Iffen we bof try git on dat boat, we's boun' git caught."

"Da's right, Gal. Youse smart in yo' haid! It's jes' me dat gits on de boat."

"Lak Ah sa'd, how dat go'n' he'p me?"

"Wal, it won' at firs'. It go'n tek time. Wha' I gots in min' is go no'th on de boat an' git settled sumwhar, git a job. It prob'ly tek sum time, but whin Ah kin save up 'nuf money, den Ah sen's fo ya. But, iffen Ah don' git sum o' Mista' Gerald's clo's, den Ah might's well not try. Cum on, Gal, Ah needs yo' he'p!"

Bessie stood looking off into the distance for what seemed to Tolly a very long time. Then she looked back toward the house and then toward the barn. Finally she looked at Tolly's face and asked, "Wha' clo's ya need?"

Tolly had not realized until that moment he was holding his breath, waiting for her answer. Out of sheer relief, he threw his arms around Bessie and held her close. When she stiffened, he jumped back awkwardly and forced himself to assume a casual demeanor again. "Not much. Iffen ya kin git jes two o' ever't'in', da's all. Pants, shirts, socks, shoes. Ah don' know iffen da shoes go'n fit, but dey go'n haf ta do. An' ah needs a belt."

"Whin's ya wan' dos tin's?"

"Soon's ya kin git 'em ta me."

"Ah can' do it all at one time. Ah has ta hide t'ings unda mah dress. Whar' ya wan' me put 'em? Miz Wallace, she won' lak me foolin' wi' Mista Gerald's t'in's. Ah t'in'k she skin me 'live iffen she catches me."

"She won' catch ya, Bessie. Ya knows how ta do t'in's. Jes' 'member, der's not many days left. So, git wha' ya kin quick as ya kin. Iffen ya jes put t'in's under th' back po'ch steps, Ah kin fin' 'em Ah gits 'em afta dark. Dat way, nobody sees me."

"Does ya really mean it, Tolly, 'bout sendin' fo' me afta ya gits settled? Do'n' be foolin' wi' me."

"Ah ain't foolin' wi' ya, Gal. I sen's fo' ya. Soon's ah kin. Now ya betta be gittin' bak in de house 'fo' dey misses ya. Jes mek' sure ya don' say nuttin' to nobody."

"Ah won'. Ah jes hope Ah don' gits caught."

"Gal, iffen ya do it right, ya wan git caught."

He put her hand in his again, an held it for several second, then gradually pulled her toward the barn. When they reached the barn door, she pulled back, hesitating to go inside. Tolly waited for her to relax, then gently tugged at her hand again. This time she yielded to him. And hour later they both emerged from the barn, things between them forever changed.

Tolly watched Bessie walk back toward the back porch, knowing he had no intention of ever sending for her. She was not a very intelligent girl and he felt she would be a liability to him rather than an asset. If he were to ever get ahead in the world, he would have to be free to move about unhindered and unfettered. He was beginning to realize that for the most part he would have to live by his wits, and he had no idea how it might work out. But he had no qualms against using Bessie to gain his own ends. It was easy for him to justify in his mind what he was doing. After all, Bessie would be no worse off for helping him. Her situation would not change. There would be only her disappointment, and she would get over that.

For the rest of the day he stayed clear of the big house. He wondered if there would be enough time left that day for Bessie to get any of the late master's clothes out of the house. There would be enough moonlight for him to find his way back after everyone had gone to sleep. So he waited. There was too much activity in the kitchen and back part of the house for him to risk checking for the clothes during the early part of the evening. He must wait until all the lights were extinguished and then allow time for everyone to fall asleep before he dared check under the back porch steps.

This kind of waiting was a new experience for Tolly. He tried to remember if ever there was a time before when he had something important to look forward to. He could not think of anything. His days were always very much the same, one day following another in more or less the same order. True, there were entertaining distractions at times, but he could not remember a time when he felt such keen anticipation for what lay ahead of him.

At long last the house was dark and quiet. Moving about in near darkness was not new to Tolly. Stealth was almost second nature to him. The night sky was nearly clear, with only a few wispy clouds passing now and then over the crescent moon. The Spanish Moss hanging from the trees moved lazily in the lightly stirring night air. There was nothing unusual, nothing he had not seen night after night his whole life at Three Willows.

He was soon at the back of the house. He squatted down to reach under the back steps and felt around as much as he could. There was nothing there! Disappointment washed over him. He had been so sure Bessie would manage to get at least a thing or two down for him. Then he realized she might have put something under the other side of the steps and quickly checked there. He pulled out a single shoe with a pair of socks stuffed into it. Just one shoe? What did she think he could do with just one shoe? Stupid girl! He reached under the steps again, checking the area thoroughly. There was nothing else there.

There was nothing to do but hope she would bring the other shoe the next day. He followed the path to the barn, then sat down on an old stump a few yards from the door to see if the shoe would fit. He knew he must be able to wear that shoe. He held the shoe in his hand for a few seconds, rubbing the top gently. It was smooth and Tolly knew it was shiny. He had seen the kind of shoes white men wore many times. Just to own a pair of shoes like that would be pure luxury. He slapped his bare foot with his hand to brush the dirt off then slipped his foot into the shoe. It pinched. It was not a good fit.

Slowly he pulled the shoe off his foot. He let his shoulders slump and tried to think what to do. Finally, he resigned himself to the fact that if he were going to stow away on the *Sultana*, he would have to endure shoes a little too small for himself. But if he could just get into them, then it would be a small price to pay for the freedom he hoped to gain. He would wait for the other shoe and then try to learn to walk in them.

Sleep did not come soon for Tolly that night. For the first time in his life he had actually made plans for his future and then taken steps to make those plans become a reality. True, all he had so far was a pair of socks and a shoe. But it was a beginning. And if Bessie would just come through for him, by the time the *Sultana* was due back at Natchez he would have enough clothes to implement those plans.

The following night Tolly found a pair of pants and a shirt under the stairs. He was disappointed the other shoe was not there, but was well pleased to find those garments were a fairly good fit. And such fine garments they were. Tolly only wished he could have a big mirror so he could see just how good he looked in them. He was certain they made him look very handsome. But all he had for a mirror was a small piece of a broken one the white folks had discarded. It was adequate to see his face, but he could only imagine how he looked in Mister Gerald's pants and shirt.

It took a couple of days for Bessie to get the other shoe to Tolly. He saw her once when she slipped something under the back stairs, but made no attempt to contact her. He was taking no chances on their getting caught. By the last day before the *Sultana* was due back at Natchez, Bessie had been able to get all the clothes to Tolly that he had asked for, including the belt. He was finally able to put on a whole outfit. He had not realized what a difference having socks on would make in the fit of the shoes. The shoes were still a little small for him, but he knew he could manage with only a minimum of discomfort. In the meantime he found a place in the barn to store the things, a place he knew Willard was not likely to chance upon.

One thing he had forgotten was that he would need was something to carry those clothes in. He could not put them on before the family left. And even after he changed clothes, there was that extra shirt and pair of pants and socks. He knew the family would expect him to drive them to the boat, and he would have to find a way to hide them on the wagon along with the family's luggage. So, he needed some kind of a box or bag, but it must be something that would not attract attention.

The only thing he could think of was a burlap bag. He knew there were still a few of those lying around in the barn. But they had been collecting dust and dirt for a long time. How could he put those fine clothes Bessie had smuggled out of the house into one of those. Never mind. That was all there was, so he pulled one from a long empty stall.

Under cover of darkness he made his way to the well, and pulled up a bucket of water. Even though it was the bucket used for drinking water, he plunged the bag into it, scrubbing it between his hands to try to get it clean. There was not enough light for him to tell if he really got it clean, so he could only hope it would do. Without soap, he knew it would not be very good, but if it would not get his new clothes dirty, that was all he wanted. When he thought it would do, he wrung out the excess water, threw the dirty water out of the bucket and let it drop back down into the well. He did not bother to rinse the bucket, thinking it would serve the white folks right to have to drink a little dirty water.

He went back into the barn and found a nail to hang the wet bag on. Willard might find that, but it seemed unlikely and it was a chance he was willing to take. He had done all he could do to implement his plan.

CHAPTER 5

The day before the family was due to leave, Laureen was once again staring out her bedroom window, trying to cool herself from the heaviness of the April warmth. She and Florence had almost completed their packing, having packed so many things that then had to be unpacked to make room for more important things, adding fresh grief over the things they must leave in the house. As she stood there looking out and yet seeing nothing, lost in her memories of a distant time in the past, a slight movement near the barn caught her eye and drew her attention once more to the present. The movement had seemed furtive. She looked harder and saw nothing more at first. But as she continued to scrutinize the area where she thought she had seen movement, sure enough, there was young Gerald, flattened against the wall of the barn, nearly hidden by high weeds that were a constant reminder of the pitiful condition of their plantation.

As she watched she could see Gerald moving ever so slightly from time to time, inching his way toward the barn door. "Why would that boy be sneaking around like that?" she wondered to herself. Gerald was usually a quiet, obedient boy, but his attitude had grown a little disrespectful after he learned he would be leaving Three Willows. Since his father's death, he had frequently spoken of the plantation as belonging to him. Each time he did his mother reminded him that, technically, it belonged to her. And each time she did he reminded her he was the next in line to inherit and land belonged to the men in the family. Of course, at fourteen, Gerald was too young to think of the numerous things that would be involved in owning and managing such a farm.

Laureen realized her young nephew's life was being turned upside down, as were the lives of the rest of the family, so she was not inclined to be especially critical of him for his emotional outbursts of the past few days. So much was happening so quickly and she allowed for the fact that too little time had elapsed for him to adjust his thinking.

But this was something she decided she wanted to investigate. So she eased downstairs and out onto the back porch. "Gerald, Gerald!" she called. She could not see him from the lower elevation of the porch, but she knew he would be able to hear her. She waited a moment then called again. Almost at that moment he came into view on the weed-chocked path, running a little.

"What is it, Aunt Laurie?" he asked her, not even out of breath.

"What were you doing at the barn just now? I could see you from my room and it appeared as you were sneaking around. Why?"

"Oh I wasn't really sneaking, Aunt Laurie. I was just trying to listen to Tolly talking to himself and I thought he'd quit if he knew I was there."

"Tolly! What was he saying that interested you so much?"

"Well, Aunt Laurie, it was the strangest thing. It didn't sound like Tolly at all. He didn't talk the way he usually does."

"Why, what do you mean, Gerald?" she asked, but she thought she knew the answer to that. Tolly had demonstrated to her that he knew how to talk without sounding like a slave.

Gerald answered, "He didn't talk the way slaves talk, like he usually talks. He sounded more like we do, like he had some education." Then Gerald looked at his aunt in a quizzical way and said, "Tolly can't read, can he?"

"I don't believe so," she answered. "But that doesn't mean he can't learn how to speak properly. Tell me what he was saying."

"It was the strangest thing. He was saying things like, 'Good evening. I'm very pleased to meet you. How do you do? My name is Terrance Wallace. I hope you're having a good day.' Things like that. And, where do you suppose he got the name Terrance Wallace? And something else. Everything he said came out real slow. Like he had to think how to say every word."

"Well if he were speaking the way we do, then I suppose he was having to think about how to say each word."

"What do you suppose it means, Aunt Laurie?"

"I don't know, Gerald," she answered. But a thought was forming in Laureen's mind and she did not like it. She would not tell what she was thinking to anyone, not even Tolly, but she determined to watch him very closely until they were on the boat. It was too bad they would have to use Tolly to drive the mule to the boat, and not once but twice, because the trunks would have to be taken to town then the wagon would have to return for the family, since there was not room in the wagon for so many trunks as well as all five members of the family.

The more Laureen thought about that the more uneasy she became. Tolly was planning to make his move, of that she had no doubt. "Well, let him do what he likes," she thought, "as long as he gets us and our luggage to the boat tomorrow." But, she felt it was very risky now. She did not want to miss that boat. It was too important they get there on time. If Tolly took the luggage by himself, he might not return. The luggage must go into town first, because it would make it such a long wait for the family to have to go into town so early in the morning.

As Laureen struggled with those thoughts, she realized the solution was so simple! All they needed to do was instruct Willard to accompany Tolly when he took the trunks into town. Even if Tolly refused to return with the wagon, at least Willard would bring it back. Either way they would be able to get back to town on time.

At first, when Laureen suggested to Florence that Willard should go along with the luggage, Florence objected.

"Laureen, Willard's old and tired and he doesn't need to make that trip unnecessarily."

"I know, Flo. Of course he is, but there is a lot of luggage and Tolly could use some help getting it off the wagon and left where it won't be in the way while the wagon comes back for us. Send him along with Tolly, Flo."

"Why are you concerning yourself with what happens to Tolly, Laurie? You've never paid much attention to what I assigned the slaves to do before? Why now?"

"Oh I don't know. Maybe I'm just a little uneasy. Now that it's time to go, I'm afraid something might happen. Maybe Tolly won't come back once he gets into town with the wagon. Something could go wrong. He could hurt himself. Something. I just think it would be a good idea to have Willard go with him."

"I think that if Tolly were going to run away, he would have done it when that last group left right after the fire. Don't you?"

"If we were staying on here then I'd agree with you. But I don't feel too easy about him now. He could be thinking we should take him with us. I know for certain Bessie would rather go with us. You've seen how pouty she's been with us ever since she found out she couldn't go, so perhaps he thinks that same way, too. Oh just humor me in this and send Willard with him when the luggage has to go in tomorrow"

"All right, Laurie, if it means that much to you. They can both take the luggage into town. I want them to get started by daylight. That should give them enough time to get back here and get us to the boat on time."

"Thank you, Flo. I know I'm probably just being a worry wart, but I don't want anything to go wrong. I want us to be on that boat tomorrow! We've worked so hard to get ready to go and it would be such a shame to see all that work go to waste."

"Well we could take a later boat, Laurie. It won't be the end of the world if we miss the *Sultana*. I don't know why we got so fired up when that letter from Zinnia came and we thought we had to do this right away. You'd think our lives depended on our being on that very boat tomorrow!"

Laureen felt comforted, knowing there would be someone with the wagon the next day to make certain it returned for the family after delivering the luggage to the wharf. She hoped young Gerald would forget about overhearing Tolly practicing "white" talk. If Florence learned about it, she could make an issue of it and frighten Tolly into leaving before the trunks were taken to the boat. The family needed him for that one last task.

As the dawn was beginning to make itself known the next morning, the family and servants were busily working at getting all the trunks loaded onto the wagon.

"I don't know, Flo," said the wide-awake Laureen. She had been up for quite some time, too excited to sleep until daybreak. "Do you think this old wagon is going to be able to handle all this weight. These trunks are heavier than I thought they'd be."

"It has to carry them," Florence replied determinedly. "It just has to. We've packed only bare essentials and I don't see how we can possibly leave anything else behind."

Tolly and young Gerald were doing most of the work of loading the luggage into the wagon, with Pansy doing her customary act of supervising. Willard and Bessie were wresting with some of the smaller pieces. After much groaning and struggling, all the pieces were loaded, with the heaviest ones sitting over the back axle.

Florence had told Willard the evening before he was to accompany Tolly with the luggage. This was not to his liking and he said so. "Miz Wallace, ya knows Ah don' hev much stren't' to he'p with dose hebby trunks. Tolly, he'll 'spect me ta do mech as he do, and Ah can'. If'n ya sen's me wi' 'im, Ah'se go'n git hurt!"

"I'll talk to Tolly about that," Florence reassured him. "He knows you don't have a lot of strength. I'll tell him to get someone else to help him unload the luggage. There are always people hanging around the wharf. If they won't do it without payment, then he can tell them I'll give them something when I get there. But you stay with him and make certain that he doesn't obligate me if he doesn't have to."

"Yes,m, Miz Wallace." Willard said no more, but he clearly was not happy with this new turn of events.

As the sun was about to show itself above the trees, Tolly and Willard mounted the wagon and turned the mule down the driveway toward the road into town. It would be nearly three hours before they would return for the family. As Laureen stood at the edge of the yard and watched them go, she seemed to realize fully for the first time how drastically her life was changing. She seemed to sense she would likely never come back to Three Willows and take up her life as she had always known it. Three Willows had already changed, and certainly not for the better. Now with all the family leaving it, it would change some more, but they would not be there to change with it. They would change in a different direction, so life there could never be the same again. A sense of sadness came over her in a way that she had never experienced before. Three Willows was the only home she had ever known. In the past she often thought she might marry some day and move away, but to have everyone walk away and leave it to whatever fate might overtake it was almost too much for her to bear.

She turned to look at the house once again, that once stately, beautiful mansion that was now marred so horribly by the burned portion of the south wing. Oh, how she hated the Yankees afresh for that. Her sadness turned to anger, slowly growing so intense that it frightened her. At that moment she felt she could do anything to the Yankees, not even stopping short of killing them, and it would not bother her conscience at all. In fact as she stood there mourning the loss of her home, she thought she would actually welcome such an opportunity.

Suddenly, she realized she was alone in the yard. Florence had returned to the kitchen and was directing last minute preparations of food for them to take on the boat and Laureen was doing nothing to help. She scolded herself for allowing herself to wish for things that probably could never be. So back into the kitchen she went, hoping Florence would not scold her for her absence.

She need not have worried. Florence had her hands full with Little Adelle, who had decided to throw a temper tantrum at being awakened so early in the morning. Florence had instructed the family she wanted to feed everyone and get all the last minute things finished as quickly as possible, so they would all be ready and waiting when the wagon returned for them. She assured them the captain of *Sultana* would not wait for them. More than that, they did not know exactly when the boat would arrive at the dock. So the family needed to get there as early in the day as they could.

CHAPTER 6

Tolly wanted so much for the mule to pull the wagon faster. He wanted to get away from Three Willows as quickly as he could. He guessed correctly why Willard was riding into Natchez with him that morning. He did not know which of the two women suspected what must be on his mind, but if he had to name one of them, it would be Miss Laureen. There was just something about that woman that got under Tolly's skin. She was never unkind to him, so he had a hard time putting a finger on exactly what it was. He was convinced she was not quite the upstanding lady most people believed her to be. He had glimpsed a side of her only a few days ago that he never saw before and it intrigued him. Oh she had covered it up well enough and then made certain he was not able to see it again, but he knew it was there. If only he could find some way to exploit it.

He still planned to be on the *Sultana* when it left Natchez that day but, so far, had been unable to formulate a good workable plan for doing it. Perhaps it was just as well Willard was sent along with him. He might not have returned for the family had he brought the luggage into town alone. But since Willard would report his absence on returning to Three Willows, there was no need to create problems for himself. And there were certain to be problems if he failed to return on that wagon.

Suddenly another thought occurred to him. Since they obviously no longer trusted him completely, would he even be asked to drive the family to town, or would they leave him at the plantation and have Willard do the driving on that last trip. That thought alarmed him. He did not want to have to walk back to town from the plantation. He sighed. There was nothing to do but to wait and see how it worked out.

Willard broke in on his contemplation. "Wha' ya so quiet 'bout dis mo'n'n, Tolly? Ya ain't sa'd t'ree woids since we been on de road."

"Ah jes' wonder'n' wha' T'ree Willers go'n' be lak wid all de fam'ly gone now. Lot diff'rent, Ah 'spect."

"Me'be, me'be not."

"Ya go'n' move to de big house now? Ya kin if'n ya wants to, Ah rec'on. Won' be nobody 'roun' to say ya ken't."

"Not me. Ah'se stayin' right where Ah been all 'long. Ah rec'on ya can, tho', if'n ya wan's to."

"Nah, Ah can' see no reason fo' dat. Let de gals hev it if'n dey wan's it."

Both men fell silent again, and Tolly was lost in his own world of fantasy about what life was about to be like for him. The sun had risen well above the trees and the morning was beginning to warm up. The dew was rapidly evaporating from weeds and grass that pushed against the edge of the road, as though trying to find a way to expand into the rutted ribbon of brown. Tolly kept urging the mule on in spite of the unusually heavy load he was having to pull. The boards in the wagon bed creaked with age and wear. If only it would continue to hold together for this and one more trip.

At long last they reached Natchez. Tolly pulled the wagon up as close to the wharf as he could get it and found someone in charge so he could ask where to put the luggage, explaining he would have to return to Three Willows to collect the boat passengers, since there was not enough room on the one wagon to transport luggage and passengers at the same time. He was shown the place and soon had it all stacked neatly in as small an area as he could manage. He had found a teenager to help him, but did not offer to pay him to do it. Willard sat on the wagon seat, never moving, let alone offering to help.

All the while Tolly was unloading luggage, he was looking around at the layout of the wharf and trying to find a place to hide from any curious eyes until the last second before slipping aboard the boat without being detected. There was a small outbuilding that looked promising. After eliminating all other possibilities, he finally decided it offered him the most hope for acting on his plan. At least it would have to do. He had managed to slip his burlap bag containing the late Gerald Wallace's clothes onto the wagon without being noticed. And the teenage boy helping him to unload the wagon paid no attention as Tolly slipped the bag down in among the trunks. If Willard saw it, he made no comment.

After all the luggage was stored on the wharf, Tolly casually sauntered close to the old shed. The door was ajar, the hinges having rusted so badly the door never completely closed. It looked unused. That would make the perfect place to store his bag then perhaps later to change into Master Gerald's clothes. Just as casually Tolly strolled back to the luggage, picked up his bag, trying not to appear to be doing anything he shouldn't, and went back to the shed. Carefully, slowly, he glanced around to make certain no one was watching, and quickly put his bag inside the shed, just out of sight. He looked toward the wagon. Willard appeared to be dozing, so he felt certain no one had paid any attention to him. He was determined to get on that boat. It was too bad the boat would arrive in broad daylight instead of at least affording him the cover of darkness. But there was nothing he could do about that.

Tolly had overheard some talk that the *Sultana* was going to take on a load of newly released Union soldiers when they reached Vicksburg. Those men had been prisoners of war in the Andersonville and Cahaba prison camps. Tolly wondered if there might be some way he could use that bit of information to his advantage. He resolved to say nothing about it to any of the others.

Soon after he began to formulate his plan, seeing a chance of success, remote as it might be, he returned to the wagon and Willard and they endured another miserable ride back to the plantation.

About half an hour before Tolly and Willard reached Three Willows, Florence stationed Pansy in a rocking chair on the front porch to watch for the wagon's return. Then Florence asked each child to walk around the house one last time, looking closely at each room. She wanted to give them that chance to entrench in their minds whatever memories of the only home they had ever known they might want to preserve. After that, there was nothing to do but sit quietly and wait. At least she and Laureen sat quietly. But the children were too used to activity to sit for long. They were quickly engaged in a game of hide and seek, with Florence cautioning them to try not to get their clothes dirty, as they needed to stay as clean as they could.

"Just remember there will be dust on the road and the wagon will stir it up, and some of it will get on us. Most likely we will all be somewhat dusty by the time we reach town, but I suppose there's no help for that. But I would like us to get there as clean as we can. So try not to get dirty before we even leave the house."

Laureen had mentioned to her how muddy the streets were in town, but the mud did not reach all the way out to Three Willows.

"We'll try, Mama," answered Doreen as she disappeared around the side of the house to hide once more.

Florence sighed, and said to no one in particular, "There's only so much I can do. If they get dirty, I think there's just nothing I can do about it and they'll simply have to go the way they are." But she called to them to come back to the back porch, since the wagon was due back home any minute.

At long last the wagon came in sight, and the moment it did, even before it could turn into the driveway, Pansy was on her feet, calling, "Miz Wallace, dey's back!"

She did not need to say it twice. Florence was listening for precisely that signal and quickly gathered her children to the yard.

By the time the wagon reached them, Florence was directing the children where they would sit. She had brought out a patchwork quilt with her to spread on the rough boards that made up the floor of the wagon. The quilt would at least keep the dirt on the floor boards off the children's clothes. It would also prevent splinters from those boards from digging into their flesh.

Both Tolly and Willard left the wagon seat and Tolly began helping the children onto the back of the wagon. Florence spoke to Willard, saying, "I guess this is 'Goodbye,' Willard. I've already said 'Goodbye' to Pansy and Bessie. Tolly can drive us into town. There's no need for both of you to go this time. Besides, there's barely room for three on the wagon seat and certainly not for four. Take care of yourself and the others."

Laureen watched in surprise as a tear slid down Florence's cheek. "She actually has some feelings for that old man," she thought. "I never would have suspected!" Laureen remembered that all four of the servants who were left at Three Willows had been there when Florence married Gerald and came to live there. So she was saying 'Goodbye' to almost everything that had been familiar to her for the last fifteen years.

Florence stiffened when the tear spilled onto her cheek and

quickly brushed it aside. Laureen thought she could almost tell what Florence was thinking at that moment. Certainly she did not want anyone to see her cry. In fact, Laureen could not remember ever having seen Florence cry.

"Are you ready, Laureen?" Florence said sternly as she walked to the front of the wagon, and waited for Tolly to help her up to the seat.

"Yes, Flo, I'm as ready as I'll ever be. Let's go!"

Once again the old mule was going down Three Willows' driveway pulling the wagon. Florence had inspected the wagon as the children were climbing aboard. She had said to Tolly, "This left rear wheel seems to be quite wobbly. Do you think it will hold together long enough to get us into town?"

"Ah don' kno', Miz Wallace. It' gittin' wus all de time."

"Well we'll just have to hope it lasts that long. We have to do with what we have. If it will get us into town, then that's all I care about. After that you can do whatever you like with it. I have too much on my mind to worry about it. And if it breaks down along the way, well, then I think we'll just have to deal with it then. I'm not going to try to cross bridges now that we may never come to." With that she let Tolly help her onto the wagon seat.

Laureen had not intended to be maneuvered into the middle position on the wagon seat, but there she was, in spite of her good intentions. She did not see how it happened, but she was certain it was Tolly's doing. She could not object out loud without making Florence wonder why. And that was the last thing she wanted, to have Florence asking questions about her reactions to anything Tolly said or did. So she accepted what she must. She would ride the next three miles seated next to Tolly.

Sitting so close to him, much closer than she had only a few days ago when they had gone to town together, she soon felt the stirrings of the same feelings she felt that day. This man was young and good looking, could easily pass for white. Through the sleeve of her dress she could feel the hardness of his arm muscles as the handled the reins of the mule. She determinedly looked straight ahead, not daring even to glance in Tolly's direction. Even so Laureen knew Tolly was not oblivious to her either. She knew she was revealing altogether too much of her emotions to him in spite of her determination not to do so. It was putting her at a disadvantage with him. And he would be quick to look for a way to exploit that advantage. He was too quiet. Laureen could only guess about his thoughts and knew she must not give him even the slightest means to take advantage of her.

The children, trying in vain to find a comfortable position in the back of the wagon, had fallen into squabbling among themselves, particularly Gerald and Dora. Adelle was still a little young to understand what they were arguing about, but she never wanted to be left out of anything the older children did or said, so she tried to get right in the middle of it. As a result Florence's attention was centered on her children, trying to mediate their arguments and keep them more or less quiet. Otherwise she might have noticed the tension between Laureen and Tolly and wondered about its cause.

By the time the wagon finally reached Natchez, the late April day had grown quite warm. With no shade to temper the heat for the passengers on the wagon, the ride had become an ordeal for all of them. Florence and Laureen had hoisted umbrellas in an attempt to ward off the burning rays, but the meager shade did little to relieve their discomfort. Both the little girls were wearing sun bonnets and Gerald had on a hat, but there was nothing to stop the heat of the sun from penetrating their light layers of clothing. It was little wonder the children were cross and fretful.

Tolly stopped the wagon under the same Magnolia tree where he had when he drove Laureen into town only a few days before. Before Florence could even get down off the wagon, Gerald asked, "Mama, could I have something to eat? I'm getting hungry."

"Oh, you exasperating boy!" exclaimed Florence. "I tried to get you to eat more breakfast. I don't have a lot of food with us and it will be expensive to buy it on the boat. Can't you wait a little while longer and then we'll all eat?"

"But I'm hungry now, Mama. Can't I please have something, just one sandwich?"

"If I give food to you, then the other children will want something, too. We need to save what we have. Please wait."

"But, Mama......." he started. However, the look his mother gave him told him that she meant for him to drop the subject.

"I want all of you to wait here while I go and get tickets for us. Perhaps someone will have some idea when to expect the boat. I hope we don't have to wait too long. Tolly, help me down and then come with me."

Laureen was suddenly feeling resentful that Florence had unceremoniously taken control and left her sitting in the wagon as though she were one of the children. But it was typical of the way Florence treated her from the time she arrived at Three Willows. On one level, Florence acknowledged that Laureen was a grown woman, but she seemed to think of it as merely a chronological thing. She never seemed to realize Laureen was also grown mentally and emotionally. If Laureen had weakened in her resolve of a few days ago to distance herself from Florence and Three Willows, that one chance bit of thoughtlessness on Florence's part now strengthened it enormously. Suddenly she stood up.

"Gerald, watch your little sisters for a while. I want to take a last look around the town," she said . "That is if I can find some place to walk where it isn't too muddy." This business of being left to sit with the children while Florence made arrangements for them to have passage on the *Sultana* was not sitting well with her at all.

"No, Aunt, I want to see some of the guys here and say "Goodbye" to them. I'll be gone only a short time. I think we have plenty of time before the *Sultana* is expected." And Gerald was out of the wagon and gone before Laureen could say any more.

"Oh, that boy!" said Laureen under her breath. "If he were my son, I'd give him a good beating at least twice a day."

"Aunt Laurie, you don't mean that," said a somewhat shocked Dora. Dora was a very sensitive little girl, in part because she had never gotten over the loss of her father. And, she was especially sensitive to any criticism of her big brother, whom she adored. She might quarrel with him several times a day, but she had demonstrated many times she would not tolerate any negative remarks about him from anyone else.

"Oh yes I do mean that," said Laurie stubbornly. "That brother of yours has gotten too big for his britches these days. He needs someone to set him straight and your mother doesn't seem to be up to it."

"Aunt Laurie," cried Dora, almost in horror. "I've never heard you talk like this about my mother before!"

"Oh calm down, Dora," Laureen hastily responded. "I didn't mean it. I suppose I'm just on edge over this move. I think we all are a little short tempered right now." She could not resist adding, "You have no room to criticize me after the way you and Gerald quarreled all the way into town this morning."

At that moment, little Adelle stood up on the quilt and started to cry. "I want my mama, I want my mama," she sobbed.

"It's all right, Honey," cajoled Laureen, reaching out her arms toward the child. Your mama will be back soon. She just had to go check on the boat for a few minutes. She'll be back soon."

Adelle welcomed the possibility of a lap to sit on after the long, difficult ride in the wagon. She stood behind the wagon seat, arms high in the air, waiting to be picked up. But, Laureen was not eager to have a wriggling child wrinkling her dress before she could even get on the boat, so said, "It's too hard to pick you up over the seat, Adelle. You've gotten to be such a big girl. But just stand here by me and let me hold you that way," she said as she twisted in her seat to encircle the child's shoulders with one arm.

Even to Laureen, Florence seemed to be gone a long time. Both little girls were getting quite quarrelsome by the time she returned to the wagon. "Well it's all settled," Florence said as she stood beside the wagon, reluctant to climb back up to sit on the hard seat. "I have tickets for all of us to stay in one stateroom. I understand the cabins are quite nice, very roomy. Ours is right off the main saloon, and very near the bow. I think we'll be quite comfortable there."

Laureen noted that Florence did not offer to give her a ticket, but kept them all. One more indication Florence still thought of her as one of the children. She decided not to make an issue of it. It was best to get this trip behind them in the most peaceful way possibly. Laureen knew she would have to take advantage of Zinnia's offer for her to stay with them. But that was to be a very temporary situation.

56

No longer than was absolutely necessary.

She said simply, "Did you get any indication as to when the *Sultana* might be here?"

"No, no one has heard anything. It could be down just below the next bend and it could still be in New Orleans for all anyone knows."

"Oh I don't think that could be true. Captain Mason told Tolly the other day he had some kind of appointment in Vicksburg and he did not want to be late. That's why he said we'd better be here because he couldn't wait for us."

"I see," she replied absently. Then suddenly noticing her son was not in the wagon, she asked, "Where's Gerald? How could you let him loose in town today of all days?" Her voice was taking on a shrill tone.

"Calm down, Flo. He's not going to get into any trouble. And, I didn't 'let' him do anything. I asked him to watch the little girls for a few minutes while I took a last look around town and, instead, he jumped out of the wagon saying essentially I could watch them myself. He wanted to say 'goodbye' to some of his friends."

"What friends?" cried Florence. "He doesn't have any friends here in town. He hardly knows anyone here."

"All I know is, that's what he said to me. I don't know where he went. Would you rather I chased after him and left the girls here by themselves?"

"No, of course not. I'm sorry, Laurie. I guess I'm just on edge right now." "Well I suppose he'll be back soon. He knows we don't want to miss the boat. Surely he'll hear the whistle when it's docking and come back, if he isn't already back. Besides I was just thinking. You know how he was already saying how hungry he was. Do you suppose you should get a little more food to take with us. It's probably cheaper to buy it in town than it will be on the boat. We're going to have to be on that boat for at least three days, perhaps four."

"Oh I don't think more than three days unless they have some kind of problem with the boat. And that seems unlikely. I hear the *Sultana* is only a couple of years old and is quite well made. We should get to Cairo in very good time," answered Laureen.

At that point, she realized Tolly had not come back with Florence. Trying to sound as off-handed as she could she asked, "What happened to Tolly? I didn't see him after he left the wagon."

If Florence thought anything of the question she did not indicate it by her manner. "Oh after I bought the tickets, he asked if there was anything else I needed him for before the boat got here and I told him there wasn't. So he went off somewhere. I don't know what he had in mind but it really doesn't make any difference, does it? I doubt he'll stay long at Three Willows after we're out of here. I only hope he stays long enough to take the mule and wagon back there. But if he doesn't there's not a thing we can do about it, is there?"

"No I suppose not," she said softly. She looked straight at Florence and asked, "Flo, do you suppose we'll ever come back here again? Three Willows has been in the Wallace family for several generations. I'd hate to think it could slip into other hands now. How does Gerald feel about it?"

"To tell the truth, Laurie, I've never talked to him much about it. He knows it is to be his one day if we can keep the taxes paid on it. But I don't know how he really feels about it. I think he hates the Yankees about as much as you do, especially since his father died in the war. Perhaps he would like to keep the plantation to prove to them he can run it even without slaves. As I said we've never really talked about that aspect of it. That boy is pretty private about what he's thinking and he doesn't tell me much, even when I ask him. He'll give me some sort of off-hand answer and I really don't get anything out of him, especially on things that matter. As you know, he likes to say it belongs to him, but I think it's just to hear me remind him that, at least for the time being, it belongs to me."

"I kind of thought that. So this may well be the end of the Wallaces on Three Willows. It's kind of sad, isn't it? My father loved that place so much. I'm sorry you didn't get to know him. He and my mother seemed to fit there so perfectly, and when I was a child, I think I thought it was the most wonderful place there could ever be. It never occurred to me that any of us might ever leave it. I thought life would go on and on just as it was. But then they died and my ideal was shattered. I sometimes wonder how my life might have been different if they had lived." She said that last in a soft wistful voice.

It's depth of meaning was not lost on Florence. To her mind Laureen was saying her life would have been much better if her parents could have finished rearing her rather than her brother and new sister-in-law. Laureen had always been a difficult burden for her to bear and she supposed that burden would continue indefinitely. Laureen had not had many opportunities to marry before and now there would be almost none. Well she was strong woman and if she must bear it, then she must. No point in wishing for something that could not be.

Time seemed to stretch on and on while they waited in vain for the *Sultana* to put in an appearance. Gerald did not come back and Florence could not help but worry about him a little. The little girls grew restless and then tired. Finally Florence realized she must give them something to eat and then perhaps they might take a nap. She knew that was stretching it a bit as far as Dora was concerned, but she could surely get Adelle to sleep for a little while.

After they ate she persuaded both girls to take off their dresses and petticoats and lie down on the quilt in just their shimmies to try to rest.

"But, Mama, I'm not sleepy," protested Dora.

"I know you're not, Child. But all I'm asking is for you to lie down and rest. I didn't say you have to go to sleep. Besides I think it would help Adelle to sleep if you lay down with her. After all she's not used to sleeping in a wagon. And it won't be so hot without your dresses. There's no one around close enough to see you so please do it for me."

With only a little more grumbling both children complied and Adelle was soon fast asleep. As soon as Dora detected this she whispered to her mother, asking to be allowed to get up again. Florence agreed it would be all right and helped her would-be-grown daughter back into her clothes.

Meanwhile Laureen had seized the opportunity to move around the town alone. There was so much mud in the streets, making it difficult for her to go anywhere without sinking into it. She did not want to ruin her shoes, so was very limited in where she could go without doing so.

The walkway toward the river dock and wharf had been built up higher than the street, so it seemed natural she would eventually find herself there. There was little activity, though, as those few people who were to board the *Sultana* had placed their luggage there and gone into town to occupy themselves there while they waited for the boat. The river was so swollen from the flooding rains much farther north, and she noticed how swiftly the water was flowing. In spite of the warmth of the day, she shivered as she looked out at its rippling current. The red silt it always carried made it look so forbidding. What lay beneath the surface of that muddy river that flowed so continuously toward the sea, that never ran out of its huge volume of water?

As Laureen stood contemplating the extraordinarily wide river she caught a glimpse of Tolly as he ducked behind a little shed at the edge of the wharf. It was quite apparent to Laureen that Tolly did not intend for her to see him. "Hmmn," thought Laureen. "I've caught him doing something he doesn't want me to know about. I guess he didn't expect me to be on the dock but I've caught him now."

"Tolly!" she called out to him.

"Yes'm, Miz Laureen," he reluctantly replied.

"Come here, I want to talk to you."

"Cumin', Miz Laureen," he said as he started toward her unconsciously looking back toward the shed.

That one look told Laureen that Tolly was up to something he wanted to keep secret. She had nothing better to do while waiting for the boat, so she was determined to find out what it was. The most likely thing was that he was going to try to sneak on the boat. And then she thought, "Well, why not? At the very least it might offer some amusement to watch him try not to be detected."

Tolly stood in front of her, and asked, very slowly and deliberately, "Did you wish to speak to me, Miss Wallace?"

Laureen knew she had not been mistaken. He was doing it again. Trying to talk like a white person. Well what did she care if he did? Her need for his services had come to an end and it mattered little to her what he did from that point forward. But she would not let Tolly know how she really felt. Instead she said, "So, Tolly. You really think you can 'pass,' do you? You have a long way to go before your speech won't give you away. The first time you get excited about something, you'll forget yourself and fall back to 'slave' talk and you'll be exposed for the fraud you're trying so hard to be. You are what you are, Tolly, and nothing will ever change that."

Tolly continued in his almost agonizingly slow voice, "You're so right about that, Miss Wallace. But perhaps you'd like to tell me exactly what that is." He was making no attempt to hide his insolence.

Laureen started to say, "Why, you're just a Nigga' slave," but caught herself. Tolly was not a slave. There were no slaves. That life was over and done with. Instead she said, "I believe you're a freed slave, Tolly. What do you think you are?"

"Well that's a good question, Miss Wallace. As you said, I'm not a slave. My mother was a Negro slave and my father was a white plantation owner. So what do you think that makes me?"

"Oh, Tolly, it makes no difference what I think you are. And please, if you're going to talk to me at all, I don't have the patience for you to translate every word you say?"

"Say dat woid ag'in, Miz Laureen. What did ya call it?" He had reverted back to his usual way of talking.

"'Translate?' Is that the word you mean?"

"Yes'm, dat's de one. Tell me wha' it means."

"Hmm, let's see," she answered. How could she explain this to Tolly so he would understand? After hesitating to give herself time to collect her thoughts, she continued. "It's usually used when people are turning one language into another one. Like the word 'yes,' in English is 'si' in Spanish. If you're used to speaking in English all the time, and are not used to speaking in Spanish, then when you're speaking to a person who speaks only Spanish, you have to really think what the Spanish word is for each English word. So you can't speak

Spanish as easily as you would English. And that's the way it sounds when you try to talk the way white people do. Like you're translating every word."

Tolly was silent for a moment, then replied, "I giss I jes' ain't had 'nuf' prac'ice. But, I'se go'n' git dere, Miz Laureen. Ya won' tell nobody, will ya'?"

"Why should I tell anyone what you have in mind to do, Tolly? It's of complete indifference to me. But I tell you this: If you stow away on that boat and they catch you, they're likely to throw you off right out in the middle of the Mississippi River so I hope you know how to swim!"

Tolly's face registered genuine surprise.

"You didn't think I knew what you were up to, did you, Tolly? Well I think maybe I'm smarter than you give me credit for. As I said I won't give your secret away. Anyway I hope you know how to swim.

He replied simply, "Oh, Ah swims real good, Miz Laureen."

"I have just one request to make of you, Tolly. I hoped you would take the mule and wagon back to Three Willows. I'm going to pretend I think you will. But if you don't intend to do that, will you make some arrangements, at least for the mule, so he doesn't stand hooked up to that wagon until he falls over and dies?"

"Yes'm, Miz Laureen. I mek' sure dat mule all right. Ya don' need werry none 'bout 'im."

"Thank you, Tolly. Now you might as well go on with what you were doing. I'm going back to the wagon for now."

She didn't say "goodbye" to him. She would not treat him as her equal. Besides she had every expectation she would see him on the boat. He would try not to let anyone else see him, but he would have no reservations about letting her see him. Such a secret was kind of exciting to her, even if she did have to share it with a colored man. That was a totally new experience for her and she spent the time of her walk back to the wagon trying to understand herself and how she felt about it.

CHAPTER 7

When she reached the wagon, only the two little girls were there. Adelle was lying on the quilt in the back of the wagon, still napping. Dora was sitting on the wagon seat, obviously feeling very "put upon" at being left there to watch her little sister. "Where's your mother?" Laureen asked her.

"She went looking for Gerald," was the response.

"You mean that boy still hasn't come back?" cried Laureen in shocked dismay. "Where do you suppose he could be keeping himself all this time?" Then she looked at Dora suspiciously. "Dora, do you know something you're not telling? Do you know what he's up to?" As Dora looked down at her hands Laureen reached up, took hold of Dora's upper arm and continued very sternly, "Look at me, Girl. I want the truth. Do you know where he went?"

"Well," she said slowly, reluctantly, "he didn't think it was fair that we're being hauled off to Missouri and not given any say in it." Then, with unexpected determination in her voice, she added, "Mother explained some of it to me, but I still don't think it's fair, either!"

"You might be right. Maybe it isn't fair. But you're going to find out soon enough there's not much in life that is fair. And that's just the way it is. When you're ten years old or even fourteen, you don't get much voice in big decisions that have to be made. But you'd better realize your turn will come soon enough, and then you'll find out it's no fun having to make them. However in the meantime, you don't have much choice but to do as you're told. Now you tell me this minute what you know about Gerald. Where is he?"

That last was said with such emphasis that Dora's eyes widened, letting Laureen know she had made her point and the child would tell what she knew. "Gerald didn't actually tell me what he was going to do but I think he was thinking about going down to the feed store and try to hide out in the back room there. But honest, Aunt Laurie, I didn't think he'd actually do it. And I didn't say anything because I thought that if we missed the *Sultana* today then maybe we wouldn't have to go."

"Oh you foolish girl," cried Laureen. "We don't have any choice! We have to get on that boat. It's going to save our lives. We have no life left to us here. We just have to get on that boat! You stay right here with Adelle, and I'll try to find your mother and maybe we can get that boy back here before the boat comes. Don't you move!" Then as an afterthought she asked, "Do you have any idea where your mother might have gone?"

"I think she said something about trying the general store. But that was soon after you left the wagon so she could be anywhere by now."

"Oh what have we gotten ourselves into now?" worried Laureen to herself. It was distressing to her to have to get out on the muddy streets, but there was just no help for it now. She would have to clean up her shoes when Gerald was found and they were all back safely at the wagon. She could only hope there would be time to find him before the boat arrived. They needed to be at the wharf by the time the boat pulled in, because it would rest there only long enough to load the boarding passengers and their luggage. Florence had said that, besides the Wallaces, there were only three more people to get on at Natchez, a young couple and their small son. Of course she had no way of knowing if there would be passengers getting off the boat, and if so, how many. In any case it would seem the *Sultana* would be stopped at Natchez for only a very short time.

She made her way across the muddy street and stepped upon the wooden walkway in front of a row of stores. She stood in the open doorway of first one and then another and then another of those stores, hoping to find Florence and tell her what Dora had said. But Florence was not there. With each failure to find her Laureen's distress level grew, until she was becoming quite frantic. At the end of the row of stores there was nothing for her to do but to go across the next street and check the livery stable. As she stood in its big open doorway, she could see only a couple of horses, survivors of the Yankees' march north as they closely skirted the town itself.

As her eyes adjusted to the dimmer light inside, she spoke to the blacksmith working on a new horseshoe off to one side of the stable, "Mr. Jacks, Did Mrs. Wallace come by here recently looking for her son, Gerald?"

He looked up, smiling in recognition of Laureen. She was always welcome there, although he had only rarely seen her. "Well, Miss Laureen! Aren't you a sight for sore eyes! As a matter of fact, Miz Wallace was here just a few minutes ago. Said that boy of hers must have forgotten the time and she needed to find him. You folks gettin' on the *Sultana* for a trip north, she said. Well, I think that's right nice."

"Thank you, Mr. Jacks. I'd love to stop a visit a while, but we must find Gerald. There may not be much time before the *Sultana* docks."

"I understand," he replied as she turned to go.

"Well I suppose the thing for me to do now is check the feed store myself. I don't know where Florence is and I need to find that boy," she mumbled to herself. She hurried on, getting farther and farther from where she wanted to be, but Gerald must be found. "Oh I'd like to give that boy a licking he won't soon forget," she said again and again to herself. "Why do boys have to be so difficult, anyway? Right now I'm very glad I don't have children of my own. It's so much easier to do things when I have no one but myself to take care of."

Laureen knew she was not being altogether rational in her thoughts, but that was not her prime concern at the moment. She would sort those out later. Right now the focus had to be on finding young Gerald. As she reached the feed store and looked inside she could hardly believe her eyes. There was Florence approaching the front of the store with young Gerald in tow. Quite literally in tow. Florence was actually leading the boy out of the store by his ear! "Well," she thought, "it's about time that Florence cracked down on that boy."

Gerald was resisting but not enough that he would pull away from his mother. He whined and complained at the indignity of what she was doing to him, but his training would not allow him to go any further than that.

"Oh, Florence, I'm so glad you found him. I've been looking all along the way here for you. How did you know where he was?"

"Mother's sometimes have instincts about these things, Laurie. When I couldn't find him anywhere else, I started thinking about what he might do. I knew he'd had an awful lot to say about not wanting to leave Three Willows, and it finally occurred to me that he might be trying to rebel. And the back room of the feed store seemed the most logical place he would choose to hide. So I came here and demanded that I be allowed to look back there. And sure enough, I found my wayward son."

"Gerald, you ought to be ashamed of yourself for all the worry you've given us. And just look at all the mud on my poor shoes," she cried. "They probably won't ever clean up to look the way they did.

Oh what's the use?" she said in complete exasperation.

Now that Gerald was found, her worry of a few moments ago readily turned to anger at the boy. She comforted herself with the thought that in only a comparatively short time he would no longer be her worry. She would get away from Florence and her children and Zinnia and all the rest of what she was fast starting to think of as her 'old life.'

The three of them walked back the way they had come in much less time than it had taken them to arrive at the feed store. Both the little girls were still in the wagon. Adelle was awake now and acting very irritable. This was such a long time to have to sit in that wagon with a stinky old mule hitched to it. The droppings at his heels only added to the stench. Even the wonderfully sweet fragrance of the Magnolia blossoms scattered over the tree failed to mask this odor.

The women were not particularly interested in sitting in the wagon any longer either. The day was growing late and they were all becoming tired. Fortunately, there was no need to wait much longer. Right at that moment they heard the whistle of the *Sultana* approaching Natchez. That was the sound they had been waiting for ever since they reached the town. Comfort at last!

"Come, Adelle, let me help you down. You, too, Dora. Let's go on to the wharf and watch the boat come in." In saying this, Florence realized it would be several minutes before the boat would actually be tied up at the dock, but the little girls had been in that wagon much longer than she had wanted them to be. It was time to let them down and do a little walking. "Gerald, carry Adelle for me to the dock, will you please?"

Gerald was fond of his little sister, even though he found her spoiled and annoying much of the time. He said nothing in response to his mother's request, but picked up the child and hoisted her on his back for the walk to the dock. It was only a short walk, so the family arrived there just in time to see the *Sultana* come into view from the nearest bend in the river downstream from Natchez.

"Oh, Mama," cried little Adelle as she saw the boat, "Is that the boat we're going to ride on? It doesn't look very big."

"Just wait, Adelle," replied her mother. "It looks small now, but as it gets closer, you'll see it's much bigger than it looks now. I hear it's 260 feet long."

"I don't know how long that is, Mama."

"Then you'll just have to wait until it gets here and you'll see how long that is." Florence could not readily think of a distance that equaled the boat, something to use as an illustration to her child. But, it did not seem important to her to try to satisfy the little girl's curiosity right then. They would be on the boat soon enough and then the child could see for herself. She was looking forward to getting into their stateroom and relaxing. This trip would likely be the last one she would take for quite some time to come and she had made up her mind to thoroughly enjoy it. She could only guess what the future might hold for them when they reached John and Zinnia's farm, so these few days would likely be the last truly pleasant days she would have. She might just as well enjoy them while she could.

As the boat gradually shortened the distance between itself and the wharf, the children began to complain. "Mama, why is it taking so long to get here?" whined Adelle.

"Try to be patient," responded her mother. "It will be here before long. I promise."

To Florence and Laureen, the anticipation of getting on the boat made the waiting time seem insignificant. All other thoughts were forgotten, thoughts of Three Willows, of the servants they did not expect to see again, even of the wagon and mule they had abandoned under the magnolia tree. A new life awaited them and, even though there was a mild fear of the unknown mixed in with the other feelings, they were both eager to get on with it. Even the heat of the afternoon sun mercilessly warming them to the point of discomfort could not diminish the anxious excitement they both were feeling.

As the boat drew closer, Adelle began jumping up and down to the point that Florence was afraid she might jump right into the water. "Gerald, get hold of that child and get her back away from the edge," Florence cried as the child's last jump put the little girl perilously close to danger.

"Oh, Mama, I don't want to have to watch her now," he whined. "I want to watch the boat." He grudgingly took hold of his little sister's hand and led her to their mother, even putting the child's hand in that of her mother's.

Indeed, the boat was worth watching. It was a beautiful side-wheeler, 260 feet long and launched only a little over two years before. It was built at a cost of $60,000.00. It had a 42-foot beam, a hold seven feet deep. It could carry 1,000 tons. The water wheels were each 34 feet in diameter. Each paddle was 11 feet long. Gerald was giving all his attention to the boat and did not want his little sister distracting him. He could hardly wait to get aboard and explore all its decks, cabins, even the hold. He had never ridden a river boat before even though he had seen several of them. The excitement he felt in actually riding on this boat made him forget his resentment at having to go north with his family, at least for the time being.

Slowly the boat eased its way alongside the wharf and several men jumped out to make it secure with ropes. The young couple with the small child had returned to stand by their luggage, also waiting to board the boat. They were to be the only other passengers in addition to the Wallaces, to get on at Natchez. Laureen wondered how many people there were already aboard and if she might see someone there she knew.

Until the war disrupted all their lives so drastically, Laureen had been to numerous parties and social functions in the Natchez vicinity and had met quite a number of people from various plantations, even people from as far away as New Orleans and Memphis. So it was quite conceivable to her there could be someone on board she might recognize. She had begun to realize she must look for any and every opportunity that might come her way to make her new life. If there should happen to be someone on board who could further her ambitions, she did not want to overlook such a possibility.

At long last they were ready to board the boat. The young family went first while Florence was watching closely the men who were taking the Wallace's luggage on board. But, eventually, they were all standing in their rather spacious stateroom. There were two beds inside and a pallet in one corner. A full length mirror adorned the back of the door and there was a small chest of drawers pushed against the far wall.

"I'm sorry you have to sleep on the floor, Son," Florence apologized to Gerald. It was the best I could do for you."

"Oh I don't mind that, Mama. Actually I kind of expected it, being the only male in the group." With only a slight pause he continued, "You don't need me for anything now, do you?" he asked. "I want to see the boat. I'd like to go and stand topside when we leave the dock. Is it all right with you?"

Dora chimed in, "May I go, too, Mama? I want to see, too."

Immediately Adelle joined in, "Me, too, Mama. Me, too."

Florence addressed Adelle first, "There's one thing I want you to understand right from the beginning. You're not going anywhere on this boat without your Aunt Laureen or myself with you." Then turning to Gerald, she said, "I don't mind if you explore the boat as long as you stay away from the boilers and the engines. That's dangerous and passengers don't belong there. So go ahead, but don't be gone too long.

"Mama, please," begged Dora. Let me go with Gerald. Please, Mama, please." The child's face had such a pleading expression on it as she searched her mother's face.

Florence could not resist. "Oh, all right But I want you to stay very close to your brother. It's safer that way."

"Oh, Mama," cried Gerald. "I don't want her tagging along with me. People will think I'm a sissy!"

"First of all, Son, it doesn't matter what people think. You know what you are and are not. Second, it's safer for two to be together. Third, Dora shouldn't be walking alone in public anywhere. She's getting to be a young lady now and needs a chaperone. And who makes a better chaperone for a young girl than her older brother? You might as well get used to that role, because it's about to become a part of your life."

Gerald grumbled then sighed in obvious resignation of himself to the inevitable. When his mother took that tone of voice with him, he had learned from long experience there was no point in arguing with her. He always lost so he might as well do as she asked. Besides, Dora was usually good company to him even if she was four years younger.

73

She looked up to him and he liked the feeling that gave him. She made him feel important.

"What about me, Mama? Let me go, too. I want to see the boat," cried little Adelle.

"No, Honey," answered her mother. "You're too little and I don't want them to have to be responsible for you right now. You have to stay with me."

As the older children ventured out to explore the boat, the two women busied themselves with unpacking the few things they expected to use on the trip. They were using Florence's estimate of three days they would be on the boat. They should reach Vicksburg before the end of the day. Laureen wondered idly what it was that was so important to the captain in Vicksburg that he had to get there in such a hurry. She did not know if he was married, so the thought occurred to her that he might have a romantic liaison planned. But it really did not matter to her what he had planned. They were all safely on the boat even though the river was much higher than usual, actually at flood stage. The boat was sound and could navigate the river without complication.

Finally Florence broke the easy silence that had developed between the two women. "I didn't realize until just now how tired I am. It must be all that activity of this day. I know I woke up earlier than usual this morning. I couldn't sleep, knowing all I had to do, and making sure the luggage got to town and all that went with that."

Laureen chimed in. "Well that ride we had to take into town was no little thing, dealing with that foul-smelling mule, the rough wagon ride, not to mention irritable children. Then Gerald's attempt to hide so he wouldn't have to get on the boat."

Florence opened her mouth as if to retort, but closed it again and took a deep breath. Then she said, "Do you think he was serious about staying behind or might that be just an adolescent boy's attempt at getting some extra attention for himself? Maybe I do need to pay more attention to him." When Laureen wisely kept quiet, Florence continued, "I guess it will have to wait until we reach Missouri, whatever he needs. Anyway for right now I intend to relax and enjoy this trip. There'll be plenty of time later on to analyze my son's feelings and actions."

When Laureen still offered no comment, Florence turned to Adelle and asked, "Adelle, how would you like to take a nap with Mama?"

"But, Mama, I already had a nap today. Do I have to take another one?" whined the little girl.

"That's right, Florence." Laureen finally spoke. "She napped in the wagon for quite a long time. Don't you remember?"

"Yes, I suppose I do, but I'd forgotten. As I said, it's already been a long day for me and I'm rather tired."

"Tell you what," replied Laureen. "Suppose I take Adelle with me for a walk around the boat. She's been in the wagon most of the day and hasn't had any time to play. You lie down and take a nap and we'll stay out of your way for an hour or two. How does that sound to you?"

"Oh, Laurie, would you?" Florence was genuinely surprised at the generous offer from her sister-in-law. Such offers did not come often. Florence knew Laureen loved her brother's children, but she had never been one to do much toward taking care of them. She had always made it quite clear she felt that was the responsibility of Florence and always made a point of leaving their care to her.

But on this day, Laureen was feeling a little more like spending time with Adelle. If things went the way she intended for them to, time was fast running out for her to be with any of the children and she would genuinely miss them when that time came. So Laureen took Adelle by the hand and quietly led her out the door of the stateroom and into the long narrow saloon that ran down the center of the boat with all the cabins opening onto it from either side. It had a few strategically placed padded narrow benches lining the walls to allow passengers a place to rest and visit. She paused a moment to admire the magnificent chandeliers that lighted the way of that fine hallway. The little dangling prisms danced with the swaying of the boat, sending tiny flecks of reflected light chasing each other across the ceiling and walls, even at times reaching the plush carpet that covered most of that hallway, revealing only a narrow strip of highly polished wooden floor on either side. Idly she made her way to a set of stairs to go up to the next deck. She wondered where the other children had got to by this time.

As she started up the stairway she became aware the boat was moving. She, too, thought she would like to watch the dock fade away, so she reached down and picked up Adelle and hurried up the stairs. Still holding the child, she made her way to the rail to watch Natchez grow smaller and smaller as the boat made its way up the river. She had almost the same feelings at watching that as she had in the wagon as they were leaving Three Willows. Would she ever see Natchez again? Would she even want to? What would the next bend in the river of her life be like? She felt she was on an adventure, her greatest one so far. She welcomed it and at the same time feared it. Of one thing she was certain, however. Her life would never be the same.

CHAPTER 8

Laureen stood at the rail for a long time, long after Natchez had disappeared from view. She was lost in thoughts of what was past in her life and possibilities for her future. She hardly noticed the fast flowing muddy water below her or the tree lined river banks so distant on either side. The beauty of the fresh green leaves on the trees was lost to her consciousness, as was the fact that the river was vastly overflowing its banks in so many places. She had even forgotten the small child standing in front of her, also trying to see out through the rails. Laureen could have been standing anywhere other than where she was and would not have realized it. That is until a man's voice, coming from only a few feet away, said, "Why, Miss Wallace. I do believe it's Miss Wallace, isn't it?"

Laureen whirled to face the direction of the voice. "I beg your pardon?" she said.

"Aren't you Miss Laureen Wallace from Three Willows?" said the man, obviously somewhat amused at her confusion.

"Do...Do I know you?" she stammered.

"Well, we've met. But it seems that you don't remember. I'm Graham Talbert, of New Orleans. We met at a bar-b-que at Hilltop Haven about the time the war started. I see I didn't make much of an impression on you." This last was said with a mocking tone in his voice.

"Oh, yes," said Laureen, recovering her composure. "I do remember you, Mr. Talbert. In fact, I very distinctly remember you. I believe my brother Gerald knew you."

"Why, yes, that's true. But you said 'knew.' Has something

happened to him?"

Laureen responded, "My brother was a casualty of the war, Mr. Talbert. He died over a year ago."

"I'm so sorry, Miss Wallace. I didn't know."

"No, you'd have no way of knowing, I suppose. Thank you for your sympathy."

"What about his family? Are they still at Three Willows? And you. Are you married? And is this your little girl?" He was smiling at Adelle, who moved to stand behind Laureen, clutching at the wide skirt that fell to the floor over the big hoops in the top underskirt, her big dark eyes almost covered from view.

Laureen looked down at the child, but did not move to bring her forward. She said simply, "This is Gerald's youngest, Adelle. Her mother and the other two children and I are on our way to visit Florence's sister in Missouri." Laureen had no intention of telling this man any more about herself or her family than was absolutely necessary. Oh, she remembered him, all right.

Gerald had cautioned her quite sternly about him that day nearly five years ago. He had been so charming and paid more attention to her than he should have. When Gerald became aware of it, he took her to one side and told her in no uncertain terms she must avoid that man at all costs. He was a river boat gambler, and that was one of his virtues! Things had a way of turning up missing wherever he went, although no one was ever able to prove he stole things. He had no visible means of support, yet he always seemed to have enough money to live a rather lavish lifestyle. He had worn out his welcome in quite a few towns along the river, and not only in the south. He was from Chicago, and in the course of time, worked his way up and down several rivers before finally reaching New Orleans. And now he was on his way back north, or at least that was what she assumed.

Laureen had felt very disappointed at the time, but was old enough to be past the rebellious stage. She was interested in finding a man to marry, but it must be the right man. She was not going to plight her course with someone with no scruples, not if she knew it in time. She believed Gerald because she knew that he, too, would like to see her settled in a home of her own, but with an honorable man. So she turned her attention elsewhere that day and soon forgot all about Mr. Graham Talbert. She never expected to see him again.

But there he was, big as life and as charming as ever. Hospitality and politeness had been instilled into Laureen from as far back as she could remember, so she was a little at a loss as to how to extract herself from this uncomfortable situation. Several possibilities were racing through her mind. She could say that Adelle needed to get back to the cabin for a nap, but that would mean Florence would not get to sleep nearly long enough. She could say she had been looking for young Gerald and Dora, but it would have been very obvious that she was not looking for anyone when Mr. Talbert found her standing at the rail. She would have to think of something else.

As she stood there, her mind racing, the two older children rescued her even though they did now know that was what they were doing. They came running toward her, Gerald crying out, "Aunt Laurie, you just have to come see what we found!" They stopped suddenly as they realized Laureen was talking to someone.

"Oh I'm sorry, Aunt," apologized Gerald. "I didn't know you were acquainted with someone on board the boat."

"That's all right, Gerald," she answered. "Mr. Talbert is a man I met briefly a number of years ago, and he recognized me a few minutes ago." She turned to Mr. Talbert and said, "Mr. Talbert, this is my nephew, Gerald, and his sister, Dora. Children, this is Mr. Talbert. From New Orleans I believe."

The children said in unison, "How do you do, Mr. Talbert?"

"Very well thank you. And how do you do?" he replied.

Then without waiting for a reply from the children, he turned his attention back to Laureen and continued, "What charming children you have here. But Southern children are almost always extremely well-mannered, aren't they?"

There he was doing it again, mocking her. This had to end. So she said to him, "I believe the children want me to go with them. There is something they want me to see. Please excuse us, Mr. Talbert." Then, taking Adelle by the hand and pulling her to her side, she said to Gerald and Dora, "Lead the way, Children. Adelle and I are right behind you."

The children were so excited, so she began to feel a little excitement, too. "Won't you tell me what it is that you're so eager for me to see?" she asked.

"No," said Dora. "We're almost there and you won't believe your eyes when you see it. We didn't even know what it was until somebody told us. Here, look at that big thing in the crate. He's somebody's pet!" she exclaimed, pointing.

As they approached the stern of the boat, Laureen could see the large wooden crate Dora spoke of. "Well, what do you know?" was all she could think of to say. An alligator on the boat. No wonder the children were excited. The crate was only large enough to contain the alligator without giving him room to move around. But he was making sounds to indicate he did not like to have his freedom curtailed in such a way. Laureen had never even heard an alligator roar before, let alone having seen one in real life. She had seen them only in pictures, and not many of those. " Why would anyone want to keep such an animal as a pet, let alone travel with it?" she wondered.

There were other animals being transported there, about a hundred horses and mules, as well as another hundred pigs. But an alligator? How strange. She wondered if other people were going north on a permanent basis, as were the Wallaces. Surely no one would take along a pet alligator if they were only going to be gone temporarily. But even so, how could it be wise to take such an animal along? Alligators were not cold weather creatures and she wondered how one would survive winters in the north. She made up her mind that if she came across the owners of the animal, she would ask them about it. That should make for an interesting discussion. A pleasant way to pass away the time. After all, there were not so very many people on the boat, at least that she had seen so far.

They looked at the alligator until they tired of it and then started to stroll along the deck for a little while. By this time the sun had sunk behind the dense growth of trees on the western bank of the river, leaving just a dark and ragged outline while the clouds above took on the various shades of strawberry, watermelon, cantaloupe, and plum.

"I think we should go back to our stateroom," Laureen finally said to the children. It's been such a long day for all of us, and I think that by now your mother will have had the rest she needed so much. We'll be quiet as we go in, just in case she might still be sleeping."

But Florence was awake and stirring about the stateroom when the rest of the family arrived. "Oh, I'm glad you're back," she said. "I was just thinking that the children might be getting hungry. I have enough food for us for tonight, but I think we'll have to eat in the dining room the rest of the way."

"Can we afford that, Flo" asked Laureen uneasily?

"Yes, Laureen, I think we can. We still have some money left, although I admit that it's not a great deal. But I've made up my mind I'm going to enjoy this trip. This may be the last thing we do just for our own enjoyment for a long, long time to come. Let's make the most of it."

Laureen was thinking, too, that life could very well become rather grim for them after they reached Missouri, so she was quite willing to live as though they were from a still prosperous plantation. She rather liked the idea of playing the grand lady, even if this were the last time. However, if things went the way she hoped, then it might not be the last time for her, after all. If Florence could be content with living a dull, drab life from now on, that was her business, but that was not for Laureen. Somehow, someway, Laureen was going to get money, and she was beginning to think that it was not so important how she got it, so long as she got it. Without money, she was nothing, just poor white trash, a term of contempt she had heard all her life. She would never have thought of it as applying to herself. After all, she was part of a prosperous family, a family with a big plantation, and with many slaves to work it. It occurred to her she had never even known just how many slaves actually lived on three Willows.

So many things she had always taken for granted. Before the war, she would have never thought about how quickly it could all change, how quickly so much could be lost. Even when her parents died suddenly and left her an orphan at such a young age, there was still her big brother to take care of her. She was still in the home she had always known. She still had all the material advantages that had always been hers. So even then, her life was not changed very drastically.

But now, all those things she took so much for granted had evaporated much like the morning mist that disappears with the burning rays of the rising sun. If she were ever to have them again, she would have to reach out with all her might and take them. And if they weren't there, within easy reach, then she would have to step on anything and anyone who might get in her way. It might even mean having to use such men as Graham Talbert if she could find a way to do so to her advantage. She shuddered at the thought. How could she even be thinking of sinking so low! But then, why not?

She could remember hearing her father, so long ago, saying from time to time, "We must adjust to changing circumstances. We must look at the world the way it is, not like we would wish it to be." It seemed to be one of his favorite expressions. She had no idea what circumstances he might have been talking about. But she was well aware of her changed circumstances now, so she would feel free to borrow that page from his book. Adjust she would. Starting now!

"Flo, you'll never guess who I saw on deck a little while ago. A Mr. Graham Talbert. Do you remember him?" Laureen was hoping Florence would have forgotten him. After all, five years was quite a long time to remember so casual and brief an acquaintance. If Gerald had not spoken too much about him to Florence, then she might very well have forgotten him.

But Laureen was to be disappointed in that. "Do you mean the Mr. Talbert who was at the bar-b-que at Hilltop Haven five years ago? If that's who you mean, I can't imagine that you'd be excited to see him again."

"Oh, but Flo, that was a long time ago. I was just happy to see a face I recognized. He seemed glad to see me, too."

"No doubt," sniffed Florence. "He probably thinks he has an

opportunity to relieve somebody of some money or something. Did you tell him we don't have any now?"

"No, of course not," threw back Laureen. "I don't intend to tell anyone of our present difficulties. That's no one else's business, certainly no one's on this boat. Like you said, I intend to enjoy myself on this trip. Let people think what they will." Then she softened her voice and said, almost pleadingly, "Don't spoil it for me, Flo."

"Oh, do as you like. I guess you can't come to any harm in just the few days we'll be on this boat. We don't have any jewelry for him to steal. All that was sold long ago. And what little money I have, I'm keeping in a safe place, so I'm not worried about that. If you want to be nice to Mr. Talbert, go ahead. But why in the world you'd want to is beyond me. You know what a scoundrel he is."

"Yes, I know that. But he's somebody to talk to. And he can be very charming. Most likely he's charmed something away from somebody in New Orleans or Baton Rouge that he shouldn't have and that's why he's on the boat, going north again. I didn't have time to ask him where he got on the boat or where he's going. He asked me about Three Willows, but I didn't tell him what the real truth is. I just told him that we're going to visit your sister. I also told him Gerald died in the war."

"All right, Laureen. I suppose you know what you're doing. But please be careful. You don't have any experience in dealing with men of that sort. He might get you into trouble in a way that you least expect."

Laureen thought she knew what kind of a warning that might be, but could not express it because of the presence of the children. She would not embarrass herself or them by asking Florence to explain. Instead she drew herself up to her full height and said with much formality, "Florence, I'm 27 years old and I learned how to behave myself a long time ago. I'm not looking for trouble and I don't expect it to find me. But thank you for your concern."

Florence opened her mouth as if to reply, then closed it quickly. Then looking at her little girls, she said, "Children, sit down and let's have something to eat. I know it's still early, but I think we should all get to bed before long. Especially you two, Adelle and Dora. Now let's see what we have."

She busied herself with getting the food she brought set before the children. They were so caught up in all the excitement of getting on the boat and seeing what there was on it, and had completely forgotten all about what a long time it had been since they last ate. The smell of the sandwiches their mother was pulling out of the hamper reminded them of their empty stomachs, and soon the stateroom grew quiet as the children busied themselves with eating their dinner.

Laureen was feeling a little miffed at her sister-in-law, and could think of nothing she wanted to say at the moment.

Even Florence was content to let the silence stretch out between them. In fact she was soon quite lost in her own thoughts and ceased to notice it. What was Laureen up to, anyway? Something about her had changed, so subtly that she could not put her finger on exactly when she began to notice it. But recently. Her attitude about several things was different now. Like earlier in the afternoon when she had taken Adelle off her hands for a little while to allow her to rest. Laureen did not usually do things like that. But on the other hand, there had been no occasion for that in the past. Even when most of the slaves had run away, there were still enough left so there was at least one of them to watch Adelle when the occasion called for it. Like the time when she had caught flu last winter and had been out of her head for a few days. Pansy and Bessie had taken over the care of the children, not Laureen. So perhaps Laureen helped out this day because there was no one else to do so. Yes, that must be it. It was better not to think ill of Laureen if there was no real reason for it.

Still, it was puzzling to Florence as to why Laureen would want to have anything to do with the likes of that Mr. Graham Talbert. She remembered Gerald had taken Laureen aside and talked to her quite explicitly about him. Especially after he all the attention he paid to Laureen at the bar-b-que that time. Mr. Talbert had such a bad reputation. It was rumored that he charmed his way into wealthy homes and sometimes helped himself to their valuables. Things disappeared when he was around, although no one ever saw him take anything. And the things he must have taken never showed up in the local stores or in the homes or on the persons of local people. So if he took things, then he must have some means of disposing of them so they were never seen locally again. People tried to guess what he might be doing with the missing items, mostly jewelry, but no one was ever able to say for certain where those things were going.

But now it was such a long time since she had even thought of Graham Talbert. She had met him that one time, the same time Laureen met him, and never saw him again. So after one or two conversations with Gerald about him, he had ceased to intrude on her thoughts. Until now.

But as Laureen reminded her recently, she was a grown woman with a mind of her own, and Florence could not continue to think she was responsible for her. Laureen was so young when Florence had married Gerald, so it had been so easy to forget the girl was a grown woman now. Old habits were hard to break, and for the first time Florence realized that thinking of Laureen as a child was very much a habit of hers. Well it was time to break it. Laureen wanted to be recognized as a grown woman, and that was what she was going to do. No more advising, counseling, suggesting, or nagging. She was breaking that habit right now. If Laureen chose to make a fool of herself with that man, then so be it. It was her decision, her responsibility. But Laureen would also have to face any consequences of her actions.

Florence realized she would have a difficult time implementing this new resolve. But she was determined she would do it. She would surprise Laureen. But, then again, she wondered if Laureen would even notice. She certainly seemed to be caught up in a world of her own. Florence determined she would keep quiet and see how all this played out. For the first time, she felt part of her burden had been lifted from her shoulders. It was quite a relief.

CHAPTER 9

Morning dawned clear and sunny. There were a few wispy clouds on the horizon, but the remainder of the sky was a clear brilliant blue. Laureen rose early and went out on deck. She had not slept well the night before. Even though their stateroom was near the bow of the boat, the noise of the four big steam engines were enough to disturb her sleep. She had been tired enough to sleep, but the strangeness of the room and the unfamiliar noises combined to rob her of her much needed rest. She dressed quietly in the dim light of the dawn and noiselessly left the room. She was strangely gratified to find the deck completely deserted. She welcomed the quiet solitude. She strolled absently toward the stern of the boat, barely seeing where she was walking. She rarely was awake early enough to see the sun rise and was looking forward to the spectacle once more.

Before she realized where she had come, she heard a strange hissing, then an odd roar. She jumped. Only then did she realize that she had approached much more closely than she had intended to the alligator cage. And he was letting her know that he wanted her to back off. She gave the cage a wide berth, and continued a little farther toward all the livestock that were on board. She had always taken an interest in the animals on Three Willows, especially the horses, so she wanted to have a closer look at those aboard the *Sultana*. She picked up her skirts and eased in closer. There were bales of hay stacked a little out of the reach of the horses and mules, and she wondered if it would damage her skirts to sit down there. She was trying to make up her mind about that when she noticed a dark hump behind one of the stacks that looked a little like it might not belong there.

She approached cautiously. It only took her a moment to see for certain that it was, indeed, something that did not belong there.

"Tolly!" she exclaimed. "Tolly, wake up. It's getting light!"

The young man sat up suddenly, pushing aside the horse blanket that had served as covering for him as he slept, and looked around as though thoroughly bewildered for a moment. But he regained his bearings after only a few seconds and jumped to his feet. "Miz Laureen, ya skeered me!"

"Never mind that, Tolly. I see you made good on your plan. I thought that's what you had in mind. Well, I told you it made no difference to me. I don't know how you accomplished it and I don't care to know. But if you stay here, you'll get caught and thrown off the boat." She looked at him with amusement and added, "Most likely they'll throw you off right into the river and let you swim for it. That is, if you can!"

"Ah ain' go'n' git caught, Miz Laureen. Ah med it 'dis fer an' Ah kin mek it de res' o' de way."

"No doubt, Tolly. I don't underestimate your ability to do what you set out to do. I just have one question. Did you leave that old mule standing there under the magnolia tree, hitched to the wagon? I asked you to take care of him."

"Ah got one o' de boys dat he'pt us wi'd de trunks to say he tek 'im to the blacksmif. He tek good kere o' 'im, Miz Laureen."

"Thank you, Tolly. I'm glad to know about that." She paused before turning back and asked, "I just wondered. How far do you plan to ride this boat? I suppose you'll leave the South altogether."

"Yes'm, Miz Laureen. Ah plans ta git ta Chicago. May tek a while, but thas whar' Ah'se headin'.'"

"Well, I hope you find what you're looking for. Goodbye, Tolly."

"Could this actually be happening?" wondered Laureen to herself. Was she actually conversing with a colored man, a former slave, as though he were more or less her equal? Was the world absolutely going crazy?

She shook her head as if to clear it. She told herself that what Tolly did or did not do made absolutely no difference to her. She whirled and started back the way she had come. She did not want to see what Tolly did next. Besides, she had come on deck to be alone.

She had taken only a few steps when she realized all hopes of being alone any longer were gone. Graham Talbert was also on the deck and strolling in her direction. She knew he had seen her, so there was no way to pretend she had not seen him and go another direction. Besides, if she played her cards right, she might be able to maneuver him into inviting her to have breakfast as his guest. If he would spend a little money on her, then she would welcome his presence.

Laureen knew enough of the way the world worked to know Graham Talbert would recognize her game right away if she tried to be coy with him. After all, she knew he had dealt with women much more sophisticated than she. She would have to let him lead if she had any hope of being successful. So she would treat him with dignity, without expecting anything from him and hope for the best. With that thought in mind, she looked directly at him without seeming especially happy to see him, and said as they met, "Good morning, Mr Talbert. Did you also hope to have a little time alone this morning before starting the day's activities?"

"Good morning to you also, Miss Wallace. I did not mean to intrude into your morning solitude. If you wish to be alone then please excuse me."

"I'm sorry, Mr. Talbert. I didn't mean to be rude." Laureen was thinking fast. This was not the way she had meant the conversation to start. "I just meant that people aren't stirring yet and I assumed that if you came up here this early, you might be trying to get away from people. For myself, I woke up early and thought I'd come up here where I wouldn't wake anyone." She almost added they were all sharing one stateroom, but thought better of it before speaking.

"I think there will be plenty of activity all around us very shortly. In fact I suspect the galley is already very busy, because they'll be serving breakfast in another half hour. Miss Wallace, would you do me the honor of having breakfast with me as my guest?"

Hoping her face would not betray her, Laureen exclaimed to herself, "He did it! Just what I hoped he'd do!" What she said was, "Why, Mr. Talbert, I'd be delighted to."

Laureen hoped he did not sense too great a change in her attitude toward him between the night before and the present. She wondered if she should say anything, but decided anything she said would merely call attention to the change, and that was the opposite of what she wanted to do. Better say nothing. If he thought anything about it, then she would simply let him try to determine why the change in her attitude.

"Since the dining room hasn't opened yet, what would you like to do in the meantime?" he inquired.

"Do we have to "do" anything? Can't we just stay here on the deck until it's time to eat?"

"Of course we can, if that's what you wish to do. I only thought you might be more comfortable where we could sit."

"Mr. Talbert, I sat a great deal of time yesterday, waiting for this boat to get to Natchez. I'm used to a great deal of activity these days and I am glad of the chance to do a little walking. Unless the deck starts to get crowded, would you mind if we just walk for a little while?"

"Why no. That sounds good to me, too."

They strolled along in silence for a minute or two then Graham Talbert asked, "Did the Union soldiers do much damage to Natchez when they went through? I haven't visited the city in several years. In fact the last time I stopped in that area was, I think, the time we met at the bar-b-que. I heard they went through there. On their way to Vicksburg, I believe."

"I don't think they did nearly as much damage in our area as they did in a lot of other places, especially Vicksburg. They mostly skirted the town and hurt some of the plantations out in the country."

"And Three Willows? Did they do damage to your place?"

Laureen was reluctant to have him know the full extent of the havoc wreaked on Three Willows, so she simply said, "We suffered some damage. They started a fire but we were able to put it out right away after they left, so it wasn't nearly as bad as they intended it to be. Only one building was affected. I think they were in too much of a hurry when they came by our place to be too destructive. They went north so I assume they were going to be part of the attack forces on Vicksburg. I think the main thing they wanted from us was livestock and grain."

"Yes, they've done a lot of looting and plundering everywhere they've gone. It's so sad, isn't it? So much destruction, and for nothing, really. They just seem to have it in their heads that they want to punish the South."

"I don't know if all Yankees are that wicked but I've come to hate them all. If I could, I'd kill every last one of them myself!" Laureen was getting excited as she spoke, forgetting that Graham Talbert was originally from the North. She caught herself. "Oh I'm sorry, Mr. Talbert. I didn't mean that! It's just that we've had to suffer so much at the hands of the Yankees and it's hard not to let myself be very bitter about it."

"I understand, Miss Wallace. You don't need to apologize to me! I don't hold with what's been happening to the southern people any more than you do. But the war is over now, and all we can do is to try to get on with our lives. The South can rebuild and I have no doubt that it will. Southern people have strong minds and lots of determination. I think, in the end, they'll come out of all this better than ever."

"I don't think it will be better for a long time to come, Mr. Talbert. I think it will take several generations for the South to recover. So many families have lost every thing they own, as well as a lot of their men folk. You don't get over that right away."

"No, of course you're right about that. But there are still a lot of determined people left. You can't keep people like that down for long."

Laureen thought, "You don't know how right you are about that. And I'm one of them. And if I can ever find a way to make even a few of the Yankees pay for what they've done to us, then that's exactly what I'll do. Starting with the one I'm talking to!"

But she said only, "I suppose you're right, Mr. Talbert." Then, she stopped walking and turned to him, saying, "You know something? I'm beginning to think about breakfast. I wonder if the dining room is open yet."

"Then why don't we find out?" was the quick response.

As they entered the dining room, they could see there were already a few people who had gathered there. While it was not quite time to begin serving, others were seating themselves at the tables, ready to order as soon as the waiters appeared. Laureen glanced around to take in her surroundings. This was even better than she had hoped for. Fine china and glassware had already been placed on the sparkling white damask table cloths. The good quality silver gleamed from its very recent polish. The floorboards were freshly scrubbed. Laureen felt a sense of satisfaction sweep over her. Suddenly she knew she was going to enjoy this excursion. She told herself she could very easily slip back into this former way of life, the kind of life she had grown up with. Possibly this man, or someone like him, would be the key to her having it again.

They found a table near one side of the dining room and sat down, waiting casually for a waiter to approach. As they waited the dining room began to fill up, at first only a trickle of people coming in, but soon the crowd grew to nearly filling up all the space in the room. Laureen had no idea there were so many people on board. When the waiter came to take their order, she asked how many passengers there were and the answer was about 250.

"So many!" she remarked. "I wouldn't have thought people would be traveling right now. I thought the war had left most people without that kind of money."

Mr. Talbert replied, "Well, Miss Wallace, you're traveling. I don't know why you're surprised that others are too."

At that moment Laureen saw Florence and the children enter the dining room. "I wonder if I'm in for a scolding now," thought Laureen. But she need not have worried. Florence glanced her way, saw who her companion was, and herded her children to the opposite side of the room.

Breakfast was ordered and served. The dining room was abuzz with various conversations and Laureen was finding she was enjoying herself immensely. She could not remember ever having been able to have this kind of male companionship. Her brother had always kept such a close eye on her activities until he went away to war, and since then there had been virtually no opportunities for such. She was amazed she could feel so relaxed. Not that she had forgotten for a moment the kind of man she was dealing with. She would not let down her guard.

They were almost finished with their meal when Laureen noticed Florence was engaged in conversation with a man of perhaps thirty five, someone Laureen had never seen before. She wondered who Florence had found on the boat that she already knew. Then again, perhaps this was a new acquaintance. Laureen had never thought of her sister-in-law in that light, that she might find someone new and remarry. As she thought about it she was not certain of how she felt. Her brother had been dead for over a year, so Laureen supposed it was possible Florence could be ready to make a new life for herself with another man.

"Stop it!" Laureen scolded herself. "Just because Flo is talking to a man, it doesn't mean she's ready to marry him!" Nevertheless she determined to find out who the man was, so she placed her napkin beside her plate and said aloud as she stood up, "Mr. Talbert, thank you so very much for the breakfast. And for the most pleasant company. I hope we will bump into one another some more on this trip. But I see my brother's family is about through with their meal and I may be of some assistance to my sister-in-law with her children."

Graham was on his feet immediately as he answered her. "Miss Wallace, thank you for joining me. I too hope we, as you put it, 'bump' into each other some more on this journey. Good day for now."

Laureen carefully eased her way among the tables to reach the one where Florence and her children sat. Laureen's curiosity was greatly aroused since she had seen the man with her family, sitting there in conversation as though he belonged there. As she approached the table she said, "Florence, I'm glad to see you looking so rested this morning. I woke up early and didn't want to wake anyone, so I went out on deck and ran into Mr. Talbert. He asked me to have breakfast with him. I was sure you wouldn't mind."

"No, of course not, Laurie. But I'd like you to meet someone, Mr. Roger Wainrich." As she started the introduction, Mr. Wainrich stood and faced Laureen.

Florence continued, "Roger, this is my sister-in-law, Laureen Wallace, Gerald's sister."

And to Laureen, "Roger is a distant relative of mine, second cousin three times removed or third cousin, twice removed, something like that. I could work it out, but we're both content just to let it go as being distant cousins. I haven't seen Roger since the day Gerald and I were married. He was at our ceremony. We used to be the best of friends, back when we were children."

Roger interrupted, "I would like to think that we're still friends."

"Yes of course we are. It's just that we haven't seen each other in so many years."

"Well you still look the same," he complimented her. "I always did think you were the prettiest girl of any I ever knew."

"Now aren't you the kind one?" Florence responded, blushing.

Compliments always made Florence a little uncomfortable.

Laureen felt the need to change the subject, so she asked, "What brings you on board the *Sultana*, Mr. Wainrich?"

"Oh I wanted a change of pace and I have some business that I could use as an excuse for traveling. I'm getting off at Memphis. Florence tells me you folks are going to Cairo and on to Zinnia's for an extended stay. I think that's a real nice thing to do, especially now with things are as they are in the South."

There was something very appealing in the manner of this man. Laureen thought, " Well, if Florence has 'set her cap' for him, then more power to her. He might be just what she needs." What Laureen did not see was the look on his face that should have told her he found her very attractive.

That look was not lost on Florence, however. She was quite aware of it although she felt no jealousy. To her Roger was merely a relative and an old friend. She was very glad to see him on the boat, as she sorely missed male companionship. Gerald had left the plantation so long ago and now dead for over a year. It was so good to have a man to talk to. However if Roger were interested in Laureen, then she would do what she could to promote that.

Roger had never married, although there were many young women who would have liked to attract his attention. He enjoyed the parties, the bar-b-ques, the dances, etc. But so far, he had never found a woman who made him think of marriage. As he watched Laureen, he thought that might be changing.

"Miss Wallace," he said. "Would you like to take a stroll on the deck with me?"

Surprised, Laureen looked at Florence, who smiled and shrugged.

"Why yes, I think I would like that," she answered.

"What's happening here?" she wondered to herself. "Did I read the signals wrong?" But she said nothing more as she started out the dining hall.

On the deck they walked for a short distance, then paused at the railing. The sun was getting high and the morning was beginning to get almost uncomfortably warm. A few clouds had gathered, but there were not enough of them to make anyone think it would rain. Hopefully, they would have clear sailing for the whole trip.

Laureen leaned against the rail looking down at the red muddy water rushing past them as the boat slowly made its way upriver. "Did you ever wonder where all this water comes from?" she asked. "You'd think that after a while it would have all run out to sea, wouldn't you? And yet, it just never stops. This muddy river running to the sea. I've watched the river from time to time all my life, sometimes when it's very low, and other times when it's flooding, like now. But, it's always muddy and always swift. When you look out over it from the bank it doesn't seem to be flowing so fast. But I've always known how swift and dangerous it is."

"I suppose I never thought much about it, Miss Wallace. It's always just there and, unless it floods and does a lot of damage, why, I think I never give it any thought at all."

"I've only traveled a few times on the river before. I don't like it much. I look down at all that water rushing by beneath the boat and it gives me an uneasy feeling. Oh I think it's safe enough. We don't hear of boats sinking very often. And this boat is only a couple of years old, so I'm not worried about it. All the same I wouldn't want to find myself out in the middle of this river trying to swim."

"Well Miss Wallace, I must say you seem to be in a rather dark mood this morning."

"Oh, Mr. Wainrich, don't pay any attention to me. I just get to feeling a little 'down' once in a while. It really doesn't mean anything."

"Miss Wallace, if I have anything to say about it, you won't be feeling 'down' any more for the rest of this trip, or at least as far as Memphis where I get off the boat. And with your permission, I'd like to write to you after you get to John and Zinnia's house. Would that be all right with you?"

"Why, Mr. Wainrich, I'd be highly complimented if you would."

"Let's continue our stroll, shall we?"

As they continued on their walk, Laureen's thoughts centered on this handsome, blonde man beside her. He was a little over six feet tall and had the sweetest smile, if a little crooked, that she thought she had ever seen. He was tanned and rather muscular. She could not help but think of Tolly, with his rippling muscles she had so admired when he had his shirt off. How much like that did Mr. Wainrich look?

Much of the morning passed in such a delightfully pleasant way. Laureen did not think it strange that she did not see Florence or any of the children during that time. Actually Laureen gave no thought to any of the other Wallace family members. She was enjoying herself in a way that she could not ever remember doing before. Mr. Wainrich was proving to be very attentive and she was enjoying every minute of it.

But eventually, she thought she should go back to her cabin, feeling the need to freshen up some. When she said "Good morning." to Mr. Wainrich, it was with some reluctance. And there was obvious reluctance on his face, as well. They agreed to meet in the dining hall at noon. He did not walk her to her door

As she was descending the stairs to go back to her cabin, she realized someone was trying to get her attention. It was Tolly. He was concealing himself behind some large ropes near the stairway. He furtively motioned to her to join him. As she started to say, "Tolly! What in the world do you want?" he put his finger over his mouth to let her know he wanted her to keep her voice down.

When she got closer to him, he said, "Miz Laureen, Ah needs ya' he'p. Will ya he'p me?"

"Tolly, you just have to leave me alone now. You're going on your way whatever way that is. You're not a slave at Three Willows any longer. No one owns you now. If you're going to live the life of a free man, then do it and leave me alone!"

"No'm, Miz Laureen. Ah needs yo' he'p. An' Ah t'ink ya' c'u'd use mine right now."

CHAPTER 10

"I don't think there's anything you can do to help me, Tolly. And, I don't know that I feel inclined to help you." Then, with an exasperated sigh, she said, "All right. What is it that you want me to do?"

Tolly looked around to make sure no one was on deck, then pulled out of his pants pocket the most beautiful diamond necklace that Laureen had ever seen.

"Tolly! Where in the world did you get that?" she cried as she grabbed it out of his hand. "This is very valuable!"

"Well, Miz Laureen, Ah see'd it jes' lyin' der and it di'n't seem b'long to nobody, so I jes' picked it up."

"Tolly, that's crazy. You know that a necklace like that has to belong to somebody. Who did you steal it from?" As she spoke, Laureen examined the necklace, marveling at the way it sparkled and began to get an idea where that necklace came from. But she wanted Tolly to tell her. "Now you tell me right now, Tolly. Where did you get it?"

"Well, lak Ah sed, Miz Laureen, it wuz jes' lyin' dere an...."

"Stop that this instant, Tolly. You and I both know that no one would leave a necklace like that lying around in plain view. You stole it and I want to know where you got it. Now tell me!"

Tolly dropped his head. "Yes'm. Ah be'n keepin' ma eyes out fer sumpin' to git me started up no'th. Yestiddy Ah seed dat gent'man ya' wuz ta'kin' to yestiddy showin' it to dat one ya wuz ta'kin' ta taday, den he put it bek in 'is pocket. Well, Ah jes' followed 'im 'round, hopin' he'd drop it. An' 'e did. Ah picked it up."

Before he could say more, Laureen interrupted him. "Tolly, do you really think I'm such a fool as to think Mr. Talbert would be so careless as to let a necklace that valuable just fall out of his pocket? Now I want to know how you got it. The truth this time, Tolly."

"Well Ah guess de trut' is, Miz Laureen, dat Ah sort of he'ped m'sef to it in de night, las' night. Ah t'ink Ah need it more'n he do."

Laureen's mind was whirling. Why would Mr. Talbert have an expensive woman's necklace on a trip like this? Didn't he have a reputation for stealing jewelry? Jewelry that was never seen again by its rightful owner. So in all likelihood, this was a case of a thief becoming the victim of a theft. Well maybe it served him right. But why was Tolly involving her in this? She was about to find out.

"Do you mean you slipped into Mr. Talbert's stateroom and stole it?" she cried, horrified. "How did you get the door open? What if he heard you and woke up? Don't you know you could've even been killed. A man like that doesn't get where he is in life by being gentle and kind."

"Lock' do's is easy ta open when ya' knows how. An' Ah di'n' make no noise. An', Miz Laureen, Ah'se figger'd he done stole it in de firs' place, so he di'n't hev no mo' right to it dan me."

"Well, Tolly, now that you have it, what do you intend to do with it? If you get caught with it, they'll hang you. Or drown you, since we're on the river. I don't know which. And, even if you don't get caught, you can't sell it. No darkie has anything like that, and anyone who sees you with it will know right away you stole it."

"Ah don' wan' tek no chances on gittin' caught. Tha's why Ah need ya' he'p, Miz Laureen. '

"My help! What can I do to help you?"

"Ah wuz hopin' dat ya'd keep it fo' me fer a while. Jes' 'til no one's lookin' fo' it no mo'. No one would t'ink dat ya might hev it."

"Even if I agree to do that, Tolly, you can't ever do anything with it. Like I said, you can't ever sell it."

"Miz Laureen, if'n Ah git up no'th, in de big city, Ah t'ink Ah kin sell it. Ah'se wantin' to try."

Again Laureen's thoughts were racing. And not all her thoughts at this point were unselfish. She was wondering if there might be some way she could have that necklace for herself. The sale of such a bauble would give her enough money to make a good start toward making a life for herself on her own. Tolly must not have thought of that, or he would not have asked her to keep it. Or perhaps he had, but could see no other way to escape severe punishment if he were detected. If he were found on the boat, he would be a certain suspect. In any case, there was the necklace for the taking and she would not lose such an opportunity.

"All right, Tolly. I'll keep it," she said as she continued to admire the beauty of it. She had never owned anything remotely so lovely. She added, " No one except you will know I have it. But I don't know how I can hope to get it back to you without at least one of us being detected. You may or may not know that Mr. Talbert is heading North too. So he'll be on the boat about as long as you are."

"Well, den Ah thinks ma'be Ah gits off whar yo' does. Ah kin git on anudder boat ta keep goin' no'th."

Laureen's heart sank. That might work. She wondered, though, how they could manage such a transfer with Florence and her children present. As far as Laureen knew, Florence had no idea Tolly was on board the boat.

"We can't stand here any longer talking, Tolly. Someone is bound to see us. I need to go and put this in a safe place, anyway." Laureen had already decided the only safe place for it was on her person. She turned once again to make certain no one had come close enough to see what was going on and when she turned back to give some final instruction to Tolly, he had disappeared.

"Fine," she thought. "It's better this way." She thought perhaps the best place to conceal the necklace was to wear it around her neck. After all, the high neckline of her dress would conceal it quite completely. But then there was the problem of getting undressed at night in the room with four other people. It would be difficult to keep her secret that way. As she thought about where to keep it, she decided that the only safe place would be on her shimmy. She would find a way to sew it to it where it would be safe. She could make a pocket and sew it shut. It would not be difficult to get the privacy she needed to do that. All she had to do was express her need to be alone for a few minutes and the rest of the family would respect that. In the meantime she dropped the necklace down inside the neck of her dress, not exactly certain where it would land, but knowing that waistline of her dress fitted quite snugly and it could go no further than there. Besides she wore so many underclothes that it was bound to get caught somewhere. She would walk slowly and carefully back to her stateroom.

As she entered the saloon, Mr. Talbert came rushing out of his stateroom, which was about two doors down from the Wallace's. Laureen gave a start, then regained her composure so quickly that a casual observer would not have realized she had been startled. Mr. Talbert did not see Laureen and was about to rush past her, when she spoke, nothing in her voice betraying she suspected he had just discovered the diamond necklace was missing.

"Why, Mr. Talbert," she said in her soft Mississippi drawl. "I was just wondering where you had been keeping yourself this morning. I haven't seen you anywhere since breakfast."

Mr. Talbert stopped short, swearing under his breath. He did not bother to try to conceal the irritation he felt at her attempt to distract him. "Miss Wallace, I have something to do at this moment that is rather pressing. Please excuse me.

Laureen smiled to herself. She wondered if he were going to see Mr. Wainrich. Tolly did say he only knew about the necklace because he had seen Mr. Talbert showing it to Mr. Wainrich. Laureen's smile began to fade. How could Mr. Wainrich be mixed up in this? If he had a reputation for receiving stolen goods or for being mixed up in illegal activities, wouldn't Florence know about it? And if Florence knew about it, wouldn't she have said something to Laureen? She surely would not have appeared to encourage Laureen to get to know him. This was most confusing!

"Never mind," she told herself. "I have the necklace and only Tolly knows that. I intend to keep it that way and I intend to keep it for myself. Somehow."

She knocked at her stateroom door, on the outside chance a member of the family might be inside and in need of privacy. No one answered so she slipped her key in the door and let herself in, locking the door behind her. She went straight away to a small bag she had pushed under her bed and pulled out a small sewing kit she had put together for the trip. Before taking a needle and thread, she opened the buttons of her dress carefully, pulling the necklace away from her waist, where it had rested since she dropped it down the front of her dress. Taking no chances someone might come into the room and catch her with the necklace, she slipped it into the sewing kit. Next she eased out of all the rest of her clothes right down to her shimmy. She looked down at the folds of that last garment, trying to think where best to make a pocket for the necklace. The necklace was a little on the heavy side and she asked herself if the material in her shimmy were strong enough to hold it. She decided it was not.

Then she remembered Florence had packed a length of muslin in one of her small trunks, and wondered how hard it would be to find it. She had no idea how much time she might have before some of the family might come back to the stateroom, so she hurriedly opened the first trunk she came to. A quick search turned up no muslin. She turned to the next one. She lifted up several things, trying not to disturb anything. Her hand felt something that could be it, and sure enough, it was neatly folded and resting almost on the bottom of the trunk.

Laureen very carefully pulled it away from the other things, and lifted it out of the trunk. As she was re- fastening the trunk, she heard someone at the door of the cabin. "Who is it?" she called.

"It's Florence, Laureen. I'd like to come in if you don't mind."

"Of course, Flo. I thought it might be Gerald and I'm not dressed." Laureen quickly put the length of muslin under her bed pillow and almost in the same move, grabbed an inside seam of her shimmy and ripped it. As Florence entered the room Laureen said, "I thought I heard something ripping when I was on deck and decided I'd better check it out. I thought it must be a petticoat, but I couldn't find anything on them. I can't imagine how I could have ripped a seam in my shimmy. But I thought that as long as I've stripped down this far, I might as well sew it up before the rip gets any bigger. By the way, I haven't seen you or the children since breakfast. What have you been doing with yourself?"

"Oh, we met some interesting passengers on the boat and we've been visiting with them. There's a family of four that are going to Memphis whom we found to be quite friendly. There is a boy about Gerald's age and a little girl of eight. Very well behaved children."

"I see," replied Laureen. She was wondering how long Florence intended to stay in the stateroom. "Where are the children now?" she asked. "Is it safe to leave Adelle by herself?"

Florence bristled. "Adelle is not by herself," she shot back. "She's with Gerald and Dora and they're with the family I just told you about. I came in here to get something and I'm going right back to them. I thank you for your concern, Laureen. And it's just occurred to me that I haven't seen you all morning, either. So I might ask you the same question, what have you been doing with yourself?" There was a sharp edge in her voice.

"Well if you must know, I spent a good part of the morning with the man you introduced me to, Mr. Wainrich." Laureen thought it might be a good idea to try to soften the roughness between them, and added, "By the way, Flo, what do you know about him. Is he a gentlemen?"

"Why, Laureen! What do you mean?" she exclaimed. "Did he do something that he shouldn't have?" Laureen's ploy was working. Florence's momentary irritation was being overshadowed by this veiled suggestion.

"No, Flo, he didn't do anything out of the way," she replied reassuringly. "Only I was thinking I never heard you mention him before and it occurred to me to wonder what kind of a man he is. What can you tell me about him. I find him very attractive."

Florence seemed lost in thought for a moment then slowly admitted, "I never really knew him very well. He visited our house from time to time when I was growing up. He's such a distant relative and we might have courted, but I don't think either of us ever even thought about that. Then too, almost by the time I was old enough to be courted, why your brother showed up and I wasn't interested in anyone else after that."

"I don't suppose you know if he's ever been married."

"I can't say for certain, but I never heard of it if he was."

"Do you know how old he is?"

"Oh I think he's a year or so older than I am so that would put him in his mid-thirty's, wouldn't it?"

"I see," was the only response Laureen gave. She was hoping Florence would leave the room so she could get back to her sewing project. She looked down at the rip and glanced at her sewing kit.

After only a moment Florence spoke, "Well, I must get back to the children. I'll see you after a while." Then as kind of an afterthought, she said as she was going out the door, "I don't know if it means anything, but I heard someone say that there's a problem with one of the boilers on the boat. I think they said it's going to have to be fixed when we get to Vicksburg. That could mean that we'll be on this boat a little longer than we thought"

Laureen barely heard her. Her thoughts were focused on the necklace and how to hide it. As soon as Florence was out the door, Laureen locked it once again. She pulled the muslin from under the pillow and unfolded it, trying to think how to best use it. Finally she concluded the safest thing she could do would be to make a kind of apron of it and sew it closed around her waist. She decided not to sew the large pocket she made for it closed, but made a deep flap for it instead. That way she could get her hand inside and feel the necklace once in a while when she was in bed.

It took her several minutes to cut and sew the apron then fit it to her waist, but when she had finished she was quite pleased with the result. The muslin was strong and the seams were well done. The apron would not show at her waist, and the necklace rested at the bottom of the deep pocket in front, so it would not be discerned under all her petticoats and dress. Especially was this so since the top petticoat had hoops in it, thus keeping her skirt billowing out from her hips and legs. All in all she felt quite pleased with herself.

When she had finished she folded the remaining portion of the muslin and put it with her own things. If Florence missed it she would think of something to tell her, but she did not want to take any more time putting things back where she found them. It would not do to have anyone wonder what she was doing in her stateroom so long.

CHAPTER 11

Laureen dressed quickly, one glance in the mirror telling her there were no telltale signs of what she had hidden under her clothes. She told herself her demeanor must not give away her secret. She must act exactly the same way she had before Tolly gave her the necklace. That was going to be a very difficult thing to do, but she had already taken the necessary steps to protect the necklace and now she had to trust those steps were adequate. If they were not, then she could comfort herself she had tried. Even if it should come to light she had the necklace, she was certain she could think of something to keep herself out of trouble, even if it did not save the necklace for her. So it was back on deck for her and she would face what was ahead.

People were milling around idly on deck. Laureen wondered where Florence was, but was not especially interested in finding her. She strolled casually toward the stern of the boat with no particular destination in mind. She thought about going topside. She had not been there yet and thought she might as well see all the boat while she was on it. As she reached the stairway going up she met the first mate, Mr. Rowberry, on his way down.

He had noticed Laureen as soon as he saw her getting on the boat the day before. He supposed every man on the boat, whether part of the crew or simply a passenger had noticed her as well. With the kind of beauty Laureen had she could not remain unnoticed for long.

He spoke to her. "Miss Wallace, isn't it?"

"Why yes," she replied, a little surprised at being recognized by this stranger. "Do I know you?"

"There's no reason why you should," he answered. "I'm William

Rowberry, the first mate on this boat."

"Then I'm very happy to make your acquaintance, Mr. Rowberry," Laureen replied.

"I hope you're enjoying your journey thus far," he was quick to respond, a little too much eagerness showing on his face.

"Yes I am, thank you." Laureen was becoming amused at this man's obvious nervousness and slight discomfort. She had encountered this before and it always amused her, as well as pleased her. She was not completely without vanity. "As long as we've met, Mr. Rowberry, perhaps I could ask you a question."

"Certainly."

"I'm a little curious as to how many passengers are on the boat this trip. I was told in the dining hall this morning there are about 250. Is that correct?"

"Well, let's see, Miss. I think that sounds about right and then there are about 85 members of the crew, so, doing just a little bit of quick arithmetic, I guess that means there are about 335 people altogether. Most of the cabins are in use, and there are a few deck passengers.

"That many," said the surprised Laureen. "I didn't realize there were quite that many. How many does this boat carry when it's full?"

"We have a capacity of 376 passengers, including the crew. We've never had that many people on board at one time, but I hear we're about to. More, too"

"Oh?" she questioned. "On this trip?

"Yes, Miss. I hear tell we're supposed to get a whole bunch of Union soldiers boarding at Vicksburg."

"Yankees!" cried Laureen, feeling frightened. "What are Yankee soldiers doing on this boat? I thought the war was over!" Laureen was horrified. She had hoped to never see another Yankee soldier in her life, and now she was hearing that she was about to have to share the boat with a whole crowd of them. Had they not heard that the war was over? Were they going to take the southern passengers on the boat prisoners? Life certainly was not fair.

"Yes, Miss," answered Mr. Rowberry. "The war is over, all right. It's just that a lot of the Union soldiers have been prisoners in a couple of places not so terribly far from the River and they need to go home. There's the Andersonville prison in Georgia and Cahaba in Alabama. They're transporting them to Vicksburg to send them home.

"But why on the *Sultana*?" This was such distressing news to Laureen. "They'll be sick and dirty and vermin infested and we don't need them on this boat!" she exclaimed.

"I understand how you feel, Miss," cajoled the first mate. "But the captain is determined to take them on board, and there's just nothing to be done about it. My suggestion to you is to go into your stateroom and stay there when they come on board."

"Then how would you suggest that I get anything to eat on the rest of the trip if I do that?" she retorted.

"You do have a point," he answered. "I'm afraid I don't have any other suggestions. Unless you want to get off the boat and wait for another one to take you on the rest of your trip. You might think about doing that."

"There are five of us traveling together and I don't think we can afford to buy tickets for all of us on another boat. So I guess we're just stuck with what we have. But I want you to tell Captain Mason that we don't like it one bit."

"I'll be happy to pass on your complaint, Miss Wallace, but I don't think it will make any difference. The captain is very determined to take on those soldiers. I think he's getting paid pretty good to do it and he wants the money."

"I see," she said, accepting defeat.

"Well, Miss Wallace, it was nice talking to you. I have work I must do but I hope we run into each other again before you have to leave the boat. Good day." And he was gone.

Laureen sat down on the bottom step to digest what she had learned from the first mate. If the boat could carry only 376 passengers and there were already about 335 on the boat, then that left room for only 41 soldiers. But, hadn't Mr. Rowberry just said that there were to be a lot more than the boat was supposed to carry? She wondered how many more that would mean. Laureen felt like crying. This news was so distressing to her. But crying would do nothing except make her eyes swell and her face look bad. She must make the best of whatever came her way. She stood up resolutely. She thought she probably should find Florence and tell her what she had learned. Then she thought better of it. Why should she tell Florence? There was nothing Florence could co about it.

Besides, Florence did not completely share her hatred for Yankees. She was ready to put the war behind her and try to go on with life. But Laureen nursed her hatred, not realizing that she was only upsetting herself and in no way getting any kind of revenge on the Yankees. As her hands rested in her lap, she felt the necklace through the layers of fabric and was reminded of the treasure she had momentarily forgotten.

Suddenly she brightened. It occurred to her that if the captain were getting money by transporting Union soldiers, then perhaps there might be some way she could profit from all that, too. At the moment she could not imagine any way to make that possible, but she would give it her full attention for the next several hours and perhaps something would come to her. She might make it work. There had to be a way to take advantage of those Yankees.

She had not seen them and had no idea of the pitiful condition that most of them were in. Military prison camps were totally beyond her field of experience. She knew nothing of the dreadful condition of those camps, both those in the North as well as those in the South, and that for so many of the prisoners who found themselves in such camps how they became nothing more than death camps. She could not know there was not enough food or blankets or shelter, let alone enough medicine and the other necessities she had taken for granted in her own life. She was thinking only of some way to make those Yankees pay for what they had done to the South in general and Three Willows in particular.

She sat where she was for a little while longer, pondering this new idea. She was so lost in her own thoughts and did not at first notice the two men who had come to stand behind the stair, engaged in an intense conversation. One was the captain of the boat, Captain Mason. She did not know the identity of the other man but she soon learned his name, Nathan Wintringer, then later learned he was the chief engineer. The two men were completely absorbed in what they were saying and did not see Laureen sitting on the stair..

As soon as she became aware of the presence of the two men, Laureen's first thought was to make herself known to them. But since they were so completely oblivious to her, she decided to keep still and see what she might learn from them. Her natural curiosity made her

114

wonder what they could be talking about that would have them in such a huddle. She heard Mr. Wintringer say, "But, Captain, this is serious. We can't expect to get to Cairo with that boiler the way it is. You have to listen to me."

Captain Mason responded, "Mr. Wintringer, I don't have time for that kind of thing right now. I'm supposed to take on a load of Union ex-prisoners bound for Cairo, and I aim to get there in time to take them aboard. If I don't get them, they'll be put on another boat and I can't afford to lose the fares. I've had that boiler repaired and it should last as long as I need it to."

"No, Captain Mason, that's just the point. It won't last. You have to get it fixed, and the sooner the better."

"I think, Mr. Wintringer, you are just being an alarmist! The boiler can't possibly be as dangerous as you say it is. I told you, I've already had it repaired."

"Captain Mason, I don't care if you've had it repaired a dozen times, or if it's brand new. That boiler is dangerous. It needs to be shut down right now. You haven't looked at it but I have and I know what I'm talking about. It has a leak in one of the seams. We have to get it fixed and we have to do it now. If you aren't willing to do it then I'm leaving the boat immediately."

Laureen was alarmed. A boiler unsafe? On the *Sultana*? Such a possibility had never even occurred to her before. She knew there were four boilers on the boat. She had watched them work when she had been walking around on the boat soon after the Wallaces boarded it the day before. So if they lost one boiler would they not still have three left? At the worst that would only mean they would travel a little slower. So then, why was Mr. Wintringer making such a fuss about getting it repaired?

But the captains reaction to that threat was quite surprising. "Mr. Wintringer, I'd like very much for you to stay with the boat. I need your help. I'll tell you what. You stay on the boat and I give you my word that when we get to Vicksburg we'll get the boiler fixed. Will that satisfy you?"

"Not entirely, Captain. That boiler needs to be shut down now and repaired and we're almost 10 hours away from Vicksburg. But I guess that will have to do. That is, if your word includes doing it right. We'll have to find a boiler maker. I hear there's a good one in Vicksburg. His name is R. G. Taylor. You'll allow me to find him and bring him on board for an inspection of the boilers, all of them, and to make whatever repairs he deems necessary? Say so now, because if you don't, I'm leaving the boat as soon as we reach Vicksburg."

"Yes, yes, of course," replied Captain Mason, knowing he had no intention of keeping that promise. He had every intention of losing no more time than was absolutely necessary at Vicksburg. He had pressing matters of a different nature there and that boiler was not high on his list of priorities.

The two men turned and each went in a different direction, leaving Laureen to wonder what it all meant. She supposed, at the worst, it would mean that they would be delayed at Vicksburg. Now there were two things that might cause them delay. Laureen sighed. She supposed that they were not in any great hurry, so what could it matter if it took a few more hours to reach their destination? She might use the extra time to get better acquainted with Roger Wainrich.

But there was one thing that bothered her about that man. Tolly had told her he had seen Graham Talbert showing Roger Wainrich the diamond necklace she now had in her possession. Why would he have done that? She had no doubt Mr. Talbert had stolen the necklace. Possibly in New Orleans. Why was he showing it to Mr. Wainrich? Was Mr. Wainrich a man who would knowingly buy stolen property? That was a possibility she had to consider. After all, Mr. Wainrich did say he was going to Memphis on business. What kind of business? Why had she not asked him that question? Certainly it was a logical one.

And as she thought of Tolly, she wondered where he was. How was he keeping out of sight since there were so many people on the boat? She knew no one would likely recognize him, even if they saw him. Suddenly it occurred to her he must be letting people think he was a white passenger on the boat. He could get away with that, if he did not let anyone engage him in conversation. But that would be extremely difficult to do, since the passengers were a friendly sort and most were keenly interested in why everyone else was on the boat.

Laureen did not have to wait long to have that question answered. She left the stairway and eased her way over near the rail, forgetting her original intention of going topside. She slowly walked toward the bow of the boat, enjoying the fresh morning air. She wanted some time to observe the passengers without having herself observed. How little she knew that she was rarely unobserved. Her beauty was too striking for people not to notice her. Nevertheless, she stood with her back to the rail and looked around at the activity going on near her. She watched the little groups of people engaging in conversations, laughing at some silly joke, getting serious at times. Children were playing hide and seek and other things children always find to do to amuse themselves.

All at once she realized she was looking at Tolly! He was standing near the far side of the deck from her, with a small group of men. At first Laureen was horrified! What was he doing? They would have to know he was not a white man. But as she watched, almost stunned,

117

she concluded he was "passing" himself off to them as a white man, and seemingly with complete success. He was pretending to be unable to talk. He was making all sorts of gestures with his hands, and the men he was "talking" to seemed to be able to understand him. So that was it. Well she always knew Tolly was smart. And he had come up with a way to conceal his background that she would never have thought of.

Laureen almost laughed out loud. She wondered if he could keep it up for the whole trip. Tolly may not have thought about the fact there were very few people around with that kind of handicap and that the people on the boat would soon be talking about "that man who can't talk." He would attract quite a bit of attention to himself with this stunt.

Another thing Laureen wondered about concerning Tolly: Where had he gotten the clothes he was wearing? Those were not the clothes he wore at Three Willows. But then, there was something familiar about those clothes. It had been so long since she had seen them on Gerald, but it dawned on her Tolly was wearing her late brother's clothes. That put another question into her mind. How had he gotten them out of the house and when? Florence kept a pretty close eye on everything, and yet she had not mentioned that any of Gerald's clothes were missing. It was becoming apparent to Laureen she had greatly underestimated Tolly. She would not make that mistake again.

CHAPTER 12

Mr. Talbert had watched Laureen as she walked to the rail and stood against it. He could see that she was watching someone rather intently, but he didn't realize she hadn't see him. She started as he spoke. "Excuse me, Miss Wallace," he began. "I thought you saw me approaching, but obviously you did not, since you look so surprised to see me."

"No, Mr. Talbert, I didn't see you coming. I had my mind on something else and didn't notice. And speaking of not noticing, I saw you a little while ago as you were coming out of your stateroom. You seemed very distracted. Is everything all right with you now?"

"Wha'?" he said, taken off guard for a moment. He had meant to question her about what she found so amusing in watching some of the other passengers. He had noticed the smiles dancing on her face as she watched Tolly talking with the other men, and wondered what she saw that she found so humorous, since he could not determine just what or whom she was seeing. But he was not quick enough to question her about it before she mentioned his earlier distraction on coming out of his stateroom. All thought of asking her about that was immediately wiped from his mind. "Oh yes," as he caught himself quickly. "I thought I had misplaced something important. But I do remember seeing you. I'm sorry if I failed to speak. Such a beautiful woman as yourself should never be ignored." This last comment was made with a bold twinkle in his eye, a twinkle not lost on Laureen.

Laureen asked, "I take it you found what was misplaced?"

Mr. Talbert looked at her intently. He normally could read women easily, finding most of them very naive and gullible. This one was different. She seemed to be mocking him, even flirting with him.

119

There was something he could not quite fathom going on behind those tantalizingly expressive eyes of hers. He could not imagine she knew about the necklace as he had not spoken to anyone on the boat about it except Mr. Wainrich. He recognized immediately she was toying with him. But why? Oh, well. He might as well amuse himself with her. That would easily cover his intense watchfulness of all the passengers to see who among them might be acting suspiciously. Someone had his necklace and he intended to find that someone and transfer it to his possession again. Even if he had to hurt someone in the process.

Mr. Talbert was not normally a violent man, but this necklace was valuable enough to make him become so if the situation called for it. And at this moment, he was in no mood to negotiate. As soon as he learned where the necklace was, then he would use whatever means were called for to retrieve it and do so immediately.

He studied Laureen's face for a few seconds, then replied to her, "I hadn't misplaced anything at all. I only thought I did. Just some papers I need in a business deal I'm working on. But they turned up right where I'd left them. Funny thing about me. Sometimes I can look right at something and not see it."

"What kind of business are you in, Mr. Talbert?"

"Why, Miss Wallace. I didn't know your cared!" His voice was at once flirtatious, combined with a little bit of sarcasm in it.

"Mr. Talbert, I'm always interested in people. I find them very interesting. I enjoy learning about them, knowing what they do, how their lives turn out and trying to figure out if their lives might have been different if they had done certain things differently from what they did, and why?"

"Well, aren't you the complex little lady?" He was laughing at her again, not even trying to conceal it from her.

But Laureen felt that she had the upper hand in this little game. After all, she knew where the necklace was and Mr. Talbert did not. Oh he was a cool one, all right. No wonder he was so successful at what he did. She thought he must not lose too many items the way he had lost that necklace. And Mr. Talbert had still not told her what kind of business he was in. That fact was not at all lost on Laureen. She decided it might be better to let the matter drop.

"Did you know this boat is going to be delayed for a little while in Vicksburg?" she asked, easily changing the subject. "I heard the captain and Mr. Wintringer talking about it a little while ago?"

"Mr. Wintringer? I believe he's the chief engineer, isn't he? What's the delay all about?"

"I heard Mr. Wintringer telling the captain one of the boilers has a leak in it and that we can't go on until it's repaired. The captain was rather impatient about it all, but Mr. Wintringer was insistent that it has to be repaired right away, so the captain said they would get it done in Vicksburg. He seemed quite reluctant about it, though. I have no idea how long it will take, but I would assume it will mean at least some delay, wouldn't you?"

"Hmm," was the only response Mr. Talbert made to that bit of news. After several seconds he added, "I'm not quite certain in my own mind whether it was good news or bad news. I really do need to review those papers I mentioned and this might give me just the time I need."

He remained silent for some bit, until Laureen began to be uncomfortable. "Mr. Talbert?" she said.

"What? Oh, I'm sorry. I was just thinking that if we're going to be spending extra time in Vicksburg, then there might also be enough time for me to look up an old friend there. Someone I haven't seen for a long time. Perhaps I'll speak to the captain about that. In fact, I think I'll do that now. He should have some idea of how long the delay will be. Would you excuse me, Miss Wallace? I'm sure we'll see each other in the dining room in a little while."

"Of course."

Laureen decided she had spent enough time standing against the rail and she began to stroll along the deck, nodding to the passengers she met who were also out for a walk. The sun was warm, the cloudless sky such a deep blue, and it felt good to her to look out across the muddy water so full of red silt to the distant bank slipping by. Now and then through a break in the trees she would see someone walking behind a plow pulled by a mule and know he was getting ready to plant his crop. Occasionally there would be a small cluster of houses in the distance. But mostly what she saw were huge trees in full green foliage lining the banks of the mighty river. They grew so close together, appearing to be an impenetrable wall rising from the river banks. As she watched them slowly passing by, Laureen shuddered, a feeling of foreboding washing over her like an unexpected flash flood. She turned her head away from the bank and concentrated on where she was walking and the people she was meeting.

She began to wonder where the rest of her family were, as she felt she would surely see at least the older children on deck. Even Tolly had vanished from view during the time she was talking to Mr. Talbert. Eventually she began to feel hunger pains gnawing at her stomach . It must be time for the noon meal.

As she stood in the doorway of the dining hall, she looked around for a familiar face. Her glance fell upon Florence and the children, along with Mr. Wainrich, all seated at a table near the far wall. Almost at the same time, Mr. Wainrich glanced up and caught her eye. He motioned for her to join them, which she was all too happy to do. As she approached the table, he stood and pulled a chair from the table to help her be seated.

"Miss Wallace, I was hoping that you'd be joining us for dinner," he said. "I don't know how I've missed seeing you all morning."

"I don't know, either, Mr. Wainrich. I was in our stateroom for a short time mending a rip in my garment, but, mostly, I've been wandering around on the deck. And speaking of that, I've learned something that might interest you. Actually, two things."

Florence broke in. "I hope what you plan to tell is something the children will enjoy hearing." Her meaning was not lost on Laureen.

"I don't know if they will enjoy hearing what I learned, but I can assure you what I heard is not something tender ears shouldn't hear."

Florence relaxed visibly. Laureen wondered why Florence might think she would tell something that might be inappropriate conversation in the presence of young people. Did she think that little bit of association with Mr. Talbert had corrupted her already?

"What did you hear this morning, Miss Wallace?" asked Mr. Wainrich. "If you think we will find it interesting, then I'm certain we shall. Please tell. You said two things?"

"Yes and I don't know which is the more important of the two. The first thing I heard was that we will be taking on a lot more passengers at Vicksburg. All Yankees!" She fairly spat out that last word.

"I don't understand," replied Florence. "As I understand it, we still have room for quite a few more people on board and I would think that some of those on board now will be getting off at Vicksburg. How many more are you talking about?"

"Mr. Rowberry didn't say exactly how many, but…"

Florence interrupted. "Who's Mr. Rowberry?" she asked.

"He's the first mate on the boat."

"How in the world did you happen to meet him?" Florence questioned.

"'Happened' is the right word, Florence. It was purely by chance this morning that I bumped into him. Anyway, he recognized me and we started talking. In the course of the conversation, he told me we are taking on a lot of Yankee soldiers at Vicksburg. A lot more than the boat is legally supposed to carry."

"I don't understand," murmured Mr. Wainrich.

"Well, I don't really understand, either," added Laureen. "But Mr. Rowberry said that since the war is over, all the Yankee soldiers who have been in prison camps are being sent home. He mentioned Andersonville and Cahaba prisons that are being emptied and all the prisoners being sent back North."

"And," persisted Mr. Wainrich, "are you saying we are taking on board this boat all the prisoners from both those camps?" His voice sounded very worried.

"Mr. Rowberry didn't say we're going to have *all* those prisoners on this boat. What he said was that we are supposed to have only 376 passengers on board, including the crew, but we'll have a lot more than that when those prisoners come aboard. Disgusting, isn't it?"

"I wonder where they'll all sleep," mused Florence.

"I wonder if the boat can safely carry so many passengers," said Mr. Wainrich. "After all, there must be a reason why there is supposed to be a limit of 376 people." He turned to face Laureen directly and asked, "Are you certain that was the figure Mr. Rowberry said? 376?"

"Yes, Mr Wainrich. He definitely said 376. I know I'm not mistaken about that. And I got the impression he thought there might be a lot more than that when all those Yankees come aboard. I suppose there could be 500 or more, the way he talked."

"Well surely the captain must know what he's doing. He wouldn't take on more people than he thinks we can safely carry." This comment was from Gerald, who had been quietly sitting, listening to the grownups talk. He had been taught to never interrupt adult conversation but he was rapidly approaching adulthood himself and he knew it. He felt he could add his thoughts without being disrespectful in this instance.

No one chided him. In fact this reassuring comment was welcomed by all of them. They did not like to entertain the thought they could be in danger in such a short time.

Mr. Wainrich said, "I'm sure you're quite right Gerald. After all, the captain is aboard this boat too, and he doesn't want anything dangerous on his boat." Then, turning back to Laureen, he said, "Miss Wallace, I believe you said there were two things you had heard that might interest us. What was the other thing?"

"Oh yes. I heard Mr. Wintringer tell Captain Mason there is a leak in one of the boilers on the boat. He seemed most concerned about it, although Captain Mason didn't think it was so important. But Mr Wintringer was ready to leave the boat over it."

Again Florence broke in with a question. "Wait a minute, Laurie, who is Mr. Wintringer?"

"Mr. Wrintringer is the chief engineer."

"And did you just chance to meet him, too? How is it you're meeting all these people on this boat?"

"I didn't meet him, Florence."

She was about to explain but Florence cut in, "Then how is it you know about the boiler leak if he didn't tell you?"

"I was about to mount the stairs to go topside when I overheard Captain Mason and Mr. Wintringer in conversation right behind the stairs. They never knew I was there. Captain Mason wanted to dismiss the whole thing, saying he had already had the boiler repaired. But Mr. Wintringer said it had sprung another leak and he would not continue on this trip unless Captain Mason agreed to get it repaired properly."

"When are they going to do that?" Mr. Wainrich asked.

"Well it sounded like Mr. Wintringer was insisting that it be done right away, but Captain Mason promised him that if we could just go on to Vicksburg, he would get it done there. So it looks as though we're going to be in Vicksburg for quite a while. I don't know how long it will take to get all those Yankees on board, or how long it will take to get the boiler fixed. But my guess is that we might as well be prepared for a long wait."

"I doubt that it will make so much difference to us, Miss Wallace," said Mr. Wainrich.

"What do you mean?"

"Well judging by the speed we've been making so far, we won't reach Vicksburg until tonight and we should be sleeping while they're doing all those things. Getting the extra passengers on board and having the boiler repaired."

"I didn't realize we were that far from Vicksburg," said Gerald. "Why is it taking so long?"

"I think it must be because the river is so swollen from the flooding up farther north. You must have noticed how wide it is now. And how swiftly it's flowing. When the current is so strong then the boilers have to work harder for the paddle wheels to propel us upriver. It's just slower going up river than it is going down river."

"Yes," he replied, "I know that. It's just that I didn't realize we were so many hours out of Vicksburg. I was kind of looking forward to seeing it in the daytime. I've never been to Vicksburg before."

"Well, Son," cut in Florence. "I think you won't get to see much of it this time. If you're hoping to visit Vicksburg, then it will just have to wait until another time. I don't want you to be wandering around a strange city alone at night."

"Yes, Mama," said the disappointed young man. And it was disappointing to him. He had not said anything to anyone before, but he was intensely looking forward to being in Vicksburg. He even entertained the thought he might find something there that he could use to keep him from going on to his Aunt Zinnia's in Missouri. Those hopes had just been dashed. Well there was always Memphis. Perhaps they would be in that city during the daytime. He could always hope so.

The small group enjoyed a leisurely meal and pleasant conversation. They sat there as the dining hall filled up, and continued to sit there as it began to empty again. Finally Florence stood up and asked to be excused. "I need to get Adelle back to our stateroom for a nap," she explained.

"We don't need to go too, do we, Mama?" asked Dora.

"No Dear, you may stay here if you like. Or go out on deck if you prefer. Just stay together and out of trouble."

"Oh, Mama," she whined. "We always stay out of trouble."

"I know you do," laughed Florence. "But mothers are expected to say such things to their children. Just try to stay out of our stateroom for the next hour or so, will you. I want Adelle to have at least that long to sleep and it will be harder for her to sleep in a strange bed with too much activity around her."

"All right, Mama. We can find plenty to do without disturbing you."

With that all four of them left, leaving just Mr. Wainrich and Laureen sitting at the table. Laureen decided to pursue a subject of interest to her.

"Mr. Wainrich, I've sort of renewed an acquaintance of mine from many years ago on this trip. A Mr. Talbert. I never knew him very well. Do you know him?"

"No, not really. I've only just met him on this trip."

"Oh," replied Laureen, obviously disappointed.

"Why do you ask, Miss Wallace?"

"Oh, I was just wondering what kind of business he's in. He made some reference to some business papers he mistakenly thought he'd misplaced, but he didn't say what kind of business. I was just curious. And it occurred to me to wonder if you knew."

"I'm sorry that I can't help you there. As I said I only met him for the first time as we were preparing to get on this boat. We both got on at New Orleans. But I got the impression from what he said at the time, that he was leaving more because he had to rather than because he wanted to."

"How's that?" asked Laureen, her interest definitely piqued by that remark.

"Well I think he must be a gambler, and I got the definite impression he won something in a card game that he wasn't supposed to win and the loser was taking it pretty hard. So hard, in fact, that he was trying to take legal action, saying it was stolen."

"How could he say it was stolen if it was a fair loss?"

"It appears that it was a city councilman who lost his wife's diamond necklace and the man didn't want to face the ire of his wife."

"And so he reported it to the police as stolen," she finished flatly for him.

"Yes that appears to be the situation. He would like to sell it in case the police catch up with him. He doesn't want to be found with it on him."

"How ironic," thought Laureen. "Well he doesn't have to worry about that now. Tolly took care of that." She was enjoying this turn of events enormously. It was such a shame she could not share the joke with Mr. Wainrich.

"Is it very valuable?" she finally asked. "Have you seen it?"

"Actually I have seen it," he answered. "He showed it to me yesterday, hoping I might want to buy it. It's very beautiful. But I have no need of such an expensive bauble. There's no woman in my life. He's asking quite a lot of money for it, and I just don't want to tie up that much cash in that way at the moment. Not that I don't think it's worth his asking price, and probably a lot more. But I don't need it. And I learned a long time ago that something is not a bargain, no matter how cheap, if you don't need it!"

"No," murmured Laureen in agreement. Well that cleared up that question.

She brightened. "Really, Mr. Wainrich, I don't know how we're going on at such length about Mr. Talbert. I'd much rather talk about you. You said you got on at New Orleans? And you're going to Memphis on business? Tell me about yourself. All I really know about you is that you're a distant cousin of Florence's."

"There's very little to tell, Miss Wallace. I have a farm some distance east of New Orleans. I raise a lot of sugar cane there and a little cotton. It originally belonged to my grandfather, then my father, and now to me."

"That must mean that your father is no longer living. I'm sorry."

"Thank you. That's right. He died a few years before the war started, but my mother is still living. We live alone in the same house my grandfather built. It's not as big as some of the plantation houses, but it's quite large enough to meet our needs."

"Do you have brothers and sisters, Mr. Wainrich?" inquired Laureen.

"No, Miss Wallace. I'm an only child. I've always wished for a little sister but I was the only child that blessed my parents union. I know they were disappointed when things worked out that way. I think my mother particularly always wanted a daughter." Then, his face taking on a more serious look, he said, "Perhaps this is being somewhat impertinent, but I can't help but wonder how it is that you aren't married. Florence told me you never had married. Such a beautiful woman as you..."

He stopped short, his face taking on a look of embarrassment. "Oh please excuse me, Miss Wallace," he stammered in confusion. "I didn't mean to say that. I don't know what came over me."

"It's quite all right, Mr. Wainrich." Laureen wanted to put him at ease. Such genuine compliments were rare for her these days, and it pleased her to hear what he had just said. "I don't blame you for wondering why I've never married. But the answer is quite easy. I've never found anyone I wanted who also wanted me. So here I am, a maiden aunt living off the charity of my sister-in-law."

"Oh, Miss Wallace, don't say that. I'm sure it's not like that at all."

"You're very kind, Mr. Wainrich, but I assure you that it's exactly like that. When my parents died the property all went to my brother and now that he's dead it all belongs to Florence and will go to Gerald. Her two daughters could wind up just like me so she is very charitable toward me. Until the war brought poverty to us she had never indicated she found it to be a burden. But poverty does things to people, brings out the worst in them. She tries very hard but sometimes things get next to her and then it comes out that I'm just one more mouth for her to feed."

"I'm so sorry, Miss Wallace. That dreadful war has done things to all of us in one way or another, I'm afraid."

"Yes, that's true. Florence must have explained to you about our situation and why we're on our way to Missouri. I haven't said anything to her yet, but I've made up my mind I will not stay with her sister very long. I'm going to find some way to support myself and make a life apart from Gerald's family. I think it's better if I do. Much as I hate the Yankees, I may have to go north in order to do it."

"Have you ever thought of going south? I mean, really far south, like New Orleans? The war didn't hit that area as hard as it did so many other places. You might find something you'd like there."

"No, Mr. Wainrich, that thought never even occurred to me. If I had thought there might be something for me there, I would not now be heading north. I'm not sure I would fit in with all those Creoles there."

"We're not all Creoles in New Orleans, you know. And if you went there, it would give the two of us a chance to get to know one another. Now that I've met you, I'd surely like a chance to get better acquainted, Miss Wallace."

There was such an appeal in his eyes it made Laureen catch her breath. This had not happened to her before. This was an attractive man, a very attractive man, and he was interested in her! All she could think of was that they had only one day more on the boat together, two at the most, depending on how long the delay in Vicksburg might be. Without hesitation she resolved she would make the most of that time. This just might be the answer she had been looking for.

CHAPTER 13

Suddenly, Laureen realized she and Mr. Wainrich were the only people remaining in the dining hall. She could hardly believe so much time had passed as they talked and everyone else left the room. Such fantasies she was entertaining as her conversation with Mr. Wainrich continued. But this had gone on long enough. She said, as she stood up, "I do believe the help would like to clear our table, Mr. Wainrich. As you can see, everyone else has moved on to other things, and I think we should leave, too. Don't you?"

As he, too, rose, he answered, "Well I wouldn't want to keep the hired help from doing their job. Shall we go out on deck?"

"Yes, if it's not too warm. Perhaps I should get my parasol from my room. I think it's been more than an hour since Florence took Adelle in for a nap. Shall we go?"

It was only a brief walk from the dining hall to Laureen's stateroom. While Mr. Wainrich waited in the saloon, Laureen quietly let herself into the room she shared with her family. Florence was reading as she sat in a chair next to the bed where the three-year-old lay sleeping, and when she saw Laureen, she put her forefinger to her lips to caution Laureen to be quiet. Laureen nodded to her to let her know she understood, then eased over to a corner of the room where her parasol rested against the wall, picked it up, and just as quietly as she had entered the room, left it, gently closing the door behind her.

"That didn't take you long," said Mr. Wainrich, as she emerged from the room. "Shall we go up now?"

"Adelle is still sleeping, so Florence and I didn't talk. If you don't mind, I think I'd like to go topside. It might be less crowded there because there's no shade there."

"That seems like a good idea to me, too. I'd rather spend my time with you than the other passengers." He was silent for a moment then he said, "Speaking of other passengers, are you aware there is a man on board who can't talk?"

Laureen's heart seemed to stop! So he had noticed Tolly. But he had no way of connecting Tolly to her. She recovered her composure almost immediately and Mr. Wainrich did not see the change that had so briefly come over her face. She said, "That must explain a little scene I witnessed ths morning."

"Oh? And what was that?"

"There were several men standing in a group and one of the men, quite a young man really, was doing a lot of gesturing. More than any of the others. And now that I think of it," she added, " I don't think I saw him actually do any talking. Of course I wasn't close enough to them to hear what any of them were saying. But that might have been the man you were talking about. Is it a very young man who can't talk?" she asked, gaining more confidence in discussing Tolly with Mr. Wainrich.

"Actually, I haven't seen him myself," he replied. "But I did hear some talk about him earlier. I mentioned him to Florence, but she knew nothing about such a man."

Talking to herself and not thinking of being heard, Laureen said, "No she wouldn't."

"What did you say?" he asked.

"Oh," replied Laureen, rather startled to realize she had put voice to her thoughts, "oh nothing. I suppose I was just thinking out loud. I'm not surprised Florence hasn't seen him. I think because of her having to take care of her children she keeps pretty well to herself. I think she's also somewhat self conscious that so many of the people on this boat seem not to have been hurt by the war like our family has."

"Miss Wallace, don't let looks deceive you. I know for a fact that a lot of these people are spending almost their last dollar making this trip. They're in just as desperate circumstances as your family is. They're leaving their homes behind them too, and for the same reason as your family. They can't afford to keep them up any longer. But you know what Southern Pride is. They're too proud to admit they're poor now, and they're spending their last bit of money to keep up appearances. When they get to where they're going they're going to wish they'd been a little bit more frugal on this trip."

"Is that what you think we're doing? Spending the last of our money to keep up appearances?"

"Well, aren't you?" he asked with such a soft twinkle in his eye that it took some of the sting out of his question. But, not all.

"Mr. Wainrich," said Laureen, as she lifted her head and with fire in her eyes, looked directly into his and continued, "I think how we spend our money is really none of your business!" Laureen would not tolerate that kind of intrusion of her privacy from anyone outside her immediate family. Mr. Wainrich had gone too far!

"Oh, Miss Wallace. Please forgive me. You're absolutely right. How you spend your money truly is none of my business. I'm afraid I just got carried away. You see I just find you so captivating, and I'm allowing myself to think of how wonderful it would be if I could be in a position to take care of you. I realize we've only just met and this trip is coming to an end so quickly. If we had met on your plantation I could have arranged things so as to court you properly. But times have changed now, and it's no longer possible to do things the way we have always thought of as being 'correct.' I just don't want to let you get away from me now that I've met you."

"Well, Mr. Wainrich, that was quite a speech. You were quite skillful at digging yourself out of the hole you had just dug yourself into, weren't you?"

"Does that mean you forgive me?" he asked plaintively.

Laureen laughed in spite of herself. "Yes of course I forgive you. How could I not, when you ask like that?"

"Good. I don't want any difficulties between us when we're just getting to know one another." They had reached topside and had begun to stroll along the outer portion of it. Laureen's wide skirt was almost brushing the rail. Mr. Wainrich thought she looked the picture of perfection with her white, ruffled trimmed parasol shading her face and shoulders. Being with her this way could almost make him think there had been no war, no poverty striking the plantations, no loss of slaves to work the land. He allowed himself to revel in the company of a woman he found so lovely, so easy to be with.

They fell silent as they strolled along the deck swathed in the early afternoon sun. It was such a comfortable silence as each one was lost in personal thoughts. Several minutes passed in this fashion, then Mr. Wainrich spoke.

"Miss Wallace, I know we've only known each other one day, but it seems as though it's been much longer than that. I know I mentioned this before, but would you mind if I write to you when you get to John and Zinnia's house? I'm going to be in Memphis for several days, then I'll be going back home. But when I get home, it would please me very much if I could keep in touch with you. I don't make these trips very often but I might think up some reason to do this again before too much longer, and next time I do it seems to me it would be the polite thing to do to go on a little farther and visit my distant cousins in Missouri."

"Yes, Mr. Wainrich, I think I'd feel very complimented if you want to keep in touch with me by letter. I'm sure I shall be feeling very lonely when I'm living at Zinnia's, away from home and all the people I've ever known. As you can no doubt see by now, we didn't even bring any of our darkies with us."

"Oh yes," he answered. "I did wonder about that. What did you do about them, or did you have any left after the war ended?"

"By the time we left Natchez we were down to four. A few had run away soon after the war started, but soon after the Yankees set fire to our house most of the rest of them left. At first we were going to bring the four with us, but two of them are on up in years and they refused to come with us. I think the two younger ones would liked to have made this trip, but Florence decided that since we were leaving two of them behind, then we could just leave them all." She was not remotely ready to confide in this man that one of them was actually on the boat with them as a stow-away, passing himself off as the white man who couldn't talk and Mr. Wainrich had actually seen. She wondered what he would say if he knew. She was quite certain that even Florence did not know about that.

She continued, "What are you doing about that on your plantation? Or do you call it a farm down there? I never even thought to wonder about that before."

He chuckled. "Either one will do. It's rather large to be called a farm, but rather small to be called a plantation. But as far as help to run the place is concerned, we use hired help. It is working out quite well. We had slaves before the war, but as soon as Mr. Lincoln freed them we offered ours a wage to keep on working for us and most of them chose to stay. And we've even hired a few others since then to replace those who left. It's mostly those who had run away from other places and then found it was not as easy being 'free' as they had expected it to be. So when we have needed more workers, it's been quite easy to hire them. Actually in one way, it works out better for us because we need extra help at certain times of the year, and we can have it this way without being responsible for the workers all the rest of the year."

"And your mother? Does she have anyone to stay with her while you're away on trips? I realize you said you don't travel very often, but what about now? Is she alone with just your hired help?" For some reason the thought of being left alone on a farm or plantation with only servants for company seemed unnerving to her.

"Oh Mama enjoys her solitude most of the time. And there's nothing for her to be afraid of, if that's what you mean. The house servants, at least most of them, have been with us for a very long time, some of them from farther back even than I can remember. They're very loyal and will look after her very nicely. She has her flowers and she supervises a large vegetable garden. She stays quite busy. She'll hardly realize I'm gone."

"I envy her then. We used to have such lovely grounds at Three Willows, but they're pretty well grown up to weeds these days. It really hurts me to think how that has changed so much. I guess nothing will ever be the same again, though, will it?"

"Laureen, don't you realize that things are always changing? Even if the war hadn't come, things would have changed. The secret to it is to be able to change with them. There's nothing to be gained by trying to live the way things were. You'll never be happy that way." Neither one of them noticed that Mr. Wainrich had slipped into the more familiar address of using her first name.

"But things were so perfect before the war. Gerald was alive, Three Willows was prospering, and life was just about ideal?"

They stopped walking and stood facing each other. He looked deeply into her eyes and asked very softly, "Were they? Were they really perfect?"

"I don't know what you mean," she said, equally softly, as she turned away from facing him.

"Yes you do. Was it a perfect life for you to be living in your brothers' house and watching his family growing up, having nothing and no one really belonging to you, in effect, living on the fringes of someone else's life?"

"Mr. Wainrich! I think you're being very unkind!" Laureen's eyes were flashing and her face was beginning to redden with anger.

"No, Laureen, not unkind. Just truthful. It's all too easy to look back at what was and see only the good part. Our memories are so very selective. They seem to want to filter out all that was unpleasant and magnify all that was good. But life as we live it isn't like that."

"I don't know what you're getting at here, but there must be some point to all this."

"Oh there's a point to it, all right." He put his hands on her shoulders and turned her to face him again. "How old are you, Laureen? Twenty six? Twenty seven? Twenty eight?"

"You really aren't much of a gentlemen, after all, are you?" she cried. "No gentlemen ever asks a woman that question!"

"I didn't ask because I want to know. I asked to make you think.

You need to have a home and family of your own and you weren't making any progress at all in that direction living in seclusion at Three Willows, were you? And each year that went by meant your chances of doing so were less and less."

"And what if I weren't? What difference does it make to anyone? At least I was happy there. We went to parties, dances, picnics, bar-b-ques, all sorts of social gatherings. It was a good life."

"But, Laureen, Three Willows isn't the only place where you can be happy. And I'd be willing to bet you weren't all that happy there. You just tried to convince yourself you were because you didn't know what else to do with your life."

Mr. Wainrich had hit a nerve Laureen did not even know was there. She covered her face with her hands, on the verge of tears. Mr. Wainrich pulled her closer to him then put both hands on hers, gently pulling them away from her face. He looked at that beautiful face turned toward his and waited for her to open her eyes. When she finally did, he let go of her hands and put his own hands on either side of her face, softly holding it up toward his, and slowly bent his own face down so that it was very close to hers. She closed her eyes again barely even daring to breathe. He waited until finally she opened her eyes, and when she did, he very slowly and gently lowered his head and let his lips touch hers.

By this time, Laureen's heart was beating so hard that the sound was pounding in her ears. Surely he must be hearing it too. No man had ever kissed her before and she had no idea it would make her feel this way. Such excitement, along with the wickedly delicious feeling she was doing something forbidden!

Mr. Wainrich did not linger with his kiss. He sensed it was her first kiss and he did not want to frighten her. "Oh, Laureen, if I've

140

offended you, please forgive me. I didn't plan that; it just happened. But I must admit I've wanted to do that since the first time I laid eyes on you." As he said that the twinkle that she had already leaned to enjoy returned to his eyes.

"No...," she said slowly. "No, you didn't offend me. I just wasn't expecting that."

"Well as I said, I didn't plan it. But I don't think you have any idea how irresistible you are. Especially when you get a little angry or upset."

"No, I don't know anything of the kind," Laureen shot back at him, recovering her composure. And she was feeling some irritation she had allowed this to happen. Along with a great deal of confusion at her own emotions. She had both wanted and been afraid of that kiss. To say the least, it was unsettling to her.

"Please understand, Laureen, I don't think there's any commitment between us. Not that I wouldn't like there to be, but I realize it's too soon after we've met for that. Even in these changed circumstances. But please don't rule such a future thing out, just because I was a little forward for a minute."

"Mr. Wainrich, right at this moment I can't afford to rule anything out of my life. I don't know what my life will be once I get off this boat. I've already told you I intend to make my own way in life as quickly as I can reasonably do so. I can't live off Florence, and now her sister, indefinitely. I do like you though and would like for us to get to know one another better."

"That's enough for me, Laureen. At least for the present. And please, won't you call me Roger? After all, we're no longer strangers to each other."

"That's all well and good, but how will I explain to Florence how we are on such familiar terms so soon after our meeting?"

"Aren't you the little hypocrite, now?"

Her eyes flashed again. "What do you mean?"

"One minute you're telling me you're going to leave the family and make your own way. You know they'll all object to that, yet you plan to go ahead. And now you can't even admit to getting to know me well enough for us to be on a first name basis." His expression suddenly turned serious. "Don't you think it's time to take a first step?"

Laureen's head shot up. He had hit another nerve, one she hadn't expected. "Yes I think you're absolutely right. We do know each other well enough to be on a first name basis. And I don't care if the whole world knows it. Roger, it is. And Florence can jump right into this river if she doesn't like it."

CHAPTER 14

Tolly decided he needed to keep a very low profile on the boat. He immensely enjoyed his one attempt to "pass," but he realized it would take only one slip and he would be exposed. He had no money to pay for his passage, should he be discovered as a stow-away. And a Negro, at that. He could imagine the captain might well just throw him overboard if he were found out. Tolly could swim, in fact, he was a strong swimmer. But he would have a very difficult time making it to shore if he were to find himself in that cold and unusually strong current of the swollen river. No, it was better to remain unseen for the rest of the journey, to the extent possible.

He kept a wary eye out for the crew members, trying to anticipate their moves and making certain he was somewhere other than where they were. In almost no time he understood how to tell the crew from the passengers, not so much from the difference in the way they were dressed, but more from the way they conducted themselves on board. The crew members moved about the boat with a definite purpose, while the passengers, for the most part, were idly whiling their time away. Some sat and visited, children played, there was even some gambling going on. He knew he must not appear to be hiding if someone chanced to see him, for that would certainly attract attention. So he moved about slowly, always erect and with dignity, keeping to the shadows, and empty spaces. He was careful not to stay in one place very long, realizing that even that could attract unwanted attention. He was also careful not to be moving on the same path always, but varied his movements so a pattern did not develop.

He needed money. He had managed to get into Graham Talbert's stateroom and remove the diamond necklace. If all went well, Laureen would give that back to him when she left the boat. He was afraid to risk going back into that room to see if there might be some money for the taking. He wished he dared to join the card games, but that was out of the question. He did not know the rules of those games. Then, too, he had no money to even get him started. But there had to be a way. It was something to be worked on. Perhaps when the boat reached Vicksburg, he might think of something there.

He found such fascination in watching the sidewheeler's huge paddles turning, often lingering in the shadows of the rigging in that area. He had allowed himself to become almost hypnotized by the constant turning of the paddles dipping into the water and out again, water slopping off each paddle as it came up out of the water. At one point, he let his interest in watching the movement of the paddles absorb his attention so much he forgot about the time passing. Suddenly he became aware of men's voices very close to him.

It was apparent the two men had no idea they were being overheard in their conversation. The first to speak was Captain Mason. "Mr. Talbert, now what is it that is so private you need to talk to me about?"

Mr. Talbert answered, "Captain, it's come to my attention that we're due to take on an assortment of Union soldiers at Vicksburg, more that the legal limit for this boat. Is that true?"

"Mr. Talbert!" replied the captain, quite taken aback. "Where did you hear such a thing?"

"Never mind that, Captain. What I want to know is, is it true?"

"Sir, I believe it isn't necessary for me to discuss the passenger list with other passengers. I'm captain of this boat, and I supervise the booking of the passengers."

"You don't seem to understand, Captain. I'm a passenger on this boat, and, as such, I'm entitled to the protection of the limitations built into this boat. If you're planning to overcrowd this boat, then I must protest. If I can't find a hearing ear from you, then I will take the matter up with the steamboat inspectors in St. Louis."

"It would appear you must not think we're in too much danger, if you expect to make it to St. Louis on this boat," the captain came back at him in a rather sarcastic tone of voice.

"I don't suppose I'll be in any more danger than you are, Sir. I would hope you would think more of your own life than to do that. Nevertheless, the legal limits were put on this boat for a reason, and I don't like the idea that you're going to ignore them."

"Mr. Talbert, we'll be docking in Vicksburg in a matter of hours. If you want to get off the *Sultana* there and continue your trip on another boat, I'll personally see to it that you have passage on any other northbound boat of your choice at no extra cost to you. But as far as your complaint's getting you anywhere with the steamboat inspectors in St. Louis, you're wasting your time. This steamboat company has a contract with the United States government to transport those paroled Union prisoners back up North, and I intend to be a part of that."

"You never did tell me how many you expect to take on board."

"That's right, Mr. Talbert, I didn't. Now if you decide you want to transfer to another boat, you just let me know." Captain Mason started to walk away, then turned to add, "By the way, Mr. Talbert. I heard something when we were about to leave New Orleans that might interest you."

"Oh, what's that?"

"I wondered why you waited until the very last minute to book your passage on this trip. Just before we pulled away from the dock, I heard something that made me wonder if I had the answer."

"I can't imagine what you're talking about."

"Oh I think perhaps you can. I can't remember just how I heard this, but it was something about a gambler who had stolen a rather valuable diamond necklace that belongs to the wife of a city councilman down there. You wouldn't happen to know anything about that, now, would you?" Captain Mason had a rather sardonic smile on his face as he posed that question.

"Certainly not!" retorted Mr. Talbert. "I'm an honest business man and a rather successful one at that. I don't need to steal some woman's pretty baubles." Then, as Mr. Talbert remembered he no longer had the necklace, he faced the captain, and said in all honesty, "I don't have anyone's diamond necklace, Captain Mason. Stolen or otherwise."

"No, of course not," continued the captain, rather sarcastically, obviously not believing him. "I suppose you're telling me that I could search your stateroom and not find it.

"Search away, Captain. I told you I don't have anyone's diamond necklace."

"No, Mr. Talbert. I don't have time for that right now. Under different circumstances, I just might take you up on that. But I don't have any legal authority to do that at the moment. But mind you, if I get a telegram along the way accusing you, I may have to search your room."

"I told you once, Captain, and I'll say it again. I don't have it. You can search all you want to. It's not there."

"Well, Mr. Talbert, I can almost believe you. I have to tell you, though, that my source in New Orleans was pretty convincing. But about your business. Just what kind of business are you in, Mr Talbert?"

"Oh I do a little of lots of things, Captain." Mr. Talbert had been thrown off balance for only a moment and was now fully recovered. "I do some buying and selling, some import, export business, I provide services for people. As I said, I do a lot of different things."

"Uh huh. And all legitimate, I suppose?"

"Of course. Why, Captain, I don't have any need to break the law. If I did, I might go to jail, and that idea doesn't appeal to me at all."

From his hidden place, Tolly could easily tell Mr. Talbert was enjoying toying with the captain. His tone of voice told that this bantering back and forth was amusing to him.

Even so, Mr. Talbert continued with the captain, "I don't mind admitting to you, Captain, that the thought of a lot of passengers being taken aboard the *Sultana* is making me most uncomfortable. So much so that I just may take you up on your offer of booking passage for me on another boat. But perhaps I'll hold off on making that decision until I find out exactly how many passengers you'll be taking on at Vicksburg."

Captain Mason left and Mr. Talbert eased over to the rail, looking down at the muddy river below, slipping rapidly by. He stood there at some length.

Tolly had not been discovered and stood absolutely still in the shadows, almost holding his breath. He hoped Mr. Talbert would be moving on to another part of the boat soon, and when he did, Tolly also would move to another place.

Mr. Talbert had boasted of being a successful business man. Tolly wondered if it was just talk, the kind of boasting all men seemed to like to do, regardless of their station in life. Tolly had heard many slaves boast in much the same way. Not about how much money they had, of course, but about other things. There was always something they could find to boast about.

But, if what Mr. Talbert said were true, then he likely had some money on him. A successful business man would surely have money with him when on a trip. Tolly could get a good view of him as he leaned against the boat rail, and he used the time to try to see where Mr. Talbert might be carrying it. Since most white men carried a wallet, Tolly thought he must have one. But, where? In his pants pockets? In his jacket? Where? There were no outlines in his clothes that Tolly could see to give it away. And Tolly realized he had never paid any attention to where any white man carried his wallet. There was no money for him, and on those occasions when he had been around cash transactions, he had not concerned himself with where a wallet was kept.

Finally Tolly concluded if he would learn that secret, then he must see him remove it to buy something. But what was there to buy on the boat?

Then he remembered. Mr. Talbert was going ashore in Vicksburg. Tolly would get off the boat there, too. If he followed Mr. Talbert, he might be able to find out where he kept his money. He would also watch to see if he carried his bags off the boat. If he did not, then Tolly might even have an opportunity to search his stateroom to see what he could find there that would be worth taking. Perhaps things were looking up for him.

After what seemed an eternity, Mr. Talbert slipped away from the rail, and disappeared from Tolly's view. Tolly waited for several more minutes before he, too, left the area. He moved away slowly nodding politely to the two passengers he met as he reached the stairway to topside. He started to go up, but changed his mind. There were fewer places up there for him to conceal himself and he was reluctant to expose himself unnecessarily to any of the passengers. So, he continued to more or less circle the deck, resting from time to time in shadowy areas.

Meanwhile, Florence had gone back into the dining room with her children. Gerald was complaining he was hungry. To Florence it seemed her son was always hungry. The dining room was a good place to sit and while away some of the time so she was willing to accompany him there. She knew she should be able to find something there for him to eat, even though it was not yet time for supper to be served. With some misgivings, Florence had allowed Dora and Adelle to go back to look at the alligator. Both the girls were absolutely fascinated with the animal. Adelle was frightened by him as well, but a peculiar fascination caused her to beg Dora to accompany her back to his cage again and again. Dora was more than willing, as she was almost as captivated by the creature as was her little sister.

Florence was willing to have them do that, having relented from her original position that Dora must always be accompanied by Gerald when away from her mother. It was too difficult to find something to keep them occupied during the long, tedious hours of the trip. The boat was moving so much slower than it had been that morning. She was getting tired of being idle, something she was most unused to. But there was nothing to do but to endure.

"Why, Mrs. Wallace," said a voice approaching her.

She turned to see that Mr. Talbert had nearly reached her table. "May I join you?" he asked.

"Certainly," answered Florence. "I could use some company about now."

"Come now, Mrs. Wallace. A beautiful woman such as yourself shouldn't be bored on a day like today."

He was teasing her and she knew it. But, she welcomed adult company, even if it did turn out to be a man of Mr. Talbert's reputation.

"What brings you into the dining hall so early?" she asked. "My excuse is that my son seems to always be hungry and we thought we might get something for him. The crew seem to be so courteous and helpful."

"To tell the truth I'm a little bored, too, and I was looking to see if there was anyone in here with whom I could carry on an intelligent conversation. And how delighted I am to find you here."

"He is really pouring it on thick," thought Florence. Nevertheless, she found it a little flattering and accepted the compliment. She replied, "I'm afraid I don't have much to contribute to an intelligent conversation this afternoon. My mind has gone rather dull with inactivity. I should have brought something to keep my hands busy, but I suppose I was concentrating too much on getting us ready to board the boat to think about what we'd do once we were actually on it."

"I can appreciate that. But I'm afraid I have a confession to make. You see, I have another motive for wanting to speak to you, Mrs. Wallace."

"I see," she said, immediately on her guard. "And what might that be?"

"I was wondering if you might have heard anyone on the boat

150

mention finding something rather valuable. The captain told me something has been lost by one of the passengers, and I told him I'd ask around and see if anyone has found anything that didn't belong to them. Have you heard of anything like that?"

"What was it that was lost, Mr. Talbert?"

"Oh the captain didn't say what it was, just that it was something very valuable, and that if anyone found it, he'd know it must belong to somebody. So I've been asking the different passengers to see if anyone found anything that wasn't theirs. Just as a favor to the captain, you understand."

"Yes, of course. But I haven't heard anything about anything lost or found. Not that I've had a chance to get acquainted with many of the passengers, yet."

"Then you haven't noticed anyone acting strangely, like they might have found something and didn't want to return it?"

"No, Mr. Talbert, I haven't." Florence said that slowly and with great dignity, almost as though she had taken offense at the question. Which, indeed, she had. She had a strong feeling that Mr. Talbert was the one who had lost something, something he was reluctant to have anyone know about, and that he thought she might have it.

"No I didn't think so," he said lightly. "It was just a thought. I mentioned it only on the off chance that you might have noticed someone acting a little strangely. But I should have known better."

"You can be certain, Mr. Talbert, that if I find something that doesn't belong to me, I'll see the captain about it immediately."

"Yes Ma'am. But, the captain is awfully busy today. He told me so himself. That's why I'm trying to help him with this little matter. So I think it would make things easier for him if you just came to me with anything you learn."

"Yes, indeed, Mr. Talbert," she thought, "I'm sure that's exactly what your motive is." But all she said was, "Yes, of course. You can count on it."

Mr. Talbert stood up, saying, "Well, Mrs. Wallace, I think I should be talking to some of the other passengers, since I did tell the captain I would. If what is lost can be found, I'd like to help in any way that I can."

"I wonder what it is he's lost that has him so worked up," Florence wondered to herself. She also wondered if he had stolen something and now had it stolen from him. "How ironic that would be," she thought.

Just then one of the dining hall crew members came with something for Gerald to eat, and a snack for Florence. The two of them busied themselves with the food and fell silent, each with his or her own thoughts.

CHAPTER 15

Florence had been in the dining hall for quite some time. She liked being there. The furnishings were so comfortable and luxurious, the table service so beautiful, and it was a very pleasant place for her to pass the time. She sat alone since Gerald quickly finished his meal and asked to be excused so he could continue to explore the boat. She readily excused him, knowing that a teenaged boy would not be confined at the table any longer than it would take him to eat his fill. As he left, she said to him, "I wish you'd check on your sisters, please. Make certain that they're all right and not getting into any mischief."

"Oh, Mama," he whined. "What possible mischief could they be getting into now. You keep saying that."

"I know, Son. I only want them to be safe. Humor me and check on them, please. It won't take you long, then you'll be free to do whatever it is you find to do on this boat that amuses you."

"All right, Mama. Do you want me to send them to you when I find them?"

"No, that won't be necessary. Just tell them where I am. I think I'll be here a while longer. If they get hungry, they can come in here."

"Maybe I'll take them a couple of the rolls. They'll like that."

He left and she was alone. Sitting there, she could momentarily forget Three Willows, even her destination in Missouri and Zinnia's home. She was happy to sit there, enjoying the comfortable surroundings and lose herself in her daydreams, a luxury that had been denied her for quite a long time by the demands of trying to keep her family surviving.

Florence had no idea she had been sitting there for such a long time, when she realized people were beginning to gather there for the evening meal. Roger Wainrich and Laureen appeared in the doorway and paused, obviously looking for someone. Laureen saw her and gave a sign of recognition, then she and Roger worked their way among the tables and patrons to where Florence was sitting.

Laureen spoke. "We saw Gerald a little while ago, and he told us this is where he left you and had not seen you since. But that was hours ago. I didn't think you'd still be here. Have you been here all this time?"

"Yes, I guess I have. I was kind of lost in thought and didn't realize so much time had passed. I suppose Gerald and the children will be getting hungry again..." She stopped suddenly, then found her voice again. "I don't think the girls ever got any lunch. They must be starved by now."

"Florence, if those children were hungry, they would have come looking for food. Don't worry so about them."

"I suppose you're right, Laureen. Still, I should have seen to them earlier."

"Well, Roger and I are hungry, now. And we thought we'd join you if you aren't otherwise engaged."

Florence frowned, a look which was not lost on Laureen. Roger noticed it, too. But both of them decided to ignore it, waiting to see if Florence would comment on Laureen's use of Mr. Wainrich's given name. She did not. Instead she said, "I was talking to Mr. Talbert a little while ago, and he had something interesting to say. In fact he said he was talking to a number of the passengers on the boat, so he may have spoken to you, too."

"No, we haven't seen him all afternoon, Florence. What's this interesting thing he said to you?"

"That the captain told him someone on the boat has lost something very valuable and he wondered if I might know anything about it."

Laureen's heart lurched but she kept still, waiting to get herself under complete control before speaking. Roger spoke up, making it easier for her to ease her inward turmoil.

He said, "What is it that was lost?"

"He never did say. All he said was that it was valuable and that if someone found it, then he would know it belonged to somebody and it should be turned in. Funny thing, though. He said the captain asked him to ask around about it, but he wanted anyone finding it to turn it in to him and let him take it to the captain. Kind of makes you wonder, doesn't it?"

"I'll just bet that if we went to the captain, he'd say he didn't know what we were talking about. I don't think there was anything lost at all, do you?" Laureen wanted the subject closed.

"Then why would he be talking about it if no one lost anything?" asked Roger.

"Oh I think that man just likes to play games with people, stirring something up," Laureen answered."

"Why would he do that?" asked Florence.

"I don't know. I don't know that man at all," replied Laureen.

"I wonder...,"mused Roger. "Hmmm. I just might know what's lost. Yesterday Mr. Talbert showed me a very beautiful diamond necklace and offered to sell it to me at a very good price. That is, at a good price if I had any use for it. But I didn't think I wanted it. He must have lost it. If so, it's no wonder that he's trying to learn if someone found it. Still, if that's the case, then why the pretense?"

"I don't know. I just know there's something not quite open and above board about that man. You know, don't you, Roger, that he has a very bad reputation concerning things like that?" answered Florence.

"No, I can't say that I do. Do you know him well?"

"Not really. But I do know about his reputation."

"His reputation." repeated Roger slowly, then continued, "Reputations aren't always accurate. I've noticed it sometimes happens that gossip gets started from an unknown source and someone's reputation gets smeared through no fault of his own. So sometimes the "reputation" is deserved and sometimes it's not. I wonder which it is in this case."

"I can't say for certain that his reputation is deserved or undeserved. But I can say this, that from the few times I've been in his company, I have not felt altogether comfortable. I always get the feeling that he's playing with words, that what he says has double meaning, that there's innuendo in much of what he says." Florence was concentrating hard on what she was saying, wanting so much to be fair. "And I do know that even though he said it was the captain who told him something valuable was missing, it was Graham Talbert who was trying to find it."

Laureen was happy the two of them had gotten so engrossed in their conversation, neither one noticed she was sitting quietly, saying nothing. Of course it was the diamond necklace in her possession Graham Talbert was trying to find. The others could guess about that, but she knew for certain. And she could not confide in anyone.

She knew within herself if she did, somehow it would become known and she would not risk that. She was determined the necklace would stay with her.

She became absorbed in her thoughts about that necklace, and she did not realize the conversation had turned toward her. She did not hear Roger ask her why she was being so quiet.

"Laureen?" he repeated. "Laureen, where in the world are you all at once?"

She started, as she realized he was speaking to her. "Oh Roger, I'm sorry. I guess I let my mind wander. What were you saying?"

"It wasn't important. I was wondering what you think of Graham Talbert. I know you've been talking to him some."

"Yes, but only a very little. He seems to be so very sure of himself. I asked him what he does for a living, but he evaded the question and didn't tell me. I think he probably deserves the reputation Florence says he has."

"Yes, well time will tell. I think we've about exhausted the subject of Graham Talbert and his necklace, don't you? Have you decided what you want to eat tonight?"

The subject of Mr. Talbert and his necklace was quickly abandoned. Laureen was delighted to have the topic of conversation go on to other things. The three of them passed a pleasant hour, with all of the Wallace children joining them within a short time.

As the meal was ending, Roger asked Laureen, "Have you any idea when we are supposed to be docking in Vicksburg? I had expected us to be there by dark."

"No I haven't heard anyone say. We're not moving as fast now as we were at first. I just supposed we had slowed down because of the leak in one of the boilers. And it's going to take a while to get that fixed, I would imagine. So we'll likely be there for a while."

"I'm hoping that they can do that while we're sleeping. I think they should be able to set up lanterns enough to see how to do it."

"I would think so," agreed Laureen.

Before long Florence excused herself, saying she wanted to spend some time with her daughters before it was time to retire to their stateroom. Gerald was allowed to continue wandering around the boat for the time being, but Florence instructed him to be in their room by 9:00 o'clock.

Laureen and Roger sat at the table for a short time longer and then wandered out onto the lower deck for a while. They had taken only a few steps when Roger said, "I hate to think we have only another day or two together on this boat. I don't know how long it will take in Vicksburg to get the boiler fixed, but if they get it done during the night then we'll be on our way tomorrow morning, and most likely will be in Memphis before tomorrow night. If it works out that way, we have only tonight and tomorrow. I would so like to have more time to get acquainted before we must part."

Laureen murmured agreement. "Well, it's not as though there's no tomorrow after that. You'll go back home and I'm going to John and Zinnia's. The river boats will still be running and we will have other opportunities to visit."

"Yes but I want us to have more time right now. I don't want to wait months before we see each other again. We have to find a way to work this out."

Suddenly, much to Laureen's surprise, Roger bent his head and kissed her, the second time that day. She had not anticipated it this time, either, but was not shocked or put off by it. In fact, she rather liked it and responded in kind. He wrapped his arms around her and held her that way for a long moment. Then remembering they were not alone on the deck, she pulled away. "What will people think of us!" she exclaimed.

"They'll think we are two grown people who care about one another and are making the most of the time we have to be together," he laughed.

"Roger! Be serious! We can't carry on like this. It just isn't done!"

"Maybe not in the past. But it's being done now." And he tried to pull her to him again, but she put her hands against his shoulders and held him at arms' length.

"No I won't behave this way. I'm a respectable woman!"

"No one ever said you weren't. And, I'm a respectable man."

"Then behave like one," she cried laughingly. "Or I'm gong to my stateroom right this minute!"

"All right, I'll behave. Don't go."

"Actually, I think I need to go in, anyway," Laureen said. "It's getting a little chilly now that the sun is setting."

"Wait until it does. Let's watch it go all the way down together. I've always loved this time of day. I've heard so many people talk about early morning's being their favorite time of day, but I like this time best. It's as though the world is settling down as it gets to be twilight, preparing for the night's rest. It lasts such a short time each day, and I like to stop whatever it is I'm doing and savor it. Watch with me. Please."

Laureen could not resist such a plea, and willingly stood at the deck rail looking off in the direction of the Louisiana shore line as the sun gradually sank. There were few clouds in the western sky, but they reflected the brilliant orange and purple of the setting sun, gradually deepening and turning to gray, as the sun sank out of sight. Lanterns were lit on the *Sultana,* and as the night began to settle in, Laureen turned to go, saying, "I really must get back to the room before I get chilled through. But I see what you mean about enjoying the twilight time. Perhaps there can be other times when you and I watch the sunset together."

"I think we can be certain there will be."

They walked along in silence after that. It took only a very short time for them to reach the Wallace's stateroom and Laureen turned to Roger as she was ready to enter, saying, "I've really enjoyed being with you today, Roger. I hate to see the day end, too, but it has and I must go inside. Sleep well and I'll see you tomorrow morning."

"Good night, Laureen," he said. Their eyes locked for a long moment and as she had expected and wanted him to do, he put both his hands on her shoulders and bent down and kissed her very gently on the lips. He did not linger, though, this time. He released her shoulders and walked quickly away.

Laureen leaned against the stateroom door, waiting for her heart to stop beating so fast, collecting her thoughts before joining Florence, knowing she would still be up.

As she entered the room, Florence looked up from the book she had been reading by lamplight. Adelle was already in bed sleeping, and Dora was preparing to join her. "Well, Laureen," she started, "it looks as though you and Mr. Wainrich are getting very well acquainted. But don't you think it's a little soon to be addressing one another by your given names?"

"I knew you'd notice that, Flo. And yes, in other circumstances, I would agree with you. But don't you see, Flo," she intoned, "things are different now. We're not back at Three Willows, with garden parties and bar b ques and ladies' teas now. The war has changed things. We don't have time for the niceties we've always been used to until now. Roger is getting off the boat at Memphis and we're going on to Missouri. Who knows how long it will be before we get to see each other again."

"I know things are changed now," replied Florence. "But there are still certain proprieties that should be observed. This man is still almost a stranger to you."

"No he's not, Flo. That's where you're wrong. We've spent most of today together, and we talked. Not about silly, frivolous things, but about important things, things that really matter. We want to see each other even after this trip is over. He's getting off at Memphis and then he'll be going back south to his home. But this is not going to be the end of it. We're going to write to each other and do what we have to do to see one another again. This simply will not end it."

"Laureen, think what you're saying! You met this man only yesterday. No matter how much you talked today and how serious the things you talked about, you don't know this man!"

"Flo, look at me. I'm 27 years old, have no money, no prospects, no future. This man is kind and gentle, owns his own plantation or farm, whichever one prefers to call it, and he's interested in me. I'm not going to turn away from him. I'm not ready to run away and marry him tomorrow. But I'm not going to discourage him from seeing me again. I like what I see of him and I want to know him better."

Florence seemed a little satisfied at what Laureen had said last. "Well if you're sure you're not going to do anything rash right away, then I suppose it's not so bad. But Laureen, do be careful. Even though he's a distant relative of mine, I've never been around him enough to really know what kind of a man he is."

"But didn't you say he might have courted you at one time? Before Gerald was in the picture?"

"Yes, but I didn't say I knew him very well. Besides, people change. I haven't seen or heard of him in years until yesterday. All I'm asking of you is for you to be careful and give this thing time so you can see what you might be getting into before you do something you wish you hadn't."

"All right, Flo. I'll be careful. But I don't intend to live off your charity for the rest of my life. Things will change. I don't know just how, but you can be sure of it."

Florence and Laureen were completely absorbed in the subject of their discussion, and they forgot all about the not yet sleeping Dora, who had been listening to her mother and her aunt in conversation. At this point she spoke, saying, "Mama, are you and Aunt Laureen having an argument?"

"Oh my goodness, Dora. I didn't intend for you to hear all that. But to answer your question, No, your aunt and I are not arguing."

"That's what it sounded like to me."

"Yes, Dear, I suppose it did. But as you get older you'll find grown people often get into discussions in such a way that it might sound to children as though they're arguing when they're really not. Your Aunt Laureen and I were having one of that kind of discussion. But we're not mad at each other." She smiled at her child, then at Laureen, to reassure Dora that all was well in her world of adults.

Laureen smiled at her, too, and said, "Jump into bed, Little One. I'm going to do the same. Tomorrow will be here soon enough, and we want to be rested and ready to meet it."

Laureen was soon under the covers, daydreaming about what her future might be with Roger Wainrich. Sleep came soon enough and her dreams were pleasant.

CHAPTER 16

Florence did not go to bed right away, as she wanted to wait until Gerald came into the room before she, too, retired. Only a few minutes after she heard Laureen begin to snore softly, Florence concluded the boat was slowing down even more than it had during the past several hours. Soon after it did she felt a bump as though the boat had hit something. Since she had not yet gotten into her bed clothes, she decided she would investigate. So throwing a shawl around her shoulders to ward off the cool night air, she slipped quietly out the door and into the saloon. Once on the deck she realized they had docked, she supposed at Vicksburg, since there were city lights in the background. It was about 8:45 p.m.

The gang plank was lowered and immediately various activities on board and ashore began. She was not sleepy and she did not know where Gerald was, so she decided to stand where she could see who went ashore and who came aboard. She knew Vicksburg was the destination of some of the passengers, and she supposed there would be others getting on the boat, in addition to the paroled Yankee soldiers that were expected to come aboard.

Meanwhile, Gerald purposely did not go to his stateroom that evening. He hoped he might have an opportunity to go ashore and find some way he could stay in Vicksburg and not have to continue with the family to Cairo. He watched intently for the lights of Vicksburg to come into view, and now felt rewarded for his vigilance. He waited impatiently for the few passengers who were leaving the boat to move away. That took a little while, because of the luggage, trunks, etc. they had to remove from the boat. The excitement they generated seemed contagious to Gerald, who was keeping back in the shadows. When the activity changed and seemed to center on the crew of the *Sultana* rather than passengers, he began to make his way toward the gangplank.

From her position on the deck, Florence saw Gerald emerge from the shadows as the last of the passengers left the boat. When it became apparent to her that her son also intended to leave the boat, she called out to him.

"Gerald! Come here!"

The boy groaned. This was an unexpected turn of events, since he supposed she was in her stateroom and probably sleeping. "What is it, Mama?" he asked in a defeated voice.

"Just what do you think you're doing, Young Man?" she demanded as he approached her.

"Oh, Mama. I just want to see the city. Let me go ashore. Please!"

"Certainly not!" she answered him in a tone that would beg no resistance. "We're all staying on this boat until we reach Cairo. No one leaves the boat before that. Do you understand?"

"Yes, Mama," answered the boy, dejectedly.

"If you want to stand here with me and watch what's going on, that's all right. But if you go anywhere else now, it must be straight to bed."

"All right, Mama. I'll stay with you for a while. But I'm surprised you didn't already go to bed. Didn't the rest do so?"

"Yes, they're all in bed. But I waited for you, and it seems it's a good thing I did, isn't it?" She looked at her son in the dim light, tousled his hair for a moment, then continued, "I know you're nearing being a grown man, Son, but you aren't there yet. Be patient. Adulthood will come soon enough, even though you may not think so right now. Stick with me for a few more years and then you'll be ready to make your own decisions about your life. But just remember, I still need you and you need me."

"Yes, Mama," he answered, but far from being convinced of the truthfulness of her words.

"Let's make a pact, you and I, right now. We'll do everything we can to help each other, work together as best we can then, when the time comes, I'll support you in whatever direction you want to go with your life. Deal?"

Gerald hesitated for a long time before he finally looked up at his mother and agreed. "Deal!" he said.

Florence would have like to hug her son at that moment, but she knew that this nearly grown son of hers would not take kindly to such a show of affection, even in the semi-darkness of where they stood, so she resisted the impulse and tried to content herself with the knowledge that when he actually became a man then he would welcome hugs from her once again.

While the mother and son were thus engaged in their own interactions, they were not aware of what was taking place on shore.

Mr. Wintringer left the boat immediately upon docking and went looking for the boiler maker to make the necessary repairs on the leaking boiler. He soon found him, the Mr. Taylor he had spoken of to Captain Mason.

Even though the hour was late, Mr. Taylor willingly left his home and family to take care of the faulty boiler. He was used to being interrupted at odd hours, for such was the nature of dealing with river boats, as they were likely to dock at any hour of the day or night.

"What seems to be the trouble with the boilers, Mr. Wintringer?"

Mr. Taylor wanted to know in his easy southern drawl.

"That's your department to determine what the trouble is. All I can tell you is that they are leaking, particularly one of them, and that I don't think it's safe to continue up the river the way they are. I know Captain Mason is quite eager to have them repaired right away. He wants us to get back out on the river as soon as we can. He's contracted to take a load of Union prisoners north and he'd like to get under way with them with a minimum loss of time here."

"Well, I'll have to have a look at those boilers before I can give you an idee of how long it will take. Could be that all they'll need is a little fixin' and could be they'll need a lot of fixin'. Just can't tell 'til I get a good look-see."

The two men made their way back to the boat and boarded it without noticing that Florence and Gerald had stationed themselves near the gangplank to observe those who boarded and left the boat.

As Mr. Taylor examined the boilers, he suddenly pointed to a large bulge on the middle larboard boiler and exclaimed to Mr. Wintringer, "My God, Man! Do you see that bulge? I don't know how you made it this far. Why didn't you get that fixed in New Orleans?"

Mr. Wintringer stiffened at the seeming insult, drew himself up to his full height and replied, "Don't you think safety of this boat is important to Captain. Mason and myself? Surely you don't think we'd have left New Orleans with the boilers in this shape. There was nothing to indicate anything was wrong when we left there. In fact it was only late this morning when we discovered the leak. That's why we're so late getting into Vicksburg tonight, because we had to slow our speed down to accommodate that leak. What I want to know is, can you fix it, and if so, how long will it take?" Somehow, Mr. Wintringer had softened his stance on insisting the boilers be repaired properly before leaving Vicksburg.

By this time Captain Mason had joined the two men at the boilers. "That's exactly what I want to know, too," he said. "I'm Captain Mason, and I need to get this boat up and running just as fast as you can get it ready."

"Well, Captain," drawled Mr. Taylor, "that boiler's in bad shape. You see that bulge right there?" he continued, pointing. That's not an easy thing to fix. We have to let the boilers cool down, then those two sheets on the boiler will need taking out and new ones put in. An' that boiler's not the only one needin' fixin'. Every one on this boat is burnt."

"Now wait a minute, Man," sputtered the captain. I don't want to wait here all night for you to fool around playing with those boilers. Just get the job done so I can be on my way."

Mr. Taylor was good at his work and knew what it would take to make the boilers safe for travel. So he straightened up as if to go. "I take pride in what I do, Captain. When I'm finished with a boiler, I know it's safe to travel. I been doin' this kind of work for 28 years and I don't do makeshift work. If that's the kind of work you want done here, then you'll have to find yourself another man to do it. Good evening, Sir." And Mr. Taylor turned to leave.

As he continued toward the gang plank, both the captain and Mr. Wintringer were close at his heels, still trying to convince him to work on the boilers. Mr. Taylor just kept walking, wasting no time in leaving the boat. Finally, Mr. Wintringer said to him, "We really need you to fix those boilers, Mr. Taylor. You can see we can't continue up the river until they're fixed. What will it take to get you back to those boilers and to do the best you can? More money? Tell you what. If you'll go back and do the job, just do the best you can, then we'll pay you double what you usually get for a job like that. Will you do it?"

Mr. Taylor paused, breaking his stride for the first time since he turned away from the boilers. "You'll pay me double? You want me to do it that bad?" He hesitated only briefly, then added, "I guess you know money's tight for everybody these days, includin' my family, since the Yankee siege of Vicksburg. I know I could sure use some these days. I'm a proud man, Mr. Wintringer, but these hard times can make pride an expensive luxury." He stood motionless for several seconds, while the Captain and Mr. Wintringer waited expectantly. Finally he said, "All right. I'll do it."

Captain Mason quickly told him, "I know you want to do the best job you can on the *Sultana*, and that's what I want too. But I just simply don't have the time to wait for you to take those two sheets out of the boiler. Isn't there some other way to fix it?"

"I don't know Captain. That's the only way I know of to really make it safe."

"Couldn't you just patch the weak area? That wouldn't take nearly as long, would it?"

"You're talkin' about an awful big patch, Captain."

"No, just patch where the bulge is. That should do it."

"Captain, I don't think what you want me to do is safe. That boiler needs a lot of work done on it."

"I tell you what, Mr. Taylor. Just fix me up so I can get this boat back out on the river, and I give you my word that when I get to St. Louis I'll have whatever repairs you think necessary taken care of. Will that satisfy you?" The captain's impatience was showing. "Meantime, I need to leave the boat and get on with some rather urgent business."

Mr. Wintringer placed his hand on Mr. Taylor's elbow, gently pulling him to one side and said in a low voice, as though he did not want the captain to hear, "You go ahead and put that patch on the boiler like the captain said and there'll be something extra for you in addition to what we already promised you. Just do your best. That's all we're asking of you."

That was too much for Mr. Taylor to resist. So he said, "All right, then. I'll do my best. But I want both of you to know that it's not the way I want it. I don't think what you're askin' me to do is safe, and if anything goes wrong, then it's goin' to be on your heads and not mine!"

"Fine!" said the captain. "Let it be on our heads. Just get the boilers fixed and we'll soon be on our way. Now if you gentlemen will excuse me, I have business to attend to in town."

With that Captain Mason left the boat to go into Vicksburg, but Mr. Wintringer and Mr. Taylor returned to the boilers so Mr. Taylor could begin his work. The repairs would take over twenty hours, even at the best that Mr. Taylor could do.

As Mr. Taylor went to work under the watchful eyes of Mr. Wintringer, he pointed to the bulge in the boiler and said that he would have to force that bulge back into line with the rest of the boiler.

"Will that take more time?" asked Mr. Wintringer.

"Yes of course that will take time. When I push it back, it has to line up with the rest of it. You can see that it's stretched and it has to go back. I'll have to work it in to make it shrink back to its original size. That's bound to take a while."

"Then just patch over it. I don't like this business any more than you do. But the captain is insisting on speed and he did give his word he'll get everything fixed properly when we reach St. Louis. I really think he's let the hope of a profitable run override his better judgment on this matter.

Mr.Taylor was annoyed that the safety of the boat was being compromised for the sake of profit. "Mr. Wintringer," he said, " I'm goin' to do this job the way you want it, much against my better judgment. Every boiler on this boat is burned. I don't think you've been usin' enough water in them. Even after I do these repairs you still won't have a single boiler here that's safe. I'm just glad you aren't askin' me to travel with you. I never did a makeshift job on a boiler before and I don't like doin' it now. I just want you to know that."

"Yes, of course. I'm taking full responsibility for what you do. You don't have to worry about that. All the captain and I want you to do is get those boilers so they'll take this boat back on the river. And just as fast as you can."

Mr. Taylor worked through the night and much of the next day, disliking what he was doing, but doing it, nevertheless, all the while consoling himself with the knowledge that the extra money would be so welcome in his family.

CHAPTER 17

Florence was about to suggest to Gerald that the two of them retire for the night, when Gerald saw Mr. Talbert approaching the gang plank. He nudged his mother, who was looking off in the distance at the lights of the city. When she saw Mr. Talbert, she spoke.

"Are you leaving us here, Mr. Talbert?" she asked.

"I beg your pardon?" he asked, since he was not expecting to encounter any of the passengers at that moment. When he saw who was speaking to him, he brought his thoughts back to the present and answered her.

"Oh, Mrs. Wallace. I didn't realize at first you were here. I would have expected you to retire to your stateroom for the night by now."

"I'm about ready to do that," she answered. "Even though it's not so late, I'm beginning to tire. Although I can't imagine why. I haven't done any work at all today. I've looked after my children, explored the boat a little, and not much else."

"Well, Mrs. Wallace," he said graciously, "I'd say that was a full time job. Not that your children need that much looking after," he added hastily, lest she assume he meant something he did not. "But taking care of children requires a mother's full attention, especially on a boat such as this. There's all that livestock back there, the alligator, and always the possibility that one could fall overboard. I can see where all that worry would be tiring."

"You're very kind, Mr. Talbert. Perhaps that's it. My son and I were amusing ourselves for a little while before retiring, watching the comings and goings of the people on the boat. Are you leaving us here? I was under the impression you were going on farther north."

"I haven't fully decided just yet, Mrs. Wallace. I've been told the boat is taking on several hundred Union solders who've been prisoners of war and now are being sent home. I've grown accustomed to the luxuries in my lifestyle and am loathe to relinquish them, even for a few days. If the boat gets as crowded as I think it might, I probably will continue my trip on another, less crowded boat."

"I see. I can't say that I blame you. Oh by the way, do you know if the captain ever found the lost item? I haven't heard anyone else say anything about it."

He gave her a blank look, then caught himself. "Oh that. As far as I know, no one turned in anything of any value they found on the boat. I suppose whoever found it, assuming someone did, decided it was "finders, keepers."

"I'm sorry to hear that. I hope it wasn't something so very valuable that it works a hardship on whoever it was who lost it."

"The captain didn't say, Ma'am." Mr. Talbert, by this time, had given up hope of retrieving his lost necklace, even though it was a substantial loss. He had learned long ago to accept the fact that in his line of work there would be losses, even substantial ones occasionally. This seemed to be one of those times.

"Well, if we don't see you again, then goodbye, and I hope you have a pleasant journey on whatever boat you're on."

"Thank you, Mrs. Wallace. You're a real lady and I wish you the best. Goodbye."

And he was gone.

"Gerald," said Florence, turning to her son, "have you had enough excitement for one night? Are you ready to go to our room yet?"

Gerald reluctantly agreed, knowing he might as well go with her, as he felt certain she would not leave him alone again that night. Even though he truly longed to leave he was unwilling to outright defy his mother.

When Captain Mason left Mr. Wintringer and Mr. Taylor, he went immediately to see Colonel Reuben Hatch, the chief quartermaster for the Department of Mississippi. Colonel Hatch was living in a spacious rooming house in a very old part of the city, a house that had originally been a private home, but whose owners had fallen on hard times and had been forced to take in roomers in order to be able to afford to keep the house. Fortunately this house had not been damaged in the recent carnage done to the city during the war.

Captain Mason wasted no time on formalities, but got right to the point. "Colonel Hatch, I'm here to arrange to transport the Union soldiers north as we agreed on when I was here last."

"Yes, Captain Mason, I remember well our agreement. In fact I was just informed by Captain Speed that we have three hundred men ready for shipment on the *Sultana*. You remember Captain Speed, don't you, Captain? He's the assistant adjutant general here in Vicksburg and he's in charge of getting the prisoners ready for shipment..."

Captain Mason broke in. "Three Hundred men!" he exclaimed. I'm expecting more like twelve hundred. You can't possibly have shipped all the rest out in this length of time!" Captain Mason was growing more agitated with each word he spoke. "What's the problem here?"

"Now calm down, Captain Mason. There's no real problem. It's just that all the men who had been prepared for shipment left on the *Olive Branch* earlier today. I think there were about seven hundred of them."

"You don't really expect me to hang around here another day waiting for you to do paperwork on more soldiers, do you? I can't run a boat like that and expect to make a profit. I want those prisoners right away, as we agreed on."

"I do know that Captain Speed would rather transport the rest of the men at the camp in just one boat. But I don't think that he can get all rolls prepared in time for you to take them on the *Sultana*. Especially since you seem to be in such a hurry to get on your way. But if you could see your way clear to wait just one more day I think we can get the men here to you."

Captain Mason growled, "I don't have time to fool around waiting on your inefficiency. Now you go and do your job the way you're supposed to. Get those men here and on my boat!"

Colonel Hatch bristled. "Just wait a minute, Captain Mason. Perhaps you'd better remember who you're talking to." Then in a softer voice he continued, "I have to admit that Captain Speed is a bit on the slow side in getting those rolls prepared and the men ready to go. Maybe the best thing you can do is to go see him yourself. If you expect to transport more prisoners maybe you can get him to move a little faster."

"Good idea," Captain Mason grumbled. "Just tell me where to find him."

After getting the needed directions the captain left the boarding house and, without wasting any more time, made his way through the dimly lit streets to the quarters of Captain Speed.

Since Captain Mason had never met Captain Speed before, introductions were in order and quickly done. Captain Mason was already out of patience with all the setbacks he was having, not only with getting the prisoners as readily as he had expected, but because of the needed boiler repairs on his boat. However he felt the need to be discreet about the latter, saying nothing of that to Captain Speed.

"I think you know why I'm here," started Captain Mason. "I've been promised a full load of prisoners for the *Sultana* at this time, and I'd like to get started loading them right away."

"Yes, Captain, I've heard that about you. And I'd like to accommodate you. Unfortunately there's nothing I can do for you."

"Now see here, Captain Speed. I said I've been promised a full load of prisoners and I expect to have them."

Captain Speed was finding Captain Mason's irritation amusing. So he smiled at him and said, "I don't know who promised you that you would be the one to transport those men. But they're not ready to go. I've done the rolls for only about 300 of them. And none of them are in Vicksburg."

"Then where are they? I thought you were supposed to have them here and ready to go."

"No, Captain. Most of them are at a camp called Four Mile Bridge, actually Camp Fisk. As the name suggests, that's about four miles from town. The rest of them are at Big Black hospital."

"Hospital!" exclaimed Captain Mason. "I don't have hospital facilities on my boat. Are they going to be able to travel by boat?"

"I think we can work things out so that they can. But back to your situation. You can see why I can't possibly put those soldiers aboard the *Sultana*, now can't you? Not if you have to leave right away." He paused for a long time, looking hard at Captain Mason. Finally he said, "I'll tell you what, Mason. If you're willing to wait a little longer,

I'll give you the whole three hundred men."

"Not just three hundred, Captain Speed," he retorted, his eyes narrowing. "My boat belongs to the Merchant's and People's Line and that company has a contract with the government to transport the Union Soldiers. I want a full load of those prisoners."

"Well maybe I could get as many as seven hundred ready. Would that satisfy you?"

"No that won't satisfy me, but I'll wait until morning to pull out. How soon can you have them here?"

"If I get to work on the rolls right now I can probably have them ready for you soon after daylight."

"All right, Captain Speed. I'll be checking on you about then."

As he left the presence of Captain Speed, Captain Mason muttered to himself, "I don't know what's going on here, but something isn't right. I can haul a lot more than seven hundred men upriver and I intend to have them. I think the next thing to do is to see General Smith. With all this activity going on, I would expect him to still be in his office. He told me on the last trip down the river that if either Hatch or Speed gave me any trouble about turning over the prisoners to the *Sultana*, that I should let him know and that's exactly what I'm going to do."

He hurried through the damp chill of the night and was soon seated in the office of General Smith, who said cordially, "Now, Captain Mason, I must say it's a pleasure to see you again. Would you like a cup of coffee? It's rather cool out there tonight, and you look like you could use something hot."

As Captain Mason nodded, General Smith poured him a cup of the steaming dark liquid, and seated himself behind his desk, a rather large and ornate piece of furniture made of dark mahogany, gleaming in the lamplight from regular polishing and the crackling fire in the fireplace at one end of the room.

"Now, Captain Mason, just what can I do for you?" he asked, smiling gently.

As was his usual way, Captain Mason got right to the point. "General Smith, no doubt you remember when I was here on my last trip down river, you told me that I should report to you if Captain Speed failed to turn over the Union prisoners to me on my return trip. I've just come from seeing him, and at first he wasn't going to give me any of the prisoners, then he said he thought he could get me three hundred. I persisted in saying that wasn't enough and he finally offered me possibly as many as seven hundred. I have been led to believe that I was to get at least twelve hundred, perhaps more. So I thought you should know what's going on."

"Hmmm," responded the General as he stroked his abundant beard, as he so often did when he was weighing something on his mind.

"General, if it's just a matter of a few more hours to get the prisoners ready, I can assure you that I'm prepared to wait. But I want you to know my steamboat line has a contract to transport the Union soldiers north, yet it is my understanding the contract is not being honored."

"In what way, Captain Mason?"

"Other steamboats not of our line are transporting those prisoners, siphoning off money that should be coming into our line. That's a breach of contract and I have every intention of reporting it. I've just learned that the *Olive Branch* took seven hundred men away from here only today, and that boat had no right to them at all."

"Captain Mason," replied the General, "try to see the situation from another point of view. Those prisoners have been promised so many times that they would be released. Each time they aren't that's a big disappointment to them. So when the *Olive Branch* was ready to go and we had all those prisoners waiting, all processed for transport, it seemed to be the humane thing to let them go. Those men couldn't care less about what boat transports them. They just want to go home and it seemed like the right thing to do to let them go."

General Smith paused and took a few sips of coffee before speaking again. At last he said, "I just thought of something, Mason. You'll get your men. There's no reason those rolls have to be prepared ahead of time. We can check the men off as they board your boat, then the rolls can be prepared as time permits. Just as long as it gets done before they reach their destination. Will that suit you?"

Before Captain Mason could reply, the general continued, "I'll send for Captain Speed and we will soon have this matter all cleared up. I don't think Captain Speed will give us any more trouble. Suppose you wait here until he comes and you can relax while I take care of some paper work.

Much sooner that Captain Mason expected, Captain Speed arrived at General Smith's office.

With no attempt to hide his irritation, Captain Speed lashed out, "I was right in the middle of something, General. I didn't realize I was still on duty this time of the evening."

"Calm down, Captain Speed. Surely you must realize I wouldn't have called you out at this hour if I didn't have something important to discuss with you. It's about the remaining Union soldiers waiting to be transported North. Captain Mason is docked here and headed north. He would like to take a full load of those soldiers on his boat. I'm asking you to see to it that the rest of them are loaded onto the *Sultana* tomorrow. I'd really like to have this whole matter brought to a conclusion. Those men need to be on their way north and the sooner the better as far as I'm concerned."

"But, Captain, I don't have the rolls prepared, yet. And there's just no way I can get all of them ready to travel tomorrow. There are only about 300 of them ready at this time. That's a time consuming job and I don't have enough help to do all that tomorrow. And even if I could get the rolls done, it still takes time to get all of them here in Vicksburg. The train won't hold all of them at once, so that means more than one load to get on the train. And some of them are in the hospital. No, Sir. It's out of the question. I simply can't do it."

"I have an idea of how it might be done, Captain Speed. It really isn't necessary to prepare the rolls before the men board the boat. That can all be done after the boat is under way."

As Captain Speed started to object, General Smith raised his hand and continued, "Now, now, Captain Speed. Hear me out. I think my idea will work. You have the names of all the prisoners at the parole camps, right?"

Speed nodded and General Smith said, "Then, is there some reason why the prisoners' names can't be checked against those lists as they board the *Sultana*, and then the rolls prepared after the boat is under way?"

As Speed was obviously about to object further, General Smith added in an almost threatening tone of voice, "Think about it before you answer."

Captain Speed realized there was no point in further objections so, accepting defeat, said, "I understand, Captain. The rolls can be prepared later."

"Very well, then. It's settled." Then turning to Captain Mason, General Smith asked, "Does that arrangement meet with your approval, Sir?"

"Quite," replied Captain Mason. "I'll be expecting the prisoners first thing tomorrow morning. And now, if you gentlemen will excuse me, I'll get back to my boat. There are a few more preparations that I want to make to get ready for the extra passengers."

With that Captain Mason left the company of General Smith and Captain Speed, going out in to the cool night air, fragrant with the spring flowers adorning so many of the yards in that section of town. Captain Mason was in a much better mood than he had been only a short time before and thought to himself, "This should prove to be a very profitable run North, after all. I don't know how many enlisted men there'll be as opposed to officers, but I'm to be paid twenty dollars for each enlisted man, and fifty for each officer. Even if the whole lot of them are enlisted men and if I get at least twelve hundred of them, that's twenty four thousand dollars. And that's in addition to the civilian passengers' fares, plus all the freight we're carrying. Yes, yes, a very profitable run, indeed, I should say."

While Captain Mason was congratulating himself over the load of soldiers he seemed to have won, Captain Speed sought out Colonel Hatch in the latter's room.

Captain Speed asked Colonel Hatch, "Do you think that all the remaining soldiers can be put aboard the *Sultana* tomorrow? I told Captain Mason they could, but I'd like you to confirm that possibility," adding, "I think General Smith is making a big mistake here. It would make so much more sense to get all the rolls prepared *before* the men board the boat, rather than do it afterward. I've been doing a good job of keeping all the records straight until now, and I'd really like to finish the job the right way. And I can't do all that in one day. It's going to take several days to get all those records down on paper. Captain Mason should just have the soldiers we can get papers ready for and let the rest wait for another boat."

Colonel Hatch was growing annoyed. "Look here, Speed, I thought we had that matter settled a little while ago. Those records don't have to be done before the men get on the boat. It can be done just as well after the boat is headed up river. Captain Mason will get that taken care of and the records can be brought back here to you. I'll mention that to him, and I have no doubt that he'll be willing to deliver them personally on his next trip down river. You can keep your 'perfect' record, and there won't be any problem at all."

Captain Speed finally conceded the rolls would have to wait.

Colonel Hatch then asked, "Will you see to it that all the remaining prisoners are brought here tomorrow and put aboard the *Sultana*? Captain Mason said he was expecting somewhere in the neighborhood of twelve hundred soldiers? Does that figure sound about right to you?"

"I think there may be some more than that, but I suppose he can handle them."

"Very well, then I suggest you get things in motion. If the *Sultana* is to be able to leave the dock tomorrow, there's a lot of work to be done. I'll let you get to it. I just need to give instructions to an assistant commissioner of exchange to get out to Camp Fisk and get those soldiers ready to travel. I expect that will be good news to them."

"No doubt, Colonel," replied Captain Speed. Since there was nothing more he could do to stop the order for the troops to be sent North on the *Sultana*, he issued an order for a special guard of 22 soldiers to go aboard the Sultana the next morning to assist in the orderly boarding of the Union soldiers.

Soon after dawn Colonel Hatch decided he needed to check on Captain Speed, to make certain that Speed was going to follow through on the agreement to send North on the *Sultana* all the prisoners who were still remaining in Vicksburg. Colonel Hatch hurried through the deserted streets, unconscious of the beautiful old mansions he was passing. Besides, most of them appeared to be nothing more than large dark shadows, as few people were stirring at this hour of the morning. Colonel Hatch had a single minded focus that he wanted to attend at Captain Speed's room.

As he reached the house and raced up the stairs, he knocked rather loudly on Captain Speed's door. Captain Speed opened it slightly, peering out into the hallway to see who might be calling so early in the morning. He had risen and was in the process of getting dressed, but Colonel Hatch did not wait to be invited inside, but pushed open the door and brushed past Captain Speed, entering the room without ceremony.

Colonel Hatch dispensed with any greeting, saying instead, "Speed, I didn't get much sleep last night, for thinking about those prisoners waiting to be sent up North. I know this goes against your wishes, sending them all on the Sultana without waiting for you to get all the rolls prepared, and I just want to make certain you're still going to cooperate on this matter. How about it?"

Captain Speed had not slept well the night before, either, and was not awake enough at that moment to have all his thoughts collected.

This matter of not having all the records in order did not sit well with him at all. He believed regulations should be followed, and to his way of thinking, there was no reason for all this urgency that was being put upon him. Nevertheless, Colonel Hatch was insisting he follow through on his orders, and he certainly outranked

him. There seemed to be no other way, than to allow the men to leave without filling out the papers properly.

He looked at the Colonel sleepily, and finally answered him. "Colonel Hatch, I made my position clear last night when I said that I believe the rolls need to be completed before we put the men on boats. I just feel it in my gut that what you and the others want me to do isn't right. I don't know how to make you understand that."

Colonel Hatch looked at Captain Speed with a steely eye, and responded, "No, Captain Speed, it is you who doesn't understand. Those men, all of them, are to be boarded on the *Sultana* today. I hope that is clearly understood. Is it?"

"Yes, Colonel, it is perfectly understood. I said last night that I'd get the men on the *Sultana* today and that's what I intend to do. But, if it's all right with you, I'll finish getting dressed first and have some breakfast."

Captain Speed's sarcasm was not lost on the Colonel, but he said nothing. He had accomplished what he came to do, that is, satisfy himself that Speed would follow through on the instructions given him to empty out the prison camp that day. He turned and left the room without another word.

Captain Speed was quite annoyed by the visit of Colonel Hatch, so he was in no hurry to finish dressing, but took his leisure, all the while muttering to himself about the unreason-ableness of what he was being commanded to do. At last he was finished, but decided not to wait for breakfast to be served in the boarding house. He thought it best to skip breakfast on this particular morning.

Instead he hired a carriage and went as quickly as he could to Camp Fisk to help facilitate getting the prisoners out of the camp and onto the train.

CHAPTER 18

Captain Mason slept fitfully during the few hours he was in his bed that night. He was awake before daylight. As soon as he was dressed, he felt the need of a drink. He was feeling that need earlier and earlier each day. Some of the passengers were making comments about how often the saw him coming from the bar. However, he had never thirsted for a drink this early in the day before. He left his cabin and headed straight for the bar. It had not officially opened yet, but no one could deny the captain of the boat access to a drink, and he gulped down a good sized slug of whiskey. Without apologies or explanation, he left the bar and went to check on how the repairs on the boiler was progressing.

Unaware of all the activity of previous evening and early morning concerning arranging for the prisoners to board the *Sultana,* the Wallace family finished eating their breakfast, and the children, particularly Gerald, begged to be taken ashore. "Mama, it's daylight now, and we'd like to get off the boat for a little while. Won't you take us into town? We don't have to stay very long."

Laureen chimed in, "Why don't you take them, Florence? It'll do them good to get off the boat for a while. In fact, I've been thinking about taking a walk into the city myself."

"I don't feel comfortable doing that, Laureen. I don't know how long the boat will be docked here and I don't want to get left behind."

"I don't know, either, but there aren't any of the Yankee soldiers on board yet and you know it won't leave before they get here. You could check with the quartermaster and see if he knows how long it will be. Besides, I think someone's still working on the boilers, and we can't leave until he gets finished."

This little bit of encouragement was all Gerald needed to make him bear down hard on his mother to take them ashore.

Finally Florence laughed. "I seem to be outnumbered here," she said. "All right, we'll go take a look at the city. But listen, all of you children, we have to keep a watch for any signs of Northern solders boarding the boat and get back here quickly. Agreed?"

"Yes, Mama," said the three children, almost in unison.

Laureen purposely did not suggest that she accompany her family in that little outing. She expected Roger Wainrich to join her shortly, and she was not disappointed. She was watching the dining hall door intently, her face showing her disappointment each time another passenger entered. She was about to conclude he would not be coming in for breakfast after all, when he finally walked through the door. She tried not to look too pleased, but she was so delighted and relieved to see him. He could see the welcoming look on her face and responded in kind.

"I'm sorry I'm so late getting in to breakfast," he explained. "Actually I allowed myself to sleep a little later than usual this morning, as I so seldom get to do that. And I'm not much of a one to eat breakfast. My appetite doesn't kick in until later in the morning and that's when I usually try to get something to eat. "You've eaten, I assume?"

"Yes, all of us. And the rest of my family have all gone into town. The children were tired of being cooped up on the boat. And they wanted to see the city for a little while."

"I think that's an excellent idea. Even with all the damage done by the war, there will still be plenty to see. Would you like to join me for a walk into town also?" As Laureen's face lighted up and she smiled acceptance, he said, "On second thought, I think we should try to find out just how long the *Sultana* will be tied up here. Wouldn't want to get left behind, you know," giving her a knowing wink. "Have you seen the captain this morning?"

"I haven't been anywhere except in here. But we might go talk to the man who's working on the boiler if he's still there. He might know how long that will take."

The two of them left the dining hall and started round to the stern of the boat to check for information, but before they could go very far they spotted Captain Mason returning from his most recent boiler inspection. Roger approached him. "Excuse me, Captain, but I'm wondering if you have any idea how long we're going to be tied up here. I'd like to go into town for a little while, but I don't want to risk having the boat leave before I can get back."

Captain Mason's irritation at being detained showed plainly on his face. But he said simply, "I'd say we're going to be here several hours yet. You should have all the time you need to see the town." And he was gone.

"Ohoooo, I wonder what's eating him," drawled Laureen. "He certainly doesn't look too happy, does he?"

"From the smell of him you'd think he'd be a lot happier, wouldn't you?" Roger shot back. "I noticed a distinct odor of liquor about the captain."

"Well let's don't waste our time trying to figure out the captain. He said we have several hours so let's take advantage of them. I've never been to Vicksburg before, so I'd like to see some of it."

"Just remember, it doesn't look the way it did. The Yankees did a lot of damage here last year when that siege lasted so long. And there hasn't been much money to fix it up yet." "I know. But we can at least walk around and look. We can imagine how it looked before the Yankees came. Besides they can't have destroyed it all. After all, it's still here."

Roger saw no reason to try to argue with her logic. He could see a pleasant several hours ahead for the two of them and he was eager to get started. Laureen made a quick side trip to her stateroom where she grabbed her parasol, then the two of them left the boat.

Soon after Roger and Laureen left the *Sultana,* another boat, the *Lady Gay,* pulled up to the dock along side the *Sultana*. It was there for only about an hour. And even though it was from the same company as the *Sultana,* and could legally transport some of the prisoners, all too soon she was ready to get under way, without boarding a single Union soldier.

But she had taken on at least one new passenger of significance, Graham Talbert. Mr. Talbert had decided to accept Captain Mason's offer to book passage for him on another boat, and the *Lady Gay* seemed to be the logical choice. She was spacious, comfortable, and not at all crowded. As he had told Florence the evening before, he had grown accustomed to his creature comforts and was truly reluctant to give them up. Especially when there was no need. He did not say any further "goodbyes" to any of the passengers on the *Sultana*. He simply went aboard the *Lady Gay* and was gone.

Meanwhile, Roger and Laureen were enjoying walking around the streets of Vicksburg, although it was not as pleasant to Laureen as she expected. She found it was one thing to know that the city was badly damaged. It was altogether another thing to view it up close. It grieved her to see some of the once-lovely old homes so damaged by the war. Much of the debris from the war was still where it had fallen.

There was a sadness on the faces of the people on the streets. Laureen could so readily identify with the feelings she saw worn on the faces of most of the adults, as she had felt much the same way until she left Three Willows.

As the noon hour approached, Roger suggested they duck into one of the little places where food was still available and find something to eat.

"Why yes, Roger, that's exactly what I'd like to do. I didn't realize I was hungry until you said that. But you must be even hungrier than I am since you didn't eat breakfast. I'd forgotten you said you'd get something later in the morning. Why didn't you say something before now?"

"To tell the truth, I forgot about it, too. When a man is in the company of such a beautiful woman he can forgot about almost everything else." He looked down at her with a large smile.

"You're teasing me again. You get quite a bit of pleasure doing that, don't you?"

"You caught me. I'm guilty."

"Actually, I don't mind. It's been too long since I had a man to flatter me."

Roger reached out both his hands and placed them on her shoulders, turning her to face him, suddenly growing serious. "Laureen, I don't mean to flatter you. I do think you're a beautiful woman. But that's all on the surface. And temporary. Someday you'll be old and not quite as beautiful as you are right now. But if you're at all the woman I think you are, then it won't matter to me one little bit."

"Roger, I....."

"Don't interrupt. Let me finish. I don't see you as a piece of perfection, in fact, far from it. But if I read you right at all, then I believe that deep down you're a loyal, level-headed person. Hardheaded at times, and frivolous at times. And yet, practical when the occasion calls for it. I think you likely can be very stubborn when you set your mind to something, but I've watched you with your nephew and nieces. I think you really care about them. So that tells me something about what kind of person you are."

This was getting more serious than Laureen was expecting, and she was at a loss as to how to handle it. Finally she tried to put a light touch on the conversation. "What gives you so much insight into my personality?" she asked, smiling coyly. "I don't think I'm all that transparent. There are lots of things you still don't know about me."

"I'm sure that's true. Like, do you snore when you sleep? Do you sleep walk? Do you tend to forget your manners when only your family is around? I'm sure there are many things I don't know. But I think I'm fast learning the things about you that I consider truly important."

"Then you have me at a disadvantage," she responded, groping for the right thing to say.

"How's that?"

"I don't think I have the ability to size you up as easily as you seem to have drawn your conclusions about me. I think I need more time."

"Laureen, I think we have all the time we need. I have no intention of putting pressure on you. You are the one who said you want to get out from under the pressure of living off Florence's charity." He drew her hand into the crook of his arm and continued strolling with her. "I think we said something about getting something to eat. Let's do that now."

Just then they heard a train pulling into town, only about two blocks away from the small restaurant they found. "I wonder if that train has those Yankee soldiers on it," said Laureen with a definite scowl on her face as they placed their order for food.

"Good chance of it," replied Roger. "Come on, we'd better get our meal and get back to the boat. Captain Mason may want to leave when they're all loaded on the boat."

"Oh I think we have plenty of time. If they're going to put five hundred men on the boat, that will take quite a while to get them on and settled in with a place to ride."

Laureen grew thoughtful, then chuckled.

"What's so funny?" smiled her companion.

"I was just thinking. If there are going to be so many men on the boat, then perhaps I'd better take my hoop skirts off and leave them in our stateroom for the rest of the trip. It's kind of hard to get through a big crowd with these skirts billowing out the way they do. Florence will be scandalized but I think I won't let that bother me."

"You see, I told you that you could be practical when the occasion calls for it."

"Yes and I'm also bold. Unwed ladies don't usually discuss their under garments with gentlemen. But I seem to be growing shameless with you."

"I've always thought Society's rules tend to be unduly restrictive. Every one knows how ladies dress, and how gentlemen dress. It makes no sense that no one is supposed to speak of it. That also applies to other subjects as well, but now is not the time to bring those up." He laughed nervously, indicating he had said more than he intended to.

"Well anyway, I think we should begin working our way back to the boat before long. The only thing is, I don't know if I want to be on the boat or off it while all those Yankee soldiers are boarding. I don't want any more contact with them than I absolutely have to have."

"You really hate them, don't you, Laureen?"

"Oh, yes. It makes me mad every time I even think of them."

"I think you're going to have to get over that. It's not good for you to hate anyone like that."

"Well, they didn't kill someone so close to you. My brother's dead because of them. Why shouldn't I hate them?"

"Listen to me, Laureen. Many of the Union soldiers were killed in that war, too. They left behind grieving widows, brothers, sisters, parents and children. Everyone has suffered. But it's over now, and it's time to try to put that behind us and get on with the business of living. If you keep on harboring such hatred, it's going to damage you much more than it will those you hate. In fact they don't even know you exist, let alone that you hate them. So all those feelings you nurture only hurt yourself."

"I didn't come out here with you to listen to a lecture. Now if you don't mind, I'd like to go back to the boat." Laureen was not one to take a scolding readily, not even from this man she was becoming so fond of. How could he seem to be so caring one minute, then taking her to task the next? It was confusing.

They finished eating and were soon walking back toward the dock. Laureen was in no mood to take Roger's arm, as she had done most of the morning. She need not have worried about that.

Roger made no move in that direction because he was a little put off by Laureen's reaction, not only to sharing the boat with the soldiers, but to his words to her. This was the second time she had bristled at him when she thought he was getting too close to her and he found it a little less than flattering.

Perhaps he was misjudging her, after all. He tried to imagine what life could be like with her if she were such a spitfire! Perhaps not so pleasant at times, he thought. He realized he had been letting his loneliness prompt him to move a little faster with her than discretion would dictate. He promised himself he would be more careful in the future. Not that he was ready to end his relationship with Laureen. But he now knew that he wanted to allow himself to get to know this woman much better before he made a lifelong commitment to her.

As they approached the boat docks, they were quite unprepared for the sight awaiting them. So many soldiers streaming from the train toward the *Sultana*. Most of them were so thin they looked like walking skeletons. Many were still suffering from unhealed injuries received during the war, or from various diseases they had contracted in the prison camps. Some were missing limbs, walking with makeshift crutches or being helped by other prisoners. Some had empty sleeves dangling loosely from their shoulders. All of them were poorly dressed, many of them in little more than rags.

"Oh, Roger," exclaimed Laureen, as her senses tried to absorb what she was seeing. "I had no idea it was so bad. Is that what our side did to those men? I've always thought about how awful it must have been for our boys who were in the Yankee prisons. But I never thought our camps might be just as bad."

"I know," he said softly as he put his arm around her waist and pulled her close to him. "That was what I was trying to tell you a little while ago. Both sides have suffered a great deal. And those men you're looking at now can tell you all about it. But they're only glad to have it all behind them and finally be on their way home. Look at their faces. You don't see resentment on any of them. All they have on their minds right now is they will soon be with their loved ones. Can't you just be happy for them and not hate them so much?"

"I don't know," she answered flatly and without emotion. " I've hated all Yankees so much ever since we found out my brother had died. But I hadn't seen anything like this. Those poor men! I just didn't know!"

CHAPTER 19

As Laureen and Roger stood watching the Union Soldiers working their way toward the *Sultana*, they had no idea there were nearly 400 men who had already boarded the boat before the train had arrived. Those prisoners had come from the hospital and needed to be located on the boat before there got to be such a crowd, in a vain attempt to make them comfortable.

One by one the prisoners from the train boarded the boat, under the supervision of Captain Speed, who had joined the men on the short trip from Camp Fisk in order to be on hand to record the number of them who were being transported. The first clerk of the Sultana was directing the prisoners to the place where they were to ride on the boat. Most of those who came in on the train were being directed to the hurricane deck, the uppermost deck on the steamer. As the men were being settled there, one of them became curious about a hammering sound coming from below. As soon as the first clerk was occupied elsewhere, the soldier went to investigate where the sound was coming from and what was causing it.

As he followed the sound to the lower deck he soon discovered that someone, actually Mr. Taylor, was working on one of the boilers, making repairs. The man stood watching for several minutes, unobserved by Mr. Taylor, who was completely absorbed in the work he was doing, and obviously not very happy about the results he was getting. Finally the prisoner had seen enough and went back to join his friends. "Listen, Men," he said. "Do you hear all that hammering noise?"

Of course they could all hear it, as the sound came from immediately below them and carried to all parts of the boat. He continued, "I checked out what's making that sound and it's on the boilers. Somebody's down there hammering the dickens out of one of them, and I think the thing's not safe. It could blow and if it does, think about where we are."

"Yeah," said one of his friends. "We'll be the first to know it."

"Know it nothing," said another one. "We'll all be blown to bits and we won't ever know a thing!"

"That's what I figure, too," said the first one. "I think we ought to move."

The others of his group agreed and they went down the stairs to the boiler deck, saying nothing about what they were doing or why. Since there were so many men already on board and more arriving each minute, they were not questioned by anyone.

As the crunch of men boarding the boat began to lessen, Captain Kerns, who was keeping a close eye on what was happening on the *Sultana*, walked to the boat and boarded it, seeking out the first clerk. When he found him, he asked, "Do you have any idea how many men you've taken on board?" he thinking that the load was complete.

The first clerk answered, "By my reckoning, there must be close to a thousand already here, and there are about five hundred more to come."

"More!" exclaimed Captain Kerns. "This boat isn't designed to carry that many passengers. Good God, Man, that's too many. We need to put some of them on another boat."

"No, Sir, Captain. The *Sultana*'s a good boat. That won't be too many for her to carry. She can carry that many easily. This isn't the first time she's had that many passengers."

Captain Kerns was not convinced, but in view of what had been taking place during the preceding night and that morning, he thought it best not to argue the point.

As Captain Kerns left the boat, he met Laureen and Roger approaching it to go on board. He nodded to them, but said nothing as he worked his way back to his office.

Laureen looked up at the hurricane deck. There were so many men milling around or trying to find a comfortable place to sit. She groaned, "Oh, Roger, how many men do you suppose have boarded? That looks like a lot more than five hundred to me."

"Yes, and to me, too. I don't know what's going on here, but this isn't right. This boat isn't supposed to carry so many passengers. I'm going to find the captain."

"Why don't you look for Mr. Wintringer instead," suggested Laureen. I think you'll get more information from him than you will Captain Mason."

"Now that you mention it, I think you're probably right. That is, if he hasn't been drinking too." He laughed, but it was not a laugh of amusement.

There were not so many men on the lower deck as yet, so they were able to make their way though with relative ease. With the sound of hammering on the boiler still ringing out, that seemed the most logical place to start looking for him. But when they arrived in that area, there was only Mr. Taylor to be seen, still trying to repair the boiler.

Roger hesitated to interrupt him, but his desire to talk to Mr. Wintringer was stronger than his reluctance to disturb the boiler maker, so he raised his voice and called out to Mr. Taylor. "Could I ask you a question?" he called. At first Mr. Taylor seemed not to hear him, so Roger called out again. This time Mr. Taylor stopped working and straightened up, looking questioningly at Roger.

"Pardon me for disturbing you, but I'm looking for Mr. Wintringer and thought you might know where I could find him."

"No," came the answer. "He comes around here every once in a while to check on my progress, but he doesn't tell me where he goes when he leaves. Sorry I can't help you." And, he turned back to his hammering.

"Why don't we try the dining hall?" Laureen suggested next. "Even if he's not in there, someone may know where he is."

"All right. That's as good a place to look next as any other, I suppose."

But they did not have to go to the dining hall, for they had gotten only a short distance away from the boiler area when they met Mr. Wintringer, coming once more to check on the progress of the boiler repair.

Since Laureen had already met the man and spoken with him the day before, she spoke first. "Mr. Wintringer, I was under the impression that we were to take on something like five hundred Union soldiers here at Vicksburg. But that crowd looks like a lot more than five hundred to me. What's going on, here?"

"You're absolutely right, Miss Wallace. We have about a thousand men on board the boat right now. And I've been given to understand that we are to take on about five hundred more. I know that's a lot more men than our permit allows, but river boats have been doing that for a long time when the situation calls for it, so there's nothing to be worried about."

"Worried! That's not the point."

"Then what is the point, Miss Wallace?" Mr. Wintringer was a busy man and did not feel like wasting his time trying to mollify a disgruntled passenger.

"The point is that we are paying passengers and have a right not to be so crowded on a boat that's supposed to carry no more than 376 people on it."

"Miss Wallace, things don't always work out just the way we'd like them to. This boat is carrying Union Soldiers back North, and you'll just have to accept that. All of us have to be inconvenienced once in a while, and I suppose this trip is your turn. Now, if you'll excuse me..." And Mr. Wintringer hurried away.

"Oh, Roger, I don't understand. He was so nice to me yesterday, and you saw how he treated me just now. How can he do that, put so many men on the boat, I mean."

"It would appear that he can do about as he pleases. I don't know if we have any recourse or not. But it's only for a day or two for you and less than that for me. If we ever get under way, we should be at Memphis tomorrow at the latest. And less than a day later you should be in Cairo."

"Don't say that!" exclaimed Laureen, standing squarely in front of him and looking intently into his face. "We're just getting to know one another, and I don't like to think that we have only one more day together, or even less than a day."

"I know. I feel the same way. But we've already talked about that and what we can do about seeing one another in the future."

Before Laureen could answer him, she saw someone standing several yards behind Roger, trying vigorously to get her attention. Tolly! She had almost forgotten all about him. But he was still there to be reckoned with. She would have to find a way to see him.

"Roger, I hate to have to do this, but I need to go back to my stateroom for a little while. I'm sure you'll understand." And, she looked at him knowingly, willing him to think what she wanted him to think.

He did. The expression on her face told him she needed some privacy. As a matter of fact, he could use a little privacy himself, so readily excused her.

Laureen looked beyond Roger and nodded almost imperceptibly to Tolly. As she turned to go in the direction of her stateroom, she was certain Tolly would follow her. She wondered what he could possibly want of her, but she would have to find out.

Laureen would have liked to take Tolly into her room, since Florence and her children had not yet returned from their trip into the city, but she would not risk having other passengers see her do that. That was considered unacceptable behavior, and she was still guided to a large degree by the conventions of the day. Having so many men aboard the steamer proved to be an advantage in one way, as they could get lost in the crowd. But that also made it even more difficult to find a place to talk and not be overheard.

As she looked around for a place, she felt Tolly's hand on her arm, gently pulling her into a shadow where the soldiers had not yet ventured. "Miz' Laureen, Ah needs ta ta'k ta ya," he began. "Ya' still got dat neckless?"

"Yes, of course, I have it, Tolly. It's safe with me. No one knows I have it. Now, what's so important for you to talk to me about?"

"Tha's all. Ah jes' been t'inkin' 'bout dat neckless an' jes' wanted ta mek sure ya' still got it."

201

Laureen was growing impatient. She had been pulled away from Roger's company, just to reassure this darkie she still had the necklace that he thought was his. Little did he know he would never see that necklace again, if she had her way about it. Laureen still had not worked out the details in her mind as to how she would keep it from him, but there had to be a way. That necklace was her ticket to independence, and she intended to use it that way.

"Now, see here, Tolly, if that's all you want then I have other things to do. I told you it would be safe with me and it is." Then she added, "I don't see how you've avoided being caught on this boat. I never thought you'd make it this far."

"Ah knows it. But, Ah'se heah and Ah'se goin' all de way. Ya' wait 'n' see!"

Laureen turned her back and worked her way through the crowd of men to where she and Roger had been talking. He was not there, but as she glanced around the boat and toward the gangplank, she saw Florence and her children returning. The children seemed refreshed and happy, although Florence looked more tired than happy. As they came on the boat, Florence said to Dora, "Dear, would you take Adelle to our stateroom and put her down for a nap? I want to visit with your Aunt Laureen for just a minute, then I'll be along. But poor little Adelle is quite tired from all the walking we've done this morning, and she needs to rest right away."

"Aw, Mama, I want to see all the Yankee soldiers. I've never seen so many before."

"I know. But do this for Mama. Take Adelle to the room. Please."

Reluctantly the child started away from the rest of the family with little Adelle in tow. Gerald had already quickly greeted his Aunt and disappeared.

When the children were out of earshot, Florence said, "I knew the train had come in, but we had walked farther from the river than I realized and had to hurry back. Laureen, so many men. I wonder if this is really wise to have so many people on this boat."

"Roger and I spoke to Mr. Wrintringer just a little while ago about that very thing. He was quite rude to us, telling us basically to mind our own business. But I think this is our business. We're paying passengers and should have some rights to retain our comfort for the whole trip. No one said anything about crowding the boat this way when we bought our tickets. If we had known about this we might have taken another boat."

"That's exactly what Mr. Talbert did, you know. Took another boat, I mean."

"No, I didn't know that. How did you find out?"

"I saw him leave the boat last night with his luggage and he told me that's what he expected to do."

Laureen let out a sigh. So. Mr. Talbert was gone. He must have given up the idea he might get the necklace back. Well that was a small part of her problem solved. She would like to share her secret with Florence, now that Mr. Talbert no longer figured into the situation. But it was too risky. She knew Florence would strongly disapprove, probably even insist she try to find a way to return it to its rightful owner. Then, too, if she told Florence she had the necklace, she would have to tell her how she got it. That would mean revealing Tolly was on the boat. No, it was best not to say anything at all about it to her.

She was silent so long that finally Florence asked her, "Whatever are you thinking about, Laureen?"

"Oh, not much. I was just wondering when the next bunch of soldiers is to be brought onto the boat. Come on, Florence, I'll walk with you back to our room. I want to get this hoop skirt off. It's much too cumbersome to keep it on with all the people on board."

"Laureen! You can't do that! Without the hoops, you dress will reveal your limbs. You mustn't!"

"They're legs, Florence. Legs. And everybody knows that every woman has them. With all the petticoats I'll still have on, no one can see them. I want to be able to walk on this boat in a little comfort, and I can't do it with the hoops on. Just look at us now, how awkward it is just trying to get through the crowd that we already have. And with more men coming, it will be almost impossible after that."

Florence was still not convinced it was a decent thing to do, but she realized Laureen was determined and she said no more. As long as she did not have to follow suit, she could accept Laureen's choice.

CHAPTER 20

Florence and Laureen walked back to their stateroom, sometimes with difficulty because of the volume of their skirts and the crowded deck, but Florence seemed much more at ease with that problem than was Laureen. The more she felt pressured, the more determined she was to be rid of the hoop skirts. As the women worked their way through the mass of men, there were wolf whistles directed at them here and there. Florence stiffened, but Laureen laughed.

"I don't find that sort of thing at all funny," bristled Florence. "And you shouldn't, either. It's insulting."

"No, it's not, Florence. Look at those poor men. They're not going to try anything with us. They haven't even seen women in who knows how long. I don't think they mean any harm. They're just glad to be out of prison."

"Laureen, what's come over you? I thought you hated all Yankees."

"Well, yes, in a way I do," she said somewhat more slowly than her usual drawl. "But Roger and I were watching these men come on the boat. As I stood with him, watching these poor men, many of them really struggling to even walk, I think I started feeling differently about them. They look like they've been though such an awful time of it. I can't help feeling sorry for them even if they are Yankees."

"You never cease to amaze me, Laureen. I just never quite know what to make of you."

Laureen laughed. "Then don't try."

Soon the door to their stateroom closed behind them, and

Laureen wasted no time in getting to that little chore of ridding herself of her hoop skirts.

Dora had lain down with Adelle to keep her little sister still, which had the desired effect. Adelle had dropped off almost as soon as she was stretched out and comfortable. Even Dora looked as though she, too, was ready to fall asleep. However as soon as the two women entered the room, she got interested in what they were doing and saying.

As she watched her Aunt unfastening her dress, she asked, "Mama, are you two going to take naps, too?"

"No, Dear," answered her mother. "You aunt is just making some changes in her attire."

"Yes," added Laureen, "and I want to do it right away. I'm expecting a friend to join me on deck in a few minutes."

"You mean Mr. Wainrich, don't you?" giggled the child. Turning to her mother, she asked, "Is Mr. Wainrich Aunt Laureen's beau?"

"I don't mind answering that, Dora," said Laureen. "Yes, I think perhaps he is. I hadn't thought about it in those terms before, but that sounds just right to me." Laureen had gotten herself out of her hoop skirts with a minimum loss of time, then excused herself to return to the place on deck where she and Roger had parted.

As soon as she stepped out the door, she knew she had done the right thing in reducing the volume of her skirts. Even though the change in the weight of her clothing was almost negligible, she felt lighter, freer, so much less constrained. And it was so much easier to get through the assemblage of men than it had been before, although without the hoops to hold her skirts billowing out from her, the skirts were much longer. Laureen had to be especially cautious to hold her skirts up with one hand to keep from tripping over them.

There were more wolf whistles, and each time she could identify the source of one, she would favor that man with a nod and a warm smile.

Roger was waiting for her. As she joined him, he pointed to the dock and said, "It looks as though you're just in time to see the next bunch of soldiers come aboard."

Sure enough, there was another line of men approaching the boat, looking much like the first ones. "I don't see anybody checking them off this time," he observed after the men began boarding the boat. When we were watching the first bunch being loaded, I could tell that there was a man in uniform who seemed to be making a note of each one as he boarded. I wonder why there's no one doing that this time?"

"I'm sure I wouldn't know," murmured Laureen. "I didn't notice that before."

"Well it's probably of no consequence, anyway."

But it was of consequence, because it meant that Colonel Hatch was unaware that those four hundred or so prisoners had been loaded onto the *Sultana*. Colonel Hatch had allowed himself to be distracted elsewhere, forgetting how quickly the empty train could get back to Camp Fisk and return with another load of men. So there were approximately four hundred men whose names were not recorded for the roll preparation that was to take place after the boat got under way.

About the time the last of that group of men were loaded onto the *Sultana*, Laureen pointed down the river, and said to Roger, "Oh look, there's another boat that's going to dock here." She watched it easing nearer and nearer the dock and observed, "I don't think I ever realized there was so much boat traffic on this river before. I mean, passenger boats. With the war and all, I'm surprised there are enough people traveling now so the boats can afford to run so much. Hardly anyone in the South has money to travel, I would imagine."

Roger smiled down at her and replied, "We're traveling, aren't we? I suppose it could be the same with other people."

"No, we're not typical. Most people aren't running away from home like we are, at least us Wallaces. I know you're not running away, but my family won't be going back, not for a long, long time. I think that's not true of most every body else. I think most people don't have any place to run away to."

"You're probably right about that. And, you could also be right about so many boats on the river having a hard time keeping afloat financially. Let's see what boat that is. Can you read it?"

As the boat pulled alongside the *Sultana*, the name *Pauline Carroll* came into focus for them. Laureen and Roger watched with mild curiosity as the boat docked and was made secure. Two men left the boat soon thereafter, looking like men with a purpose.

And indeed those men did have a purpose. They were hoping to find passengers to transport North. They went immediately to the office of the chief quartermaster, Colonel Hatch, explaining that their boat was nearly empty, and asking if there were any Federal prisoners who still needed to be transported.

"I believe there are still some prisoners out at Camp Fisk," Colonel Hatch told the men. " It's my understanding that those men are already promised to Captain Mason, of the *Sultana*. You would have seen his boat at the dock when you arrived."

"Yes, of course. We're tied up right along side it. But, Colonel, if there's any chance that we might get some of those men, we'd surely be obliged to you. You see, our boat is almost empty. We can carry as many passengers as you want to put on her. We hardly even have any cargo and we do need a load. Any men you can give us will be greatly appreciated."

"Yes, well, I think I'd better check with Captain Speed before I give you a definite answer. He's out at Camp Fisk, supervising this transfer." With that, Colonel Hatch quickly scratched out a telegram, asking about the number of prisoners, and informing Captain Speed that the *Pauline Carroll* was presently tied up at the dock and could easily be detained. He summoned an orderly and sent him off to the telegraph office with it, telling him to wait for a response.

The answer Captain Speed sent back was that all the remaining prisoners were to be loaded onto one boat, the *Sultana*.

"Well, that's that," said Colonel Hatch. "I'm afraid the *Pauline Carroll* will have to be on its way without any prisoners. Good day, Gentlemen."

The two men were extremely disappointed at being so abruptly dismissed, but were not quite ready to give up. They soon found Captain Mason and asked, "Captain, how many prisoners have come on board your boat thus far?"

"I've been told we have about a thousand at the moment, and there should be about six hundred more coming any minute. I thought the train would have already been back with the second load before now."

Captain Mason had not been present when the train did come back with the second load, so he was not aware there were already more than fourteen hundred prisoners on his boat. "Do you really think you have room for another six hundred passengers, Captain Mason?"

"Oh, easily. I've had at least that many people on this boat before, probably more. Everybody gets along just fine." He thought about what he had said then added with a chuckle, "It's not as though these men had a lot of luggage with them."

"No, Captain Mason. It's doubtful that any of those poor wretches have even one change of clothing with them. Nevertheless, we have the *Pauline Carroll* here and can share the load with you. There's no good reason to crowd all those men onto the *Sultana.*"

"Now, you listen here," stormed Captain Mason, his tone turning ugly. "Those men have been promised to me and I intend to have them. I don't have to share them with the *Pauline Carroll* or any other boat. They're going on the *Sultana* and that's all there is to it. I'd advise you not to interfere in this matter."

Disappointed, the two men left. As they were leaving, they met a doctor coming on board the *Sultana.*

The doctor said, "I've been to see General Dana, and I have his permission to remove the 23 sick men I brought on board earlier this afternoon. These men are too sick to be transported in such a crowd. I understand that more men are on their way here, and I'm concerned about the safety of my patients."

"What makes you think they're in danger, Doctor?" asked Captain Mason. "I don't see any danger here."

"Perhaps you didn't notice those men are unable to walk, that they had to be carried aboard on cots. With the kind of crowd on this boat, they're likely to be trampled to death. I won't have that on my conscience. They're coming off, just as soon as the men I've asked to help me take them off get here."

"You can't do that, Doctor."

"And just why not? I told you that I've already spoken to General Dana, who told me it was all right to take them off the boat."

"Now, see here, Doctor. Those men are already settled on the *Sultana*, and I won't allow you to take them off again. They've already been recorded as being on this boat," stormed the captain.

"Sorry, Captain, but that's not a good enough reason to let those men be put in jeopardy. They're going off the boat just as soon as I can get them off. Your record keeping is your problem, not mine."

Within a few minutes the two men who were expected arrived and went to work, removing the 23 men on cots very quickly, since they placed them on the docks as soon as they got them off the boat, and went back for more until they were all off. The doctor then made arrangement to transport them back to the hospital to await a safer means of getting them back North.

As the last of the men were removed from the boat, he saw a fairly large group of men approaching. It appeared their destination was the *Sultana*. As the first of the line of men drew near, the doctor asked where they had come from.

The answer was, "We've been released from the hospital and told to get on the *Sultana*. They said we're going home!"

The doctor replied, "Men, I know you're eager to go, but the *Sultana* already has too many men on board it. You're not well enough to travel in such a large crowd, so I want you to go back to the hospital. I'll get you a ride out of here in another day or two."

As the men started to protest, he comforted them. "I know you're disappointed, but you're going to have to trust me. I want you to get home in the best condition I can bring about. Believe me, you're not ready to travel on this boat. There's not room on that boat for you to

211

even lie down, and I don't think you can stand on your feet for the next three days. Go on back to the hospital and wait. I promise it won't be long."

With a dejected look showing on all their faces the men turned back.

CHAPTER 21

After a while Roger and Laureen tired of watching the Union soldiers board the boat, and decided to try to work their way through the crowd to the dining hall. There, they expected to be able to sit and talk with some privacy. When they reached it, with only a little difficulty, they were surprised to find how many other passengers also had the same idea. Surprisingly only a handful of soldiers had sought refuge there.

"It must be that they don't have any money to buy food, so haven't bothered to come in here," mused Roger.

"I'm glad they haven't," replied Laureen. "I'm glad to have somewhere to go where we aren't so crowded. I hope this is the last of the crowd to be loaded on the *Sultana*. I wonder if the man who's been working on the boiler ever finished."

"Listen," he said, motioning with his finger on his mouth for her to be quiet. "I don't hear the hammering now. Maybe he has finished the job by now."

"I don't care if he takes all the rest of the day and tomorrow, too," she said. "I'm in no hurry for this trip to end."

"I know. I feel the same way. And I've been thinking about that. I don't know if I can work things out to get away from my farm so soon, but do you think if I were to visit you in June, that it would be too soon? That's not the best time for me to be away, but I do want to see you again as soon as possible. Do you think Florence's sister would mind putting me up for a few days then?"

"She's your kin, so why ask me? I've never met Zinnia, so I can't say how she would feel about that. However I am inclined to think she's on the generous side, because she invited not only Florence and her children and me to stay with her and her husband, but she even suggested that those Coloreds who were left at Three Willows were welcome, too."

"I haven't seen any of them. What happened?"

"We had only four left. All the others ran away. Two of the four were getting on up in years and when the time came, they flatly refused to go. We couldn't make them because they're not slaves any more. I think the other two would have liked to come, but Florence decided that since two weren't going, then none of them would. The girl, Bessie, is only 19 and I think she was rather frightened to be left behind. But Florence thought it was better to have somebody there, that it might help to keep looters away from the place. They can work a garden and have something to eat, but she told them she couldn't give them any money. She's hoping, though, that we can find a way to earn enough to keep the taxes paid until somehow things get better and we might go back. I think she wants to hold on to the place for young Gerald's sake." Laureen's voice had gotten softer and softer as she spoke, so that by the time she stopped talking her voice was barely audible.

She sat silent for a minute or so, looking down at the floor, but not really seeing anything. Roger made no response, sensing she was lost in memories of how things used to be.

Then she looked up at him and said, very earnestly, "Roger, there's something I think I should tell you."

She looked so serious that it made him smile. "And what might that be? Are you going to confide your deepest secret to me?"

Laureen jerked erect. "Don't you dare be condescending to me!"

214

she stormed at him. There was that temper again.

"Look, Laureen, just because I find something about you amusing, it doesn't mean I'm condescending to you. If you want to tell me something, then I'm listening. But I don't mind telling you I don't find these temper flare-ups of yours amusing at all."

Laureen had been ready to explain about Tolly's being on the *Sultana*, even about the diamond necklace, but now was not at all certain that was a good idea. She kept forgetting how little she knew about this man, how very recently she had met him for the first time. He was so easy to be with most of the time, but could she trust him with such a confidence? Could she be certain that all the things he had told her about himself were absolutely true? She decided it was not the time for confidences after all.

Finally she said only, "I'm sorry, Roger. I suppose it's that I'm not used to having anyone to talk to the way you and I have been talking. I'll try not to do that any more."

"Laureen, I have started to care about you a great deal, as unlikely as such a thing can be so soon after we've met. But there it is. I do care. And I want you to realize I think you're a very special person, not one I would ever condescend to. You're someone that I would like to be free to laugh and joke with. Now tell me what you were about to say."

"No I've decided now isn't the time. I'll probably tell you some day, but not now."

"Well as long as you don't tell me you already have a husband and ten children hidden away back at Three Willows, then it's all right."

Laureen started to bristle again, but as she saw the expression on Roger's face, decided to play along with the joke. "Oh didn't I tell you about them?" she said instead, smiling broadly. "I usually get that out in the open the very first thing when I meet an eligible gentlemen. That way everybody knows where they stand right away. I love flirtations, but with such a large family back home, that's about all I can manage these days."

Roger was delighted with her sense of humor. That was another side of her he had not seen before. But he was also curious about what she almost told him. She seemed so serious when about to speak. So he said, "Seriously, Laureen, there isn't anything I need to know about you, is there? Something that might impede progress in our courtship?"

Courtship! That was a word they had not used before. It made them seem so serious. She said, "No, Roger, there's nothing I can think of. I've never been married, never even had a serious beau, never committed a crime, nothing I can think of that a woman tells a man who's getting serious about her. I have good health and know how to work hard. I don't have many social talents though. I don't play a musical instrument, I can't sing, I don't recite poetry, that sort of thing. I'm not even very good at most domestic things, in spite of the fact that Florence has tried hard enough to teach me."

"Laureen, Laureen," laughed Roger. "I don't need you to tell me your life's history. It's just that you seemed so very serious a minute ago. I don't know what you were about to confide to me, but if you say it's nothing I absolutely need to know, then I'm content to wait until you're ready to tell me. You did say you'd tell me some day, didn't you? I just hope that by the time 'some day' comes, you won't have forgotten all about it, because you did arouse my curiosity."

"You needn't worry, Roger. This is not something I'm likely to forget. And I promise if we're still seeing each other by Summer, then

I'll tell you."

"Fair enough," he said, content to let the matter drop there. This was an intriguing woman. He was finding there were more facets to her than he had realized until now. "How would you like to go back up on deck and see how the loading of the soldiers is going?"

"Yes, let's do," she said, glad of something to take their minds off the conversation they were pursuing. "By the way," she said as they left the dining hall and worked their way through the crowds and up to the deck, " you never did say anything about my hoop skirts being gone."

"I thought perhaps the gentlemanly thing to do was to say nothing. But now that you've mentioned it, I think I rather like it. Gives me a better idea of what you really look like."

"Roger!" she exclaimed. But she felt no insult. There was such sincere admiration in his voice. "One thing I didn't think of, though," she continued, "is that my dress seems so much longer now. I'm having trouble keeping from stepping on it."

"I did notice that," he said. "You'd better be especially careful with all this crowd on board. Otherwise, someone will step on it and rip the skirt right off you."

"I hadn't thought about that, but I think you're right. But if I gather it up too much, then my petticoats show."

"Let them show, Laureen. These are people you'll never see again. It doesn't matter what they think. You do what you need to do to protect yourself."

Back on the deck, they tried to find an empty space near the rail, as Laureen especially enjoyed being able to watch the activity on the dock. She also enjoyed being able to look down at the reddish-brown water of the swollen river rushing beneath them. So much soil in that water and always on the move. It was interesting to her to try to contemplate where all that dirt came from and where it would be deposited down river, most of it near the mouth of the mighty Mississippi!

But, the crowd was getting larger all the time. Even though the official records showed about fourteen hundred men had come on board, the actual figure was closer to eighteen hundred on board already. While she and Roger were trying to find a comfortable place near the rail to stand, Laureen pointed. "Look, Roger, more men coming."

"Great Guns!" exclaimed Roger. "Look at that line of men. Surely they don't intend to put all of them on the *Sultana*. They must be bound for the *Pauline Carroll*. That must be why she's been tied up here all afternoon, waiting on that load of men."

"Oh, I hope so. This boat is already more than full. I wonder how many men there are in that bunch."

"I don't know, but I'm certain there are more than can go on this boat."

They watched as the column of men came closer to the dock, then saw it halt for a little while. There were uniformed men coming and going at the head of the column, obviously discussing something relating to that crowd.

Captain Speed was among them. There was too much noise from so many men talking all at once, both on shore and on the boat, for Roger and Laureen to hear what was being said, but it was obvious that there was a disagreement taking place there.

In point of fact, there was a serious disagreement going on there.

218

"How many men do you have in this group?" asked one of the men in uniform.

"I think there are about eight hundred this time. This is all of the men. We don't have any more left out at Camp Fisk now. It's good to get them all started North."

"Yes, everyone agrees that we want them all on the way," was the reply. "But I'd like this bunch to go on the *Pauline Carroll*. As you can see, it's tied up here and ready to go."

"No," replied Captain Speed. "It's already been decided that they are to go on the *Sultana*. We don't want to separate them."

"Is there any good reason for insisting that they all go on the same boat, Captain?"

"I told you. It's already been decide that they are all to be on the one boat. My Superiors have told me to do it this way and that's the way I'm going to do it."

"I understand that, Captain Speed. But the *Sultana* is already overcrowded and the *Pauline Carroll* has no passengers. You have two majors here. At least divide the men, and let one major be in charge of one group and the other in charge of those we put on the *Pauline Carroll*."

"How many times do I have to tell you, Sir, that all the men are going on the *Sultana*. Captain Mason is ready to go and I don't want to detain him while I try to get the orders changed." With that he motioned to the line of men to continue on and board the *Sultana*.

However some of the men nearing the dock realized they were being boarded onto a very crowded boat, and began to wonder aloud why they couldn't board the other boat that was docked alongside the *Sultana*.

219

Said one of them, "We don't know which way that other boat is going. It might be going South, for all we know."

"No," said another soldier, "I heard somebody talking about it. That's the *Pauline Carroll* and it's going North. I think we ought to ignore these men here and go get on it, orders or no. If we get on the *Sultana*, we're not even going to have a place to attend the calls of nature in private. And I doubt that there are only men on that boat. Must be women on there, too. What do you think, Men? Shall we give it a try?"

Suddenly the men broke ranks and many of them started toward the *Pauline Carroll*. Before any of them could reach the other boat, Captain Speed yelled at them. "Hey, what do you think you're doing there?" he called.

One of the Union soldiers, who seemed to be taking the lead in this rebellion shouted back, "We're getting on the *Pauline Carroll*. I don't see no soldiers on her and I can see too many on the *Sultana*. So we've decided that we'll ride on the empty boat."

"Hold up just a minute before you do," he called, hurrying toward the men. When he was within talking distance he said, "Apparently you don't know what the reason is you can't ride that boat. There's small pox on board the *Pauline Carroll*, and we don't want you men exposed to that. We know you're already weak and that makes it easier for you to catch things. We're just trying to protect you, Men. Now do what we say and get on the *Sultana*. I know it's a little crowded, but you won't be on there very long. You'll be where you want to go in just a couple of days, and all this will be behind you."

The men grumbled, disappointed, but turned back to the line of men boarding the *Sultana*. As more and more men crowded on, it seemed every square inch of space was taken up by pairs of boots and shoes, even bare feet.

Laureen was beginning to wish she and Roger had stayed in the dining hall. What she didn't know was that it had filled up with men, too. When the prisoners realized there was room in there, they slipped in, trying to find a place to ride. Every where she turned, there was a sea of faces looking back at her. Laureen was almost in tears by this time. Finally Roger said to her, "Let's try to make our way back to your stateroom. We can go in there if we have to. But this is no place for you to be. As sick as some of these men are, you're likely to catch something. See if you can squeeze through right behind me. I'll try to make a path for you. Be sure you get that skirt of yours up off the floor."

Roger started pushing his way through the heavy crunch of men with Laureen right behind him. She dared not let him get away from her, so she leaned herself against his back, refusing to let anyone get between them. Slowly they inched their way toward the saloon and her room. As they were nearing the saloon, Captain Mason could be seen on the stairway leading to topside.

One of the men called out to him. "Captain, don't you think you've got too many men on this boat? Do you seriously think your boat can transport so many of us safely?"

Captain Mason snapped back, "I know it's crowded, but there's nothing I can do about that. Anyway you don't have a thing to worry about. This boat will get us where you want to go in very good time. Now try to get comfortable and relax." And Captain Mason went on with what he was doing.

"Oh, Roger," cried Laureen as they opened the door to the Wallace's stateroom, "I don't understand why there have to be so many men on board this boat. You'd think it was the only one left on the river now. I was so sure they'd put some of them on the *Pauline Carroll*. This makes no sense to me at all.

"It doesn't make any sense to me, either. I don't know how they'll all be able to even find deck space to lie down to sleep. And how will they get fed? I overheard one of the waiters in the dining hall say they have only one cookstove on board. I don't think they're bringing food on board with them, so it looks like a lot of people are going to get hungry before we get to our destinations. And that may include us."

Laureen had been so relieved to get into her stateroom where there was space to move about that she, at first, failed to think she was doing something respectable women never did, that is, visit with a man who was not her husband alone in a bedroom. Suddenly the reality of that surfaced to her consciousness. She exclaimed, "Roger, we can't stay here."

"Why not?" he demanded. "It's a lot better than being out there with all those people!"

"But..." she started, beginning to redden in the face, not knowing how to explain. "But..."

"Oh, I see," he said, smiling at her discomfort. "We're behaving 'improperly,' since there's no one else in here with us. Is that it?"

Laureen ducked her head, staring at the floor. "Well yes, I suppose that's it." Then she met his eyes and said, "I was only thinking about getting away from all those people when we came in here. And if we go back out they'll still be there. So let's stay where we are. I'm a little surprised Florence and her brood aren't here, too. Maybe they're having a hard time getting through the throng, just as we did."

Roger moved closer to Laureen, putting his hands on her arms and saying, "We wanted some privacy and now we have it. I think we should take advantage of it." He bent his head and, once again, pulled her close to him as he pressed his lips against hers.

This time, Laureen was not surprised, and as she responded to his love making, he moved his hands from her arms and slipped them around her waist, while she raised her arms to encircle his neck. It was a long embrace with neither of them wanting it to end. They did not hear the door open or see Florence standing in the doorway until she spoke.

"Laureen, what is the meaning of this?" she cried in open-mouthed dismay.

Laureen and Roger jumped apart guiltily, like children caught in the act of some mischief.

When she could find her voice, Laureen faced Florence and said, "We couldn't stand being so crowded on deck so we came back here, fully expecting you and the children to be here. But, you weren't and we decided to take advantage of a little privacy. I'm a grown woman, Florence, and I won't be scolded as if I were one of your children. Now do come in and close the door."

CHAPTER 22

Florence clamped her mouth shut and did as Laureen had bidden. With the door firmly closed behind her, she leaned against it and waited for Laureen or Roger to speak. When several seconds passed with no comment from either of them, she asked, "Do you have any idea when this boat is expected to get under way?"

Roger answered her. "I think it will likely be soon, now. We noticed a little while ago that the repairs on the boilers seem to be finished. At least the hammering has stopped. And we surely have reached carrying capacity for passengers. I don't see how they can possibly accommodate any more men on this boat."

"That's exactly what I thought before they started loading that last bunch, but when I was on deck last time they were still bringing more men on board. I really don't know where they can all ride!"

Laureen broke in. "Where are the children, Florence?"

"I left them in the dining hall but now I'm wondering if that was such a good idea. I was getting a little concerned about where you might be and if you were all right so decided to check our stateroom." As she spoke a rather sharp edge crept into her voice as she added, "It looks as though my worries for you were misplaced, though. Now I have to make my way back through all that crush of men to my children. I wish I had brought them with me when I came."

It was obvious Florence was feeling some distress over the thought of having to leave the stateroom and deal with the difficult task of inching her way back through the jungle of reeking and emaciated bodies to the dining hall where her children waited for her.

Roger studied her face for a moment then very gently put his hand on her arm and asked, "Would you like me to bring your children back to this room?"

Her response was immediate. "Oh, would you?" she asked eagerly. "I was trying to think if there was any way to make it easier, but without success. It was hard enough coming here just now and I hate the thought of having to do it twice more. I suppose that's selfish of me to be so willing to let you do what I can't bear to do myself."

"Not at all," was Roger's gallant reply. "I'm more than happy to do it for you. And, truth to tell, I can probably get through the crowd easier than you can. Gerald can help me get the girls back here and all will be well very shortly. You'll see." And he slipped out the door.

He quickly realized that getting to the dining hall would be no easy task. Quite a few more men had come on board since he and Laureen had gone into the stateroom, so he had to virtually push his way through the horde that filled every bit of space every where he looked. What had been a quick and easy stroll at the beginning of the trip was now an agonizing and time-consuming struggle. He almost had to fight for very step he took and he invariably stepped on someone's foot with almost every move he made. If so many of the men had not been so weakened from malnutrition and disease, he would probably have had to literally fight his way through. As it was they only wanted to be left alone and Roger's passing among them was just one more thing they had to endure.

Most of them were in good spirits from the thought that they were about to go home. The war was over. They were safe now and would soon be joining their families at points north. Nevertheless, the rigors of war were telling on them. They were so tired. Sickness was widespread among them, and it had been such a long time since any of them ate a decent meal. They were not been given nearly enough blankets to ward off the cool April nights, and there was not enough shelter on board the boat to protect them from the showers that invariably came this time of the year. All too many of them would have to sleep on the cold decks without any protection from the elements.

Eventually Roger reached the dining hall. His ordeal was at least half finished, but he already dreaded his return to the stateroom. As he entered the room a feeling of dismay almost overwhelmed him. Here, too, was a mass of bodies filling all available space. And the smell of the diseased bodies here was even worse than on the decks or even in the saloon that led from the stateroom to the dining hall. Roger felt as though his sense of smell was being assaulted. He forced himself to ignore it and concentrate on the task at hand. How was he going to find the Wallace children in that crowd? He looked around hoping he could find a chair to stand on, anything that would give him a means of looking across that sea of men and try to pick out a particular young man and two little girls.

All the chairs were occupied, even the tables had men sitting on them. Roger slowly worked his way to the nearest table and persuaded the men to make room for him to stand on it by assuring them that he wanted only to be able to look around the room to find three young children, and would be there no longer than would be necessary to locate them.

From that vantage point he saw them perched on a table a short distance from where he stood. Even though most of the men were talking quietly or not at all, there was enough noise in the room so he could not make himself heard above it. After calling out to the children a few times and getting no response from them, he put his fingers in his mouth and gave an ear-splitting whistle that instantly got everyone's attention. Conversation stopped and all eyes turned

226

toward the source of the whistle. The Wallace children immediately recognized the man standing on the table.

He called out to them and motioned to them to come to him. He stood where he was as they slowly and painfully approached. He stepped down and told Gerald to assume responsibility for Dora and to go back to their stateroom. He would take care of Adele. He waited for Gerald and Dora to move away then reached down and picked Adele up, knowing he would have to carry her the whole distance. It would be harder to get through that way, but she was too little to walk through such a maze of legs. It would be all too easy for someone not to see her and step on her. Roger would not risk that so he lifted her above his head and settled her on his shoulders, a position that brought squeals of delight from the child.

After what seemed to be an endlessly long time, the four of them were in the Wallace's stateroom. "I don't know how to thank you for bringing my children in here," Florence said. "I don't quite know how you managed it but I'm so grateful you did. I wish we had something to offer you in the way of refreshments, but I think we have eaten all we brought. We had only a little food in here to begin with and the children soon ate it all."

"That's all right, Florence. I don't need anything. But thank you."

Florence busied herself with getting the girls ready for bed.

Gerald was feeling very frustrated and bored. He had readily helped to get Dora to their stateroom, but now he had nothing to do. He was not ready to go to bed and his mother did not suggest it. Roger and Laureen had moved to the far corner of the room to continue their conversation. He wanted to go out of the room, but did not want to try to move around among all those men standing everywhere. Besides he knew his mother would object if he tried to leave the room. There was nothing to do but lie down on his pallet and wait for time to pass. Of course he was soon asleep, as were his sisters. It had been a long and tiring day.

In time Florence made that observation to Roger and Laureen, hinting that it was time for Roger to leave so she, too, could retire for the night. Reluctantly Roger bade both women 'goodnight,' and left the room. He was pleasantly surprised to find the saloon slightly less crowded than it had been when he had last entered the Wallace's stateroom. At his inquiry, one of the men told him quite a number of the soldiers had made their way to the upper decks.

He was almost at the door of his own stateroom when he felt the boat lurch slightly. "We must be underway again," he said softly to himself. He felt a sudden sense of dread, not quite knowing what had prompted the feeling, but he could not shake the feeling something was definitely wrong. He waited for a full minute before continuing toward his room, hoping he was only having a bad moment. When the boat continued to slide out into the river, he decided his imagination must be acting overtime and went into his room.

Once inside his room, he was unable to shake that feeling of impending danger. Without lighting a lamp he slipped across the room and opened a porthole, not knowing what he expected to see. But the night was dark and he found there was nothing he could see, except for an occasional dim light from a lantern on the western side of the river. He could hear the sound of the water lapping against the side of the boat as it slowly crept up river. The sound was not quite the same as it had been before so many passengers had come on board. It occurred to him that the change in the sound of the boat's moving up the river might be what was giving him this sense of foreboding he could not shake. In his mind's eye he could see the boat's sidewheels turning against the cold, dark current. Nothing unusual about that.

He could sense the boat was not moving as rapidly as it did before it was discovered the boilers were in need of repair. He had overheard one of the crew members telling another that the captain was satisfied with the work that had been done on the boilers, so he reasoned that could not be why they were moving so slowly. Finally he concluded they were simply carrying too much weight with all the extra passengers for the boat to move against the swift current very rapidly.

As he stood looking out the porthole, seeing nothing, he was soon lost in thought in another direction. Laureen. This woman he barely knew had turned his life of tranquility into one of intense emotional turmoil. He had met many women with beauty and charm, but this one was so different. He could not deny her beauty. He was practical enough, though, to realize that physical beauty was of very little value in the day-to-day routine of life.

He was acutely aware of the fact that she made little attempt to be charming with him. She was not rude to him but, unlike most of the women he had met of marriageable age, she seemed to be completely unconcerned about the impression she was making on him. She did not automatically defer to him, but readily made her wishes known.

In some ways she reminded him of his mother, a woman of good intelligence and with a definite mind of her own. She had worked with and supported his father in making their plantation the prosperous business it had become. A woman of that nature would certainly be an asset to him now. But how could he be sure she would work in cooperation with him and not soon be of a different mind set? Was she frivolous and extravagant? Was she lazy? If there were children, what kind of a mother would she be? So many questions for which he had no answers.

But as his mind wandered freely, he soon forgot he was looking for answers to such practical matters. This woman had become very desirable to him. It was apparent she was a passionate woman. He could almost feel what it would be like if that passion could be focused on him. To hold her in his arms, to know she belonged to him and only to him. To watch her temper flare and to be able to kiss those pouty lips to quiet her and direct her thoughts to parallel his own. To comfort her at times of disappointment and hurt. To share her laughter, to learn her moods, to see their lives merge and blend. It was exciting and, at the same time, a little frightening. But, so very appealing.

With such a jumble of thoughts crowding into his consciousness, his longing for her became so intense that he was physically in pain.

He had no idea how long he remained at that porthole, staring out into the empty blackness, trying to feed the longing in his heart and body. At length he realized he was growing chilled and uncomfortable, so he closed the porthole and felt his way to the bed. He had no need of a light to do what little he needed to do to get himself into bed. He was not actually sleepy and he expected to be awake for quite a while, nurturing the disquiet in his mind. But in actuality, he lay awake only a short while, thinking of the beautiful Laureen, before being overcome with much needed rest in a peaceful sleep.

But he might have not have so quickly gone to sleep if he could have known the thoughts that were racing through Laureen's mind at the very same time.

After Roger left the Wallace's stateroom, Florence and Laureen talked quietly for a few minutes, reviewing the events of the day. However, since both of them had private thoughts on their minds, their conversation soon lagged and they agreed it was time for them to be in bed.

As Florence blew out the small lamp near her bedside, Laureen welcomed the darkness that instantly enveloped the room. It had been an exhausting day, but she was not ready for sleep. Such a confusion of thoughts were sweeping through her consciousness. Of course they all centered on her feelings for Roger. That was the problem. How did she actually feel about this man? It was so unmistakable that he was getting serious about her. Even though they had only known each other for two days. Was that possible, for genuine feelings to develop so quickly? She had no way of knowing. This was an altogether new experience for her. She knew so little about men.

Her thoughts wandered back to several days ago, the day she and Tolly had gone to meet the Sultana on its down river run. That was the morning she had watched him from her upstairs window as he moved about without his shirt on. The memory of him stirred deep within her. The sight had been so appealing, while at the same time a little shocking, even to her. She thought about the glistening, tight skin, the muscles rippling across his shoulders and back. Did Roger look anything at all like that without his shirt? When he had put his arms around her to kiss her, she had been much too excited to think about such things. Now she wished she had not passed up such an opportunity to take note of how his body felt.

As her longing grew, she let her mind drift to what it might be like to be married to Roger. What might it be like to feel his bare arms around her, to share his bed, to wake up beside him. She felt her face growing warm as she tried to contemplate all that would go with that and was so grateful for the darkness enfolding her and, therefore, concealed the almost scarlet color of her face.

As unlikely as it seemed, she thought she might really be falling in love with this man. Perhaps tomorrow she would let him see he was becoming important to her. As she finally drifted off to sleep, her face was relaxed and bore a slight smile from her thoughts of Roger as her husband.

CHAPTER 23

The night passed quickly for those passengers who were fortunate enough to have staterooms and for the crew members who had cabins to protect them from the cool night air with its intermittent showers of rain. For those Union solders who were forced to ride on the various decks in the open air, the night proved to be of long duration. By morning they were cold and hungry. Many of them were very ill. The army had not provided even one doctor to help relieve their discomfort.

Among the civilian passengers aboard there was a doctor. When it was learned there was someone on board who could help, he was called into service and valiantly tried to do all he could to help those most keenly in need of his ministrations. However, with so many sick men on board, he was limited in the amount of relief he could give. He had little medicine with him and much of it was not what was needed to help these men.

When the sun began to peek above the eastern horizon the next morning, it was greeted with much enthusiasm by those stiff and aching men. Even as uncomfortable as they were, most felt they were better off on the boat, on their way home to their loved ones, than they had been in those terrible prison camps. At least the perils of war had been left behind. After the suffering they had endured in the prison camps, the discomforts they were experiencing on the *Sultana* were mild by comparison. And they comforted themselves with thoughts of loved ones waiting for them at home and that it was only a matter of days before they were safely back with them.

Laureen woke early, just as the light was beginning to penetrate the portholes in the Wallace's stateroom. She had slept well and had no memory of any dreams she might have had during the night. Perhaps the stirring of the many deck passengers had roused her so early. She dressed quickly and quietly, trying not to wake any of the other occupants of the room. She was hungry and wanted some time alone to think about the day just past. She decided she would not wait for her family to join her in the dining hall, forgetting for the moment how crowded the boat was and the difficulty she would encounter in getting there.

She was reminded soon enough, though, as she opened the door to men sitting and lying everywhere there was a space for someone. As she stood there with a dismayed expression on her face, one of the men caught sight of her and began nudging those nearby to make room for her. Instantly the men began to stand and open up a small passageway for her, each one nudging a companion. As Laureen worked her way toward the dining hall, she nodded her 'thank-you's to the men she passed.

As she entered the dining hall, she wondered how all those men who spent the night in there would be fed. She found her way close to the area where the lone cook stove was located and asked the cook for breakfast. Idly, she wondered aloud about how all those men would be fed from just one stove.

"Oh this stove isn't for those soldiers," was the reply. "This is for the paying passengers and the crew."

Laureen was horrified. "What are the rest supposed to do for food, then?" she demanded.

"That's not my concern," the cook shot back. "I got all I can do here to feed the passengers and crew. But I did hear someone say the soldiers had been given some food to bring with them before they got on the boat."

"What kind of food?" Again Laureen's tone was that of making a demand.

"Miss, I didn't ask fool questions and maybe you shouldn't, either. Just eat your own breakfast and let the army take care of those soldiers." With that he handed her a plate steaming with scrambled eggs and biscuits smothered in fresh butter.

Laureen looked around, but none of the tables had an empty space. She was about to try to eat her breakfast standing when a solder nearby stood and offered his place at a table. Gratefully, Laureen sank onto the small stool. But as she looked about her, she wondered if she could actually enjoy her food when all those men in the room were not getting anything to eat. She was ready to begin her breakfast when she looked across the table to meet the eyes of a young man who looked as though he had not had a decent meal in a very long time. He said nothing, but it was obvious to her that he was savoring the aroma of her food. Suddenly she no longer felt so hungry and pushed her plate across the table to him, saying, "The cook gave me much more food than I can eat. Please help me out here and take my breakfast."

With a quick motion of his hand, the young man pulled the plate to him and seemed to Laureen to almost inhale the food, as it disappeared so quickly. When he had finished her meal, she asked, "Did you bring any food on board with you yesterday?"

"No, Ma'am, I never got any. Some of the boys were given little packages just before they got on the boat but I think they ran out before it was my turn. I was one of the last fellows to get on board."

Laureen was aghast. "So you're telling me the army expects you to make this whole trip without any food?"

"Wel, maybe they thought some kind person like you might give

235

me something now and then." And the young man smiled at her in such a way that Laureen was doubly glad she had given her breakfast to him.

Laureen stood and moved away from the table a few feet. She looked at another young soldier and asked him what he was eating.

"Bread, Ma'am," he answered.

"Let me see," she requested.

As she looked at the lump in his hand, she exclaimed, "Why, that bread is as hard as a brick! Did they give you anything else?"

"Yes'm, we got a little meat."

"Let me see!"

As the young man opened up his little food package to her, Laureen was shocked. "All you have there is salt pork, and it's raw, besides. Is that what they expect you to survive on for this whole trip?"

"It's all they gave me. I think the others got about the same thing."

By this time Laureen had completely forgotten any feeling at all of being hungry. She started to push her way through the throng in the dining hall toward the door. "I'm going to find the captain and see if he won't feed these men," she said under her breath. "These men are starving and it's disgraceful not to feed them now."

As she reached the door, she met Roger. "Oh, so this is where you are," he greeted her. "I stopped at your cabin door and knocked. Florence would not invite me in, but she said you had already left. She didn't know where you went, but I think she was a little annoyed you would wander around in such a crowd by yourself so early in the morning."

"I don't know what the time of day has to do with anything," snapped Laureen. "It won't be any less crowded at noon than it is now."

"True. But I think she thinks more people will be stirring at noon and you might be a little safer."

"Roger, what in the world do you think can happen to me, regardless of the time of day or night. You see what these men look like. Most of them are so sick or weak that they can barely sit or stand. And those who aren't so weak have only one thing on their minds and that's going home. I think I'm perfectly safe."

"Yes, I think you have a point," he replied. "I was just passing along to you my impression of what Florence was thinking."

"I know," she said in a softened voice. "In her mind Florence, in some respects, is still living in pre-war days. But I know without any doubt things have changed and they won't ever be the way they were before the war. The sooner we all accept that, the better off we'll be."

"Ma'am, I think you couldn't be more right about that," said a young soldier standing next to them. "I know you weren't talking to me, but I couldn't help hearing what you said. This war has changed things for all of us, both in the South and in the North. When I joined the army I thought we'd go down South and whip all you rebels in a hurry and make you stop making your living off the backs of other men, of slaves. We weren't allowed to think of you Rebels as real people, but as little more than animals. But I never dreamed how things really were. The people in the south weren't nearly as bad as I was led to believe, that is, for the most part. And I never thought what it would be like to kill another man. Nobody prepared me for that. All of us from both sides who survived the war are going home changed men. And not necessarily for the better."

Laureen suppressed her irritation at having her conversation with Roger interrupted. She looked at the young soldier, little more than skin and bones, and let her natural compassion for someone so oppressed rise to the surface of her thinking. She smiled at him and answered, "I think I never thought of Yankees as real people, either, Young Man. I'm afraid we've all been taught to hate each other far too much. All the same, I do still resent the damage your army has done to my homeland and to my home in particular. You see, because of your army's setting fire to my house, I'm being forced to go elsewhere to live. I realize that you, personally, probably had nothing to do with it. But there it is, just the same!" As Laureen finished that last sentence, she had let real bitterness creep into her voice without realizing it.

"Ma'am, I'm sincerely sorry for what you've lost. And we could stand here all day blaming each other and our respective armies, but that won't change anything for either of us. I'm only glad the war is over now, and we can pick up the pieces of our lives and go on. I would imagine many of us will have to completely rebuild our lives. I can't help wondering what awaits me when I get home. Will Ma and Pa still be alive? Will they still have the little farm? I don't even know if my brother survived the war. He enlisted the year before I did and I have no idea where he is now."

"Where is your home?" asked Laureen.

"I'm going home to Illinois. My folks have a nice little farm back there. It's where I was born, and I never thought I'd want to live anywhere else. I'm hoping that I can make it home before another week has passed. You'd think that after three years of fighting, this last week wouldn't seem to be so long, but I can hardly wait. I just want this boat to hurry up and get there."

As Roger listened to this conversation between Laureen and the young soldier, he once again had a feeling come over him that made him very uncomfortable. He could not explain his uneasiness, but something was just not right. Something about the young man's eagerness. Something about how certain he was so very close to home. Was he? Was everything as right as it should be? Surely he must be imagining things he told himself. It must have to do with all the men on board that was causing his uneasiness. Still, the feeling persisted. He could not quite pinpoint what was wrong, but something definitely was. He tried to tell himself he was being silly, that his imagination was working overtime, that everything was under control. After all, they had been on the river all night with this great crowd of passengers without incident. He would simply have to keep his thoughts under control.

He had allowed thoughts to wander from the conversation at hand, but was brought back abruptly when he heard Laureen ask the young soldier, "Were you given anything to eat when you came onto this boat?"

"Yes, Ma'am, a little," was the reply.

"May I see what you have?"

The young solder pulled the small package out of the front of his shirt and handed it to Laureen. As she opened it and peered into its contents, she said softly, "Just as I thought. A chunk of rock-hard bread and raw salt pork. And not nearly enough of that, even if it were fit to eat."

She handed it back to the soldier, then turned to Roger and said, "I was just about to look for the captain when you came in. This is disgraceful."

"What in the world are you talking about, Laureen?" asked Roger. He was completely in the dark about the lack of provisions for food to feed all the solders on the boat.

"Roger, they don't intend to cook for all these men. The cook in the dining hall told me the stove was only to cook for the paying passengers and crew. They haven't done anything to get the soldiers fed. And just look at them. Most of them are starving. They don't need less food now, they need more. I got my breakfast a little while ago, but I couldn't eat it in front of all those hungry men. I gave it to one of them who hadn't even got the little food package that most of them got before they boarded the boat. Roger, he didn't have anything! No food at all to keep him going for the next several days. How can the army get away with that?" she cried, getting somewhat emotional at the thought.

"I don't know, Laureen. I didn't know the men weren't to be fed on the boat. But I don't know of anything we can do about it."

"Well, I intend to try! I'm going to find Captain Mason and tell him what I know and plead with him to feed these men."

"Don't you think he already knows, Laureen?"

"Maybe he does but I'm going to find him and make certain he knows and that I expect him to do something about it."

Another of the young soldiers spoke to her, saying, "If you can get the captain to give us something to eat, we'll all be so grateful to you, Ma'am."

"I'm going to try. That's all I can say."

With that Laureen left the dining hall. Roger followed. He had no difficulty keeping up with her. He remarked as they tried unsuccessfully to hurry through the crowd, "At least we can move through this crowd this morning, slow as it is. Last night it was all I could do to get to my cabin. I guess more of the men must have gone to the upper decks to find a little more space to sleep. It was rough down here last night."

"Yes, Florence said so. She was so happy to let you go to the dining hall to retrieve the children for her. And I thought that was a very kind thing for you to do, as well. I hope she fares better moving about the boat this morning."

Laureen had little idea where to go to find the captain, so decided there might be someone near the boilers and who might direct her to him. She worked her way to the stern and was rewarded to see the captain in conference with one of the officers. As she and Roger drew near, they overheard the officer say to Captain Mason, "Sir, we both know this boat is legally allowed to carry only 376 passengers. I don't know exactly how many people are on board right now, but I think we must have at least twenty five hundred. We can get them to their destination safely, I think. But there are an awful lot of men on the top deck. They need to be rather still and not do any sudden movements."

"Yes, yes, I know," retorted the captain, impatiently. "I've already been reminded that the roof could collapse. And I know that the men need to stay more or less in one place to keep the boat in balance."

"Yes, Captain. If too many of the men stand on one side or the other, the boat could capsize. That would only spell disaster for everybody. With this river flooded the way it is, and as cold and swift as it is, we'd lose a lot of lives."

Captain Mason looked at the officer coldly and said, "Then I guess you'd better see to it that there aren't too many men on either side of the boat at any given time, hadn't you?"

Laureen shivered at hearing such a cold tone in the Captain's voice. But she would not be deterred from her mission. She drew nearer the two men and said, "Captain Mason, could I speak to you for a moment?"

Captain Mason had not noticed her before she spoke. He looked toward her without trying to hide his impatience at being interrupted by a non-crew member. "Yes, yes, what is it?" he asked.

"Captain Mason, I've just been talking to a few of the soldiers on board and I've learned something very distressing that I hope you can put right."

"And what would that be, Miss?" He scrutinized her more closely and asked, "Miss Wallace, isn't it?"

"Yes, Captain, I'm Laureen Wallace. When I went into the dining hall this morning, the cook told me the stove would not accommodate the needs of the soldiers on board, that he would be cooking only for the paying passengers and the crew. When I spoke to a few of the soldiers, they told me they were given small food packets before boarding the boat. A couple of them showed me what they had. Captain, that food was not fit to even feed the dogs. There were small chunks of hard, stale bread and raw salt pork. And even if the food had been fit for human consumption, there wasn't nearly enough of it to last them for this whole trip. I thought you needed to know about this, so you can feed the men properly."

"Miss Wallace," sneered the captain, "I would have thought that you, a properly brought up southern lady, would not have cared whether or not these Yankee soldiers had enough food for this trip."

"Captain Mason," bristled Laureen, "I may be a 'properly brought up southern lady,' as you put it, but I'm first of all a human being.

And so are these men. Yankees or not. They deserve to be treated better than the way they are now. I expect you to see to it that they are properly fed. That's your responsibility as captain of this boat."

"Now see here, young woman, I don't need you to tell me what my responsibility is. I'm responsible for getting my passengers safely to their destination and little else. I think you'd best go on about your business and let me take care of my 'responsibilities.' Now if you have finished, I have much work to do. Excuse me." With that he turned on his heel and disappeared into the crowd.

"Roger, how could he!" exclaimed Laureen. "He has no intention of trying to feed those poor hungry men. I don't understand!"

"I don't, either, Laureen. But, there's nothing we can do about it. There are too many of them."

At that moment Laureen realized there was almost a sea of admiring faces staring at her. Men who had huddled in the boiler area for the warmth it provided against the coolness of the night and early morning. One very thin and threadbare young man with the scraggly growth of a youthful beard looked at her with such intense admiration that she nearly blushed.

"Excuse me, Ma'am," he said, lowering his head slightly. "I heard the Captain call you Miss Wallace. I just want you to know that all of us soldiers would like to thank you for what you tried to do for us in getting the captain to give us some decent food."

Another equally thin and frail soldier added, "You're truly a beautiful woman, Miss. I admired you when you passed by a minute ago, but what you tried to do for us made you much more beautiful than what I saw at first."

Then a third man added, "That goes for me, too. And especially so since you're a Reb...I mean a Southern lady. I would have thought all the Southerners would have hated us Union soldiers, and especially now since you lost the war."

By that time there were animated nods and open admiration coming from the whole crowd that had overheard the conversation between Laureen and the captain. One of them spoke quickly to his companion, "We don't need to go into that right now, Pete. In a way we all lost the war. We all lost things and people we cared about."

As so many of the men started to assent and try to speak at once, Laureen raised her hands to signal the men she wanted to say something, and they fell quiet again. She looked slowly at one face and then another and another, allowing herself time to absorb the true condition of those returning soldiers. It saddened her to the core of her being to see such weak, sickly, and starved men, most of them so very young.

Finally she spoke. "It's true I'm a southern woman, a woman who has for years hated all northern people with a very strong passion. But I've seen such bravery here on this boat, such acceptance of terrible circumstances, such determination to make the best of awful conditions without fighting back, that I've begun to realize that all of us are people. More or less the same kind of people. We've been shaped in our thinking largely by where we were born and the surroundings in which we grew up. I'd like to think I've learned something from seeing all of you men in the condition you're in. And I would like to think that all the people in this country have learned something about humanity, too, not just me. I'm only sorry that I wasn't able to persuade Captain Mason to give you something to eat."

"We know, Ma'am. The important thing is that you tried and for that we're truly grateful."

Laureen smiled at him and at them all. She and Roger started back from the stern of the boat, retracing their steps forward, with the men trying even harder to make a pathway for them.

As they got away from earshot of the men Laureen had been talking to, Roger said, "I'll tell you what I think. Since you already gave away your breakfast once, I want you to go back to your stateroom and wait there for me. I'm going to the dining hall and get breakfast for all of us and take it back to your room. If Florence and the children are still there, tell them to wait in the room for me. I'll be along as soon as I can. If I see them and they haven't already eaten, and I doubt they have, then I'll send them back to your room. But wait for me. We need to eat. Just because the soldiers won't get much food is no reason for us to go hungry when we don't have to. After all, they won't get our food even if we don't eat it."

"But, Roger..." Laureen started to protest.

"No 'buts', Laureen. Let me handle it. Everything will be all right." Then, he looked squarely into her face and said with a smile in his voice, "Now be a good girl and do as I tell you."

Laureen was not accustomed to having a man take charge of her in quite this way, but she had to admit to herself she liked it. Gerald had been in charge of Three Willows and was adept at managing the plantation. But he had left her to her own devices as much as he could, choosing instead to devote his time and attention to his wife and children as much as possible.

Laureen had never expected it to be any other way. But this "take charge" attitude she was seeing in Roger was most appealing. She felt she could quickly get used to it. It would be so easy for her to let him take care of her. With such thoughts in mind, she hardly noticed the little pathway the men were making for her as she made her way to her stateroom to wait for Roger.

CHAPTER 24

As Laureen entered the long, narrow saloon that would take her to her stateroom, she encountered two women she had not seen before. They too were trying to work their way through the crunch of solders who were everywhere on the boat. These women were dressed in a much flashier way than Laureen was accustomed to seeing. Both women wore richly colored short-sleeved satin dresses in solid colors, one red and the other one blue. Both dresses were cut much lower at the neck than Laureen deemed modest. Hardly the kind of dresses Laureen thought appropriate, especially for morning attire. They even had paint on their faces and rouge on their lips. She wondered how it was she did not see these women before, but was reluctant to speak to them. She still retained certain of the proprieties with which she had been brought up, including the need for introductions before speaking to strangers, even women.

But the two women had no such reservations in that regard. They seemed glad to see another female face in all that solid mass of emaciated male faces. "Good morning," said one of them. "I'm Ruby Walters and my friend here is Rosie Brooks. We're on our way to the dining hall." Then grimacing as her eyes took in the men all around, she added, "that is, if we can ever get there. Have you had breakfast yet?"

"Good morning," replied Laureen. "No I haven't had breakfast. But I have a friend who has promised to try to bring something back to my stateroom for my family and me. That's where I'm going now."

"I wonder if there'll be any food left for us, with so many people on this boat to feed."

Laureen quickly decided that there was no point in explaining the food situation to them in the hearing of the soldiers, so she simply said, "I've heard there's enough food for the passengers. You might as well find out. By the way, I'm Laureen Wallace. How is it that I haven't seen you on the boat before?"

"We boarded at Vicksburg last night and went straight to our staterooms."

"How ever did you find rooms in all this crowd?" Laureen's voice reflected the surprise she felt.

"We had reservations for staterooms," answered the woman who had been introduced as Rosie. She continued, "I think, though, we would have booked a different boat if we had known there were to be so many passengers on board. It would have been so simple to go a little sooner on a boat that might not have been so crowded. But we waited as long as we could so we wouldn't have such a long wait in Memphis. When we booked passage on the *Sultana,* we had no idea it would be carrying all these soldiers."

"Memphis is where you're going?" asked Laureen. "Do you have family there?" She was more than a little curious about who these women were.

"Oh no," laughed Ruby. "We're theater people. There are ten of us altogether. We're on our way to do our next show."

"So that explains the gaudy clothes and face paint," thought Laureen.

Ruby continued, "If you're getting off at Memphis, maybe you'd like to come and see us. We're pretty good, even if I do say so myself."

The thought was appealing to Laureen since she had never seen a stage play. The thought even crossed her mind about the possibility she could do something like that to support herself. Even though working as an actress was not considered a proper occupation for respectable women. Still it might be a possibility for her. Another option to be contemplated. She absolutely must find a way to make it on her own. Of course the diamond necklace still tucked away on her person made her feel much more secure about her future than when the decision was made to board the *Sultana* and go to live with John and Zinnia.

"I'd really enjoy seeing you perform, Ladies," she said, "but, unfortunately, I won't be getting off at Memphis. My destination is farther north. But I wish you well." She nodded to them and continued on toward her stateroom, leaving them to find their own way to the dining hall.

Laureen finally reached her room and was not at all surprised to find Florence and the children waiting there. "Oh, Laureen, I don't know what to do," Florence almost whined as she looked back from staring out the she porthole she had been sharing with Gerald. "The children are hungry and so am I, for that matter. But after that ordeal I went through last night trying to get the children from the dining hall back to here, I don't have the heart to try to take them back there. How did you get through?" Then her tone changed as she continued, "Where have you been, anyway? When I woke up you were gone. I was worried about you. Did you go to breakfast?"

"Well in a way I did."

"I hardly know what that means, Laureen. How can you go to breakfast 'in a way?'"

"I haven't eaten anything yet," explained Laureen. "I went to the dining hall and was able to get breakfast. But they aren't going to feed all the soldiers on board and one of those young men, no more than a boy really, looked so very hungry. He was sitting across the table from me and I didn't have the heart to eat in front of him, so I gave him my food. He ate it so quickly, as though he hadn't had a good meal in a long time, and I suspect he hadn't."

"So where does that leave us? Must we all give away our breakfasts? I don't expect my children to have to go hungry for the rest of this trip." Florence was beginning to get irritated at the thought.

"It's all right, Florence. Roger has gone to get breakfast for all of us. He's going to bring it back here to our room. He said for us to wait here until he gets back."

"How can he bring food through all that crowd? One can barely walk even without having something to carry."

"It's a little easier this morning. I think more of the men must have gone up topside, because I was able to get through without quite so much difficulty as last night. But I'm a little concerned about one thing. I think we must be rather top-heavy now. I heard the captain telling one of the officers to keep a close watch on the men and to see to it that they keep an even distribution of the men all over the boat. They talked about the possibility the boat could capsize if too many men moved to one side or the other."

"Oh dear," moaned Florence. "If it's not one thing then it's another to unsettle us. Never have I wanted a trip to end as much as I want this one to be over."

Laureen said nothing. She viewed this with such mixed emotions. She too felt her safety was less than secure on the *Sultana* and would like to be off the boat. But that would mean her time with Roger would be at an end and she was most reluctant to part from him. What a dilemma! She was grateful she had no choice in the matter. As it was she would merely have to see it through as the trip unfolded. She would have the rest of this day and likely most of the next to be with him before they reached Memphis. Then Roger would leave the boat and she was very uncertain whether she would ever see him again. True, he had talked of their seeing each other in a matter of some months, but she could not be certain he would still feel that same way when he returned to his home and the familiar routine of his life.

Also she could not be certain she would remain with John and Zinnia for those months in between her arrival and his proposed visit. She had every intention of making her own way, away from the rest of the family. As those thoughts floated around, she remembered the two women from the theater troupe she met a little while beforehand.

"We have some interesting passengers on board, Florence. You'll never guess. There's a group of actors traveling to Memphis. I met two of the women a few minutes ago."

Gerald was looking out the porthole all the while the two were women were talking, but when he heard Laureen say there were actors on board, he turned and said eagerly, "Actors! How many? What did they look like? Do you think I could meet them?"

Laureen laughed at the youthful enthusiasm. "Slow down, Gerald. We're not going anywhere just yet. I met two of the women who told me their names were Ruby Walters and Rosie Brooks. They said there were ten of them altogether. They were very friendly. As for what they looked like, well they had on very pretty dresses and they kind of stand out in a crowd. If you see them I think you'll know who they are." At that she looked at Florence and winked, hoping Florence would see the humor in it, which she did not. "Of course, I didn't meet any of the men, so I can't say what they look like."

Florence broke in. "Do you mean to say the women don't look

251

respectable, Laureen?" Without waiting for an answer, she turned to Gerald and commanded, "You listen to me, young man. You stay away from those people. Actors, indeed! As if we didn't have enough things to think about without having to worry about a bad influence on our children."

"Look, Florence, I don't think you have anything to worry about there. There are too many people on this boat for anyone to have much of an influence of any kind on anyone else. So don't be too hard on the boy."

"I'll thank you to not interfere with how I deal with my children, Laureen. I've noticed your own behavior on this trip hasn't been the example to young people it should be."

Laureen bristled. She was trying so hard to keep an even temper, especially with Florence. And they had managed to get along reasonably well since they left Three Willows, but when Florence let her tongue get a little sharp with Laureen, then Laureen instinctively lashed back. "And just what's wrong with my behavior on this trip?"

Florence was about to tell her, when she saw the shocked faces of her two little girls looking up from the floor where they had been playing quietly and decided this was not the time, not in front of her children. She said instead, "I think you already know, and if you don't know by now, then it wouldn't do any good for me to tell you."

Laureen's quick intelligence had caught the reason Florence did not say what she wanted to. She, too, did not want to quarrel in front of the children so decided to let it pass. The close confinement with Florence and the children was making them all irritable but it would soon come to an end. She could endure a few more days and then they would be off the boat.

As the silence stretched out between the two women, Gerald was growing more and more uncomfortable. He searched his mind for something to say that would break it. Unfortunately, all he could think of had to do with the actors traveling on the boat. Finally he asked, "Aunt Laurie, you said there were ten actors on board. When did they get on the boat and where are they sleeping? I can't imagine there's any more room for people like that with all the soldiers here."

"Those were my questions, too, Gerald," Laureen answered. "It seems they boarded some time last night, but I don't know exactly when. I didn't see them, but then I wasn't watching all the time the soldiers were being loaded. As for where they're sleeping, one of the women said they had reservations for staterooms. So those must have been kept empty for them until they were on the boat. When I saw the two women a little while ago, they were on their way to the dining hall to see if they could get some breakfast. If they do I hope they're able to eat it. I know I couldn't eat mine," she said, repeating what she had told them a short time before.

"Laureen, you never cease to amaze me," broke in Florence. "You've always hated all things Yankee. Especially since the war broke out. And now you seem to have nothing but sympathy for all these soldiers. For all we know the very one who killed Gerald may be on this boat.!"

"I suppose that's true," replied Laureen slowly. "I think it's unlikely, but possible. I grieve for Gerald, too. It's just that the war is over now and, for the first time, I've seen the Yankees as ordinary people, like the rest of us. All these men have been starved in the Southern prison camps, they're sick and dirty, and it doesn't make me feel very proud of our side. I know the Yankee camps weren't any better in the way they treated our men. And that's exactly what I'm talking about. Look how both sides have suffered at the hands of the

253

other. All I want now is for it to end. I want to be able to get on with our lives in some kind of normal way. We've hated each other long enough."

"Oh, Laureen, you're such a dreamer! Don't you know there won't be anything normal about life in the South for a long time to come? The Yankees won the war and they're not going to let us forget it."

"No, Florence, I think you're wrong. I've talked to some of these men and all they want is to go home to their families and their homes and pick up their lives again. They don't want to gloat. If we can all be like that, we **can** get back to something close to normal lives."

"IF, Laureen, IF. That's the whole point. The men on this boat are only soldiers. They're nobodies in the larger scheme of things. They're poor boys with no influence, just wanting to go home. They're not politicians, or policy makers. You don't see any of **those** people on this boat. But, **they're** the ones we have to be concerned about. I think it will be a long time before we can go back to Three Willows and expect to have any kind of real peace. And by that time, there may not be much of it left for us to go back to. The house will go down fast now, with no one there to even try to keep it up."

Laureen was silent for some time, letting the words Florence spoke sink in. She had not thought about things that way before. Perhaps Florence was right in her assessment of things. Laureen could only hope not. But if she were, then it was all the more important to Laureen for her to be able to go her own way. She wondered if she would ever go back to Three Willows. Indeed, she wondered if any of them ever would. As that thought crossed her mind a chill swept over her like a cold blanket being wrapped around her, almost smothering her.

As she struggled to shake off that feeling, Roger opened the door without knocking, bringing breakfast to the family. Exactly the tension breaker they needed at that moment.

CHAPTER 25

By the time the group finished eating, all of them were in a much better mood. Young Gerald was growing quite restless. "Mama," he asked, "do I have to stay in this room for the rest of this trip? There's nothing to do in here and I'm tired of staring out at the river." As he finished speaking, his voice took on the tone of a whine.

"Gerald, where do you think you can go on this boat now? Almost every inch of space has a man standing on it. You have more room to move about right here than you'll have anywhere else if you leave the room." Florence's distress over how much freedom, if any, to give her son at that moment was quite apparent.

"I know, Mama. But at least there are people to talk to if you'll let me go. Please, Mama? Please?"

Florence turned to face Roger. "What do you think, Roger? You were just there. Do you think Gerald will be safe mingling with all those sick and dirty men? The smell of them alone is almost more than I can bear. I'm reluctant to allow him to risk 'catching' something. I'd hate to take a sick child to John and Zinnia's."

Roger's tone was gentle as he spoke. "I know you want to protect your son, Florence. But that's not always possible. I suppose there's a little risk from some of the illnesses the men have. But I think most of them don't have diseases that are contagious. For the most part they're suffering from malnutrition and exposure. I think it might be good for the boy to mix with the men. He'll have an opportunity to learn something of the horrors of war. Boys that age often tend to glamorize it and not think about all the suffering and death that goes with it."

As Roger spoke the frown on Florence's face deepened, so he

added, "Well, Florence, you did ask me what I thought. If you hadn't wanted an honest answer, you shouldn't have asked."

"True enough," she replied as her frown turned to a slight smile.

Then turning to Gerald, she said, "Well, Son, I'm going to listen to a voice I hope is wiser than mine and let you go out of the room. I know you'll be a man before many more years have passed and you need to learn how to use good judgment by then. So start now. But check back here around noon. All right?"

"Yes, Mama, I will," said the boy as he started toward the door.

"No, Dora, don't even ask. You're not going with him," said Florence as Dora got to her feet and was looking at her mother with an imploring expression.

As her face reflected the disappointment she felt, and then defiance, the ten-year-old said, "What makes you think I want to go with him, anyway? I don't want anything to do with all those sick Yankees!"

"That's good. Because we're staying right here in this room for the rest of the trip. So, try to find something with which to entertain yourself." With that she moved to the side of the room, sat down and picked up the book she had been reading earlier.

"Laureen, we might as well move about on the boat some, too," said Roger, taking her arm and escorting her to the door.

"But," she protested, "there's no place to go where there aren't people. There's less privacy on the decks than there is in here."

"I think Florence needs some time alone with her children," he answered. "Humor me and go with me."

The door closed behind them, and they inched their way down

the narrow saloon with the crystal chandeliers hanging from the ceiling swaying slightly, throwing tiny flecks of light dancing across the walls and over the faces and shoulders of the men sitting and standing there. "Where are we going?" Laureen wanted to know.

"No place in particular just out on the deck," he answered. "I think if we keep moving, we'll find that we can talk with a measure of privacy. In any case, it's better than sitting in the room where Florence and her little girls will listen to everything we say."

"Yes, you're right about that."

As they made their way onto the main deck, Laureen was quite surprised at the deference all the men were showing to them. The soldiers all seemed to make a special effort to give them room to pass. She could not have known how quickly the word spread throughout the boat of her attempt to persuade the captain to provide food to the soldiers on board. The soldiers seemed to take delight in telling each other of the beautiful southern woman who was not afraid to take on the captain of the riverboat in behalf of the Union soldiers. The fact that she was unsuccessful in her attempt did not seem to matter at all to them. It was the fact that she tried that made such a strong impression on them.

Finally Roger said, "Laureen, I feel as though I'm escorting a celebrity. These men are certainly admirers of yours."

Laureen had practically forgotten her encounter with the captain earlier that morning, so she responded, "Oh, you're imagining things, Roger. They're merely being polite."

One of the young men overheard that exchange and spoke up, "No, Ma'am! We heard about what you did this morning. Every soldier on the boat knows about it by now. You tried to help us,

Ma'am. Nobody's done that in a long time. We don't forget that!"

"Thank you, Soldier," she nodded to him. Then as they advanced a few more feet, she turned to Roger and laughed, "Well so much for any private conversation. No matter where we go, whatever we say is going to be heard by others."

"It does look that way. I'll tell you what. Let's see what it's like back where the animals are. Maybe there won't be so many people there."

They continued toward the stern of the boat, grateful for the space the men made for them as they passed. Laureen wasn't paying much attention to the faces of the men by that time, so it took her quite by surprise when she looked at one of the men and found herself staring straight into the eyes of someone she recognized. Tolly! She started and her mouth opened. She caught herself just before blurting out his name.

Roger, still holding onto her arm, noticed that something had surprised her, and tried to determine who or what it was. But Laureen quickly recovered her composure. Tolly's steely-eyed gaze gave no indication that he had recognized her. Even though Roger's eyes quickly swept over the faces of the men in the near vicinity, he could see nothing that would account for Laureen's surprise.

Tolly had gotten out of the fine clothes he had been wearing the last time she saw him and was wearing clothing that more closely resembled what the soldiers had on. Laureen absently wondered where he got them. She correctly guessed he was again up to something, but she had no idea what it might be. She wondered if he were still pretending to be unable to talk. Almost instinctively, she allowed her free hand to rest on her stomach where the pouch holding the diamond necklace still lay. Reassured she gently moved her hand away and smiled up at Roger's face. He was still looking around the crowd and missed the whole gesture, for which Laureen felt very grateful. Her secret was still safe.

Finally Laureen and Roger reached the area where the horses, mules and pigs were penned. Sure enough, there weren't so many people there. "If we stay against the rail," smiled Roger, "I think the smell of the animals won't be so bad. I think we can endure it for a while. And I'd really like to have some time alone with you. All right?"

Laureen nodded and they leaned back against the rail. "Did you have something in particular that you wanted to say, Roger?" Laureen asked.

"No, not really. I simply want to spend some time with you. Just the two of us. Does that seem so strange?"

Laureen absently turned toward the water, seeking the fresher air. "Look, Roger. There's a big tree almost submerged that we came awfully close to," she said. "I wonder if there are more of them in the river. With the water level this high, it must be hard to see them. I'd never even thought about that before."

"Look at the bank over there," he said, pointing. "What do you see?"

"I don't see anything but trees."

"That's the point. Trees. And when the river floods, like it is now, don't you think some of those trees wash into the water? Sometimes the floods even cause the river to change course. And that new course is bound to be full of trees that get submerged."

"Then the trees and snags could be anywhere in the river!" she exclaimed. "Even right where we go."

"I know, Laureen. I've heard that the pilots really have to watch for them and try to remember where some of them are. They can tear the whole bottom out of a boat if it hits just right."

"Do you think we're in any danger?" she asked, becoming somewhat apprehensive.

"We're always in danger, Laureen," he replied, amused at her concern. "Anywhere we go, anything we do puts us in danger. But yes, I'd say we're in a bit more danger on the river than we would be in a wagon or a buggy. But if we never do anything we think might be a little more dangerous than that, we won't do much in our lives, will we?"

Laureen said absently, "Maybe someday they'll figure out a way to get all the trees and snags out of the river and make it safer for travel."

"Yes, wouldn't that be good? But I suppose when they do, then there'll be something else for us to worry about, don't you think?"

The two of them passed a good part of the morning in light conversation. Even though they weren't discussing topics of great importance, both of them felt that it was time well spent. They were getting better acquainted and for once, Laureen's temper did not flare up.

Gradually the day passed. By late afternoon, a few scattered buildings could be seen on the eastern bank of the river. Laureen wondered if they were nearing Greenville and if they would be stopping there. She remembered that it was the next settlement of any size north of Vicksburg. Although there was still a huge stack of wood to fuel the boilers, she could tell it had grown considerably smaller than it was when they left Vicksburg.

Soon thereafter, when Mr. Wintringer was making one of his

frequent checks on the boilers, Laureen approached him and asked if the *Sultana* would be stopping at Greenville to take on more wood. He gave her a quizzical look and replied, "There wouldn't be much point in that, Miss Wallace. There's nothing left of Greenville."

"What do you mean, Mr. Wintringer. I thought it was a good sized town."

"It used to be, Miss Wallace. But the Union soldiers burned it to the ground."

"But why?" cried Laureen. "Just when I'm beginning to think the Union soldiers weren't so bad, after all, and then I hear something like this!"

"The way I heard it was that the Union solders were in a boat and it got within firing range of the shore and some of the people in Greenville fired on it. Nobody got hurt but it really made the soldiers mad. So to get even, they went ashore and burned the whole town down. Darn shame, too. It used to be a good place to get wood."

"What about all the people who lived there? Doesn't anybody care about them?" Laureen was feeling horrified.

Mr Wintringer answered, "I suppose they're just trying to make it the best they can. Some died in the fires, but I think most survived. I'm sure you realize war does a lot of damage. I don't know what the answer is, Miss."

Roger broke in, saying, "My guess is they'll rebuild it, Laureen. The reason it was there in the first place is that it's the highest point on the Mississippi side of the river between Vicksburg and Memphis. And it's too great a distance from Vicksburg to Memphis not to have some town in between. Anyway, there's nothing you can do about it, so there's no point in worrying about it.

So, Laureen tried to content herself with the hope that the people who lost their homes had found shelter somewhere. She remembered how close her own family came to being totally without a place to live and felt grateful the fire had been confined to the one wing of the house.

As the boat moved slowly up the reddish-brown silt-filled river, the day passed all too quickly for Laureen. Much before she was ready for it, she realized the sun was gradually sinking in the western sky. She and Roger had stayed together almost every minute, moving about the boat a little now and then, but mostly staying near the animals. From there they could not see the setting sun but they could tell by the little sparkles of what looked like fire reflecting from the ripples in the water that the sun would soon be below the horizon.

"I really wish we could have gotten a better look at Greenville, or what's left of it," she said at last. "I know we were too far away from the shore. But it makes me so angry that those Yankees would burn a whole town down, just because somebody took a shot at them." It seemed that her temper was making itself manifest, after all.

"I told you, Laureen, to try not to worry about it. Save your energy for things you can do something about. Greenville isn't one of them."

"I know, Roger. I know. But I do wish we could have been closer to the bank so I could see what it looks like now."

"You might better rethink that wish, Laureen. Why do you suppose the pilot has kept us in the middle of the river most of the time?"

"I don't know. Maybe it's because the water is deeper in the middle. Maybe there aren't as many snags in the middle."

"I can think of another very good reason. Mosquitoes. If we get very close to the bank, and especially this time of day, they'd be swarming all over us. Remember how bad they were in Vicksburg?"

"I guess I had forgotten that. Well, I guess I'm glad we're in the middle of the river, after all."

CHAPTER 26

By early afternoon the next day, the *Sultana* was approaching the western bank of the river to dock at Helena, Arkansas. This time, the wood supply could be replenished, only it would not be necessary to pile as much on the boat, since they would be stopping at Memphis next and they should be able to reach it by the time it was dark, or very shortly thereafter. Then, it was only a short distance back across the river to Hopefield, where they would be able to take on a load of coal.

The wharfboat at Helena was a busy place and a professional photographer chanced to be there, looking for something to photograph, something he could sell to a newspaper or magazine. When he glanced at the *Sultana* approaching, he gasped.

"What is heaven's name are all those people doing on that boat,?" he cried, to no one in particular.

The dock manager was hurrying by, but paused long enough to answer his question. "The *Sultana* is transporting Union soldiers back north. They've been in prison camps. Is this the first time you've seen that? It's been going on for the past few weeks."

"I've seen it before," he replied, "but never so many on a single boat. Maybe this is the picture I've been looking for." He began to set up his camera to try to get the best angle that would include the whole boat and still show that it was so loaded with people. He knew he would likely get only one chance to do that as the boat came into position at the dock.

One of the Union soldiers on the Hurricane deck was watching the activity an the bank and saw there was a man with a camera setting things up and realized he was about to take a picture of the *Sultana*.

"Look, Fellows," he cried. "We're going to get our picture took!"

Others nearby heard him and word quickly spread throughout the decks that a photographer appeared to be about to take a picture of the *Sultana* and its passengers. The men were excited over the idea they might be included in the picture and many of them began to make their way to the port side of the boat.

Captain Mason was just coming out of bar where he had been seen often since the boat had left Vicksburg. He sensed more than felt the boat was beginning to tilt slightly. "What the.....?" he started, so surprised that he did not even finish the question. Then he started to shove aside the soldiers who blocked his path. He had to find the reason why the men were in danger of capsizing the boat. As fast as the mass of men would allow, he pushed to the port side of the boat. He had kept at his disposal a small megaphone ever since he took so many men aboard the boat, and was so grateful at this moment that he did so.

As he tried to race through the mob, he asked, to anyone who might answer him, "What in blazes is going on here? Why is everyone moving to the side of the boat?"

Most of the men had no interest in answering him, remembering he refused Miss Wallace's attempt to persuade him to provide food for them. Finally, one young man said sarcastically, "Don't you know, Captain? We're about to have our picture taken."

"I don't know what you're talking about," retorted the captain. "Picture taken, indeed."

"That's right, Captain," spoke up another soldier. "There's a man on the wharfboat with a camera and it's pointed toward us."

As the captain reached the deck and neared the rail, he could see that the soldier was telling the truth. He put his megaphone up to his mouth and shouted into it. "Everybody! Move back to where you were. Now! Do it now! This boat is about to turn over! Get back to where you were!"

By the time the captain began shouting to the men, the boat was visibly tilting and the men realized that what the captain was saying was probably true. The problem was that those men who had the most room to move, those remaining on the starboard side, were slow to move. And, with so many men on the upper decks, the boat was quite top heavy.

After what seemed to be an agonizingly long time, the men were able to restore the balance on the boat and it began to level itself again. In the meantime, the photographer was able to get the picture he wanted and was quite happy to have been on hand to record what later proved to be quite a historical event.

One couple, passengers on the boat, having reached their destination, disembarked. Within a short time, the wood was loaded and the *Sultana* was under way again.

The Wallace family spent that day much as they had the day before. Florence kept herself and her daughters in their stateroom, while allowing Gerald to more or less come and go as he pleased. Laureen and Roger moved about the lower deck, staying largely near the stern of the boat, talking of ordinary matters. With each hour they spent together, their feelings for each other grew and they could almost feel the minutes slipping away and the time drawing ever closer to when they must part.

Laureen wished with all her heart she could slow down the passage of time, but it could not be. The seconds, minutes, and hours ticked away and much too soon the boat was slowing down as it drew near the wharfboat at Memphis. Darkness had enveloped the boat some time beforehand, but neither Laureen nor Roger were conscious of when it came.

The lanterns flickered on shore, with the reflections dancing on the little ripples in the water. The *Sultana* eased against the wharfboat, and bumped into it with a slight jar. Roger and Laureen reluctantly made their way toward the planks being lowered to allow the passengers to leave the boat. As soon as the planks were in place, the troupe of actors seemed to appear out of nowhere and were the first people off the boat.

As Laureen watched them leave, she felt a little sadness that she had not been able to get better acquainted with the two women she met the morning before. Also, that she would not be around to watch them perform in the theater. But, most of her sadness stemmed from the knowledge that Roger would also be leaving the boat and she would have to continue on her journey without his company.

The actors were not the only ones waiting in readiness to leave the boat. Many of the soldiers were eager to escape the crowded conditions on the boat and enjoy a little freedom and purer air. The men pushed against each other to the extent that some were in danger of being trampled, so great was their desire to leave the *Sultana* behind them for a while. Shouts could be heard from some of the first ones to get off that they had found a tavern near the river, so for several minutes there was a constant stream of men heading in that direction, even though most of them had no money to spend. Neither Roger nor Laureen noticed that Gerald was among the men getting off.

As the steady stream of the crowd getting off the boat diminished to a trickle, Laureen's sickening dread of seeing the last of Roger intensified. Both of them grew silent as they watched the activity of the men leaving. Finally, Roger spoke. "Laureen, come off the boat with me for a while," he implored. "I know there's a lot of cargo to be unloaded, so it will be here for a while. Come with me, please. We can at least get something to eat, and you can take something back for the rest of the family."

Laureen hesitated for only a moment before agreeing to Roger's proposal. It would be good to get away from the stench of the animals and soldiers. The smell had even penetrated their staterooms to some extent, so there was no place left on the *Sultana* to be completely free of it.

"Let's don't venture too far from the boat," she pleaded as they started to leave. "We really don't know how long it will take to get everything done. I'd hate to get left behind."

As Roger took her arm, he put his mouth close to her ear and whispered, "Would that really be so bad, Laureen?"

"Yes, Roger, it would," she said with much more firmness in her voice than she felt.

As they left the boat and walked along the rough cobblestones, Laureen was glad for the support Roger was giving by holding onto her arm. The stones were a little damp, and Laureen was not so sure of her footing after being on the boat for the last three days.

Soon they were seated inside a small restaurant Roger knew about, located right off the main street that led from the wharfboat, one that served good food and afforded them a little privacy. It was the first real bit of privacy afforded them since leaving Vicksburg two nights before.

While Roger and Laureen were enjoying their meal and conversation, there was much activity going on aboard the *Sultana*.

All 120 tons of the sugar, as well as the wine was to be unloaded. As the crew went to work moving the sugar, word passed among the soldiers left on board that there was a little money to be made by those who were able to work if they would help unload the sugar. Quite a few of the soldiers responded to that call and were soon hard at work.

By the time that word was passed around, though, many of the soldiers had already left the boat. To Tolly, this seemed to be the opportunity he had been waiting for. He had not known what it was, but he saw an occasion to earn some money and perhaps end up with even more he had not earned.

Tolly was used to hard work, so he readily presented himself to one of the officers to help unload the sugar. Without paying much attention to him, the officer told him where to start picking up the bags of sugar and where he was to take them. Without hesitation, Tolly went to work. He moved among the soldiers, easily lifting the bags and delivering them to the designated location. Back and forth he went, saying nothing, quickly establishing something of a rhythm to his work.

One of the soldiers picked up a bag of sugar to hoist it onto his shoulder, but because of his weakened state of health, missed his footing, stumbled and dropped the bag. It broke and some of the sugar spilled.

Another solder working alongside him said, "Just leave it, Man. Don't say anything. Pick up another bag and act like you don't know anything about that broken one. Nobody here will say anything."

The soldier did as he was told and ignored the broken bag. But, it did not go unnoticed for long. Two of the soldiers who were sitting nearby, too weak to help move the bags of sugar, were not too weak to slip into the cargo area and begin scooping up handfuls of sugar and eating it. To those two starving men, that sugar seemed to be a godsend. As they helped themselves, even some of the men who were working paused long enough to grab a handful for themselves. As he walked away, one of the men remarked, "I don't think I ever tasted sugar that good before."

Slowly the bags of sugar disappeared from the cargo hold and then the wine had to be unloaded. By that time, some of the soldiers had exhausted their limited amount of energy and were unable to continue helping with the heavy wine barrels. They approached the officer and asked to be paid what they had coming. Tolly was very aware of who was working and who was tiring out. He kept his head down, continued with the unloading, and made himself as inconspicuous as he could. He even pretended that he, too, was growing tired, and worked with much less energy than he had at first.

As the crowd of workers became fewer and fewer, he decided he would not return to the boat. Things were going too much his way for him to risk discovery. Besides, he thought he might accomplish his goals more readily off the boat. He did not ask for his pay, but waited for those who did to leave the boat. Most of them also went into the tavern that the first men off the boat had found. Tolly knew he had less chance of being found out if he mingled with the larger group of men, so he slipped into the tavern behind several men who had just been paid off.

Slowly, slowly, he moved through the crowd, ever watchful of where the money was changing hands and where it was being put back on the person of the one buying drinks. Before long, Tolly had relieved quite a number of the men of their newly earned funds. As the drinks flowed freely, no one seemed to notice.

Some of the men were getting very boisterous. A couple of them had already passed out and had their heads down on the tables. The tavern keeper was used to this kind of conduct, and appeared unconcerned. The only thing different about that particular night was that there were so many more men in the tavern than was usual.

All at once, one especially tall man shouted, "Some no good theivin' varment has stole my money. I had two dollars on me and now it's gone. And, I'm going to tear this place apart if I don't git it back right quick!"

That got the tavern keeper's attention immediately. "C'mon, Yank. Nobody's stole your money. You probably dropped it on the floor and didn't notice."

With that, the men began to look down, each one hoping to find the missing two dollars. Tolly took that as his cue to leave the tavern. He had hoped to relieve a few more of the men of some of their money, but now that someone had become aware his money was gone, he would not dare take any more. The problem was that he was all the way across the room from the door. He could not simply walk to the door. That would attract too much attention to himself, something he was trying to avoid at all costs. So, he made no move to leave at first.

As the men continued to try to find the missing money, he moved into an opening in the crowd, and paused several seconds, pretending to look on the floor along with the others. Then another spot opened up near him and he moved into that. By this time, the soldiers had concluded the money was not on the floor and the tall man was getting loud again.

"By God, somebody in this room has my money and I want it back," he yelled at everyone in general and no one in particular. "I'm ready to break somebody in two if I have to," he added.

"Look, Yank," said the tavern keeper. "Even if someone did take your money, there's no way to know who it was in this crowd. Calm down, and I'll give you a drink on the house. Will that satisfy you?"

"I don't know," grumbled the soldier. "Two dollars will buy a lot more than one drink." He paused for a minute, then added, "Make it two and we'll call it even."

The tavern keeper was more than willing to give the soldier two drinks if it would help to keep the peace.

Meanwhile, Tolly was getting closer and closer to the door. No one had noticed him. Finally, he reached the door and slipped out, unnoticed he thought. But, just as he left, one of the soldiers at a table near the door asked his companion, "Who was that fellow who just left? I've seen him before, but I don't think he's a soldier. Do you know who he is?"

"Someone from the *Sultana*, I think," was the reply.

"Something just registered with me. I never did see him buying any drinks. Did you?"

"Can't say that I did. But, then I wasn't really paying any attention to him. Not everybody in here has bought drinks. What're you getting at?"

"Well, if Old Lean and Lanky over there really did have two dollars stolen, then that fella could be the one who stole them."

His companion thought about it several seconds, then added, "If he stole money from him, what about the rest of us? Do you still have yours?"

Both men quickly felt for their money. The first man was reassured to find his was still where he had put it, but his companion came up empty-handed when he reached for his own money. "I think we got us a durn thief in our midst," he exclaimed. "Maybe we'd better pass the word around and see how many more men have been robbed."

Even before either of those two men could say anything, they were overheard and men all through the tavern were checking to see if they still had the money they had gone in the tavern with. Unfortunately, all too many of them came up devoid of their money.

Fortunately for Tolly, most of the men had not noticed him and could not later identify him. But, the two angry men who had seen him could. They could only hope that their chance to do so would soon come.

CHAPTER 27

Young Gerald had not asked his mother for permission to leave the *Sultana*. He had not been in the Wallace's stateroom when the boat docked in Memphis, and when he saw so many of the soldiers leaving the boat, he decided he would be among them. He had wanted so much to leave the family, had not even wanted to get on the boat at Natchez, and saw this as his opportunity to escape to freedom. He simply worked his way into the gang of men leaving and was off the boat before anyone knew where he was.

He had no money, so knew there was no point in going into the tavern where so many of the soldiers were. He wondered how they could have money enough to buy drinks after being in a prison camp for so long. So, he passed on by the tavern and decided to take advantage of the opportunity to explore the city. The streets lights threw long shadows and there were not enough of them for him to see as well as he would have liked, but at least he could breathe air that did not reek of sick and unwashed bodies. And, just as important, he was not brushing up against those bodies with every step he took. He breathed deeply. Fresh air and freedom were a little heady.

With no particular destination in mind, Gerald wandered around the city for quite some time, lost in his own thoughts. Eventually, it registered with him he did not know exactly where he was or how to get back to the *Sultana*. Not that he necessarily wanted to get back to the *Sultana*, but he did wish he had paid more attention to his surroundings as he walked. He had made so many turns by then so he was unsure in which direction he was going.

In time hunger pains began to remind him it had been quite a long time since he had eaten. Also it began to dawn on him he had no place to sleep. He turned another corner and saw a large hotel ahead of him. It was well lit and he could see quite a few people moving about. In fact, the place seemed to be bustling with activity. As he got closer, he noticed a group of people dressed a little differently from what he was accustomed to seeing, women in bright and revealing clothing, men in fancier suits with bolder stripes and plaids than he had seen before. A large wagon with mules hitched to it was waiting while men were unloading all sorts of trunks and assorted baggage from it. Could that be the group of actors Aunt Laureen had mentioned the morning before? He tried to remember the names of the two women she said she met. If only he had paid a little more attention! Ruby? Yes, that was it! Ruby Walters and Rosie Brooks. Those were the names.

A plan began to form in his mind. This could be what he was looking for all along. He approached one of the men who was in the process of pulling a heavy trunk, plastered with bright stickers from various cities, from the back of the wagon. "Excuse me, Sir," he said a little timidly.

The man paused, letting the weight of the trunk remain mostly on the wagon. "What can I do for you, Sonny?" he asked pleasantly.

"Uh, are you one of the actors that got off the *Sultana*?"

"Why, yes, so I am. Johnny Sparks' the name. From Chicago. And to whom do I have the pleasure of speaking?"

"Uh, my n-name's Gerald Wallace," stammered the boy.

"Glad to meet you, Gerald. And why are you inquiring about my being on the *Sultana*?" "Well, uh, you s-see it's this way," started Gerald. He had never had a problem with stammering before and was having a difficult time understanding why he should be doing so now. He had never felt so intimidated in speaking to anyone ever before.

That must be the reason. He continued, "I was on the *Sultana*, too, and my aunt told me about m-meeting two ladies who were part of a troupe of actors riding on the boat. I thought if they were here, I'd like to m-meet them."

"Son, you're as nervous as a rabbit on the path of a rattlesnake. Take it easy. I won't bite you," he said, smiling indulgently at the boy. "Now, what did you say the names are of those two ladies you want to meet?"

The obvious congeniality of the man went a long way toward putting Gerald at ease and the stammering let up. "I think my aunt said their names are Ruby Walters and Rosie Brooks. Are they here?"

"They sure are, Young Man," he said, laughing. "Right over there." He pointed to a small group of women standing near the door of the hotel. Ruby is the one with the yellow hair and Rosie is the one with the red hair." Then, kind of as an aside, he added softly, "Did you ever see hair that color before?"

Gerald looked more closely at the women and at their elaborate coiffures and stated with a measure of surprise in his voice, "No, Sir! I never have." He thought about Laureen's blonde hair, but it was darker than that of Ruby Walters, whose hair was almost the color of gold. So gold, that he knew at once that it did not grow naturally that color. He wondered momentarily how she made it look that way.

And, even more surprising was the red color of Rosie Brooks' hair. Again, he had seen red hair before. There were several members of a family on a neighboring plantation near Three Willows who had red hair. But not the brilliant red that resembled the color of fire he saw on this woman.

Johnny Sparks was watched Gerald's reaction to the women with much amusement. He had guessed immediately this was a boy who had never been away from home very much. "Well," he said, "don't stand there gawking. If you want to speak to those women, then go on over there where they are. They won't bite you," he chuckled.

Gerald swallowed hard and started toward the door of the hotel. The women were absorbed in their own conversation, and hardly noticed the approaching boy until he spoke.

"Um, I'm looking for Miss Ruby Walters and Miss Rosie Brooks. The man at the wagon, Mr. Johnny Sparks, directed me here."

The women stopped talking and looked at the young boy. He was dressed nicely enough, reasonably clean and certainly mannerly. But, at this time of the evening, what could such a young boy be wanting with two actresses who were checking into a hotel?

"I'm Ruby Walters," said the golden haired lady. "What can I do for you?"

"Um, I just got off the *Sultana* right after you did." He paused.

"And?" asked Ruby.

"Uh, I think you met my aunt on the boat." He was having a hard time finding the right words to explain his mission.

"We met quite a few people on the boat, Son. Who is your aunt?" This question was from Rosie Brooks.

"Her name is Laureen Wallace. I think she said she met you in the saloon yesterday morning when you were on your way to breakfast." He had at last found his voice and was trying to get all the words said as quickly as possible.

"Laureen Wallace," mused Ruby. "Oh, yes, I remember her. Very pretty woman. Said she had given her breakfast away because she couldn't eat in front of all those hungry men. Is she with you?"

"No, but I wanted to meet you. I never did see you on the boat." He did not add that his mother had told him to stay away from the actors, even if he had come across them.

"And, why do you want to meet us?"

"Well, our house at Natchez got damaged by fire during the war, and my mother is taking my two little sisters and my Aunt Laureen to Missouri to live with her sister and brother-in-law. I don't want to go with them, but I need a job. I thought that an acting troupe might could use some help carrying luggage and things to do with the theater." Again, he rushed to get all the words said as quickly as possible.

"What did you say your name is, Son?" asked Ruby.

"Gerald. Gerald Wallace."

"Gerald, have you ever seen a theatrical production?" As the boy started to shake his head, she continued, "Have you ever even been inside a theater?"

"No, Ma'am. But, everyone has to have a first time inside one," he said very earnestly.

Rosie Brooks cut in. "Give the boy credit for being quick on his feet," she laughed. "He's right about that."

"True," laughed Ruby. "How old are you, Gerald? Are you sixteen, yet?"

Gerald thought he could pass for sixteen, so he said, "My birthday was over a month ago. Can you give me a job? I'm willing to do anything you need doing. I'm strong and I can learn what needs to be done."

"And, you say your mother's on the *Sultana*? Going to Missouri? Does she know you followed us here?" Ruby was firing the questions at him too rapidly for him to answer any of them.

Finally, she said, "I think we should talk to her before making a decision about taking you on."

Gerald had let his eyes drop down to look at his feet as the first questions came his way, but his head jerked up at that last statement. "No!" he exclaimed. Then, realizing he had given himself away, he said slowly, "I wish you wouldn't do that. She wants me to go to Missouri with her and the girls. It's just that there's nothing for me to do there, no way for me to get a job. My aunt and uncle live on a farm and my guess is they're just barely making it without five more mouths to feed. I think my Aunt Laureen doesn't expect to stay there very long, either. She hasn't said much, but I can tell by the way she acts."

"Well, Gerald Wallace, we'll have to think about this," said Ruby. "Besides, the decision isn't up to us. You were talking to the person who can hire you when you first got here, Johnny Sparks. He's the one who does the hiring for the troupe. Do you think the *Sultana* will be tied up here in Memphis all night? It was in Vicksburg all night, so it probably will be here all night, too. It's kind of a long way to go back there tonight, but I really do think we should talk to your mother before making a decision. Why don't you go back there and sleep on the boat tonight and we'll let you know first thing in the morning if we can use you in the troupe."

Gerald's heart sank. He knew if he spoke to his mother, she would refuse to let him leave the family. But, he had no other place to sleep, and he did not relish the idea of sleeping out in the open. The air was damp and he thought it would probably rain before morning. So, he could think of nothing else he could do, other than find his way back to the boat.

The problem was he had no idea how to get back there. He was afraid that if he asked the actors, they would not only laugh at him, but would conclude he was too incompetent to hire as part of their troupe. A boy who could so easily get lost in the dark.

He turned away and started to retrace his steps, at least as many of them as he could remember. Within a very short time, he realized he was hopelessly lost. He kept walking, trying to stay on the more lighted streets. He had no idea how long or how far he walked, when he realized he must ask for directions back to the river front and the *Sultana*. There was a little café with lights on inside, so he decided to duck in there where surely someone could give him directions.

Inside, he could see tables and chairs, most of them devoid of customers. He had never been inside a café before and was not certain what was expected of him. He did not try to sit down, but waited just inside the room, hoping someone would come and speak to him. His eyes were already used to the dim light, from being on the streets outside, so he looked around, hoping to find someone who would take notice of him.

Finally, a middle-aged man wearing a large, not too clean apron, realized he was standing expectantly near the door, and approached him, saying, "Is there something I can do for you, Young Man?"

"Yes, Sir. I can't remember which way back to the river. Can you direct me?"

As their voices broke the quiet of the café, Laureen stood up from a table near the back and gasped, "Gerald! What in the world are you doing here?"

Gerald's heart sank. Of all the places where he might have asked for directions, it would have to be the one where his Aunt Laureen was! But, there was no help for it now. She would see to it that he would soon be back on the *Sultana*. His hopes were dashed!

"Aunt Laureen! I didn't know you were in here. I've been trying to see some of Memphis and I must have gotten lost. I guess I don't know how to find the river, again."

"I suppose you don't realize how close you are to the river, then," she said. "You're only a few blocks from there." She stood in the doorway, pointed to the main street and added, "Go back out there, take a right and keep going. You'll come to the river in just a few minutes. Mr Wainrich and I will be going back shortly. So, you can tell your mother we'll be along soon and she need not worry about us."

"Does that mean both of you will be getting back on the *Sultana*? I thought Mr. Wainrich was only going this far."

"He is, Gerald. He won't be getting back on the boat. But, he'll walk me back there so I don't have to be on the streets alone. Now, run along."

"Aunt Laureen, before I go, do you suppose I could get something to eat? It smells so good in here and I haven't had any supper."

Laureen was aghast. "It's late, Gerald. You must be starved. I'll have a sandwich made for you so you can take it with you."

She summoned the man in the apron, who by this time had picked up a broom and began sweeping in the back of the room.

Within a few minutes, the sandwich was made and in Gerald's hand. Then there was nothing for Gerald to do but go back in the direction of the river. It was decision time for him. Should he get back on the boat and go to Missouri or should he try to find another place to sleep and wait for the boat to leave. If he chose not to go back to the boat, then he would have no clothes or anything else that belonged to him other than what he had right at that moment.

As he contemplated the various aspects of what was involved in making his decision, another possibility occurred to him. Perhaps he could get back on the boat, let everyone assume he was going to Missouri, and when the others were sleeping, he could take his things off the boat and go back to the hotel where the acting troupe were housed. The more he thought about it, the more that seemed to him the sensible thing to do.

CHAPTER 28

At the time Gerald approached the river and the *Sultana*, he paid little attention to the fact that some of the soldiers were beginning to drift back toward the boat. Those who had participated in unloading the cargo soon spent in the tavern what little money they had. When became apparent they stopped buying drinks, the tavern keeper let it be know to them that they should leave and make room for paying customers.

As he neared the river, he had not quite made up his mind whether he would board the boat or not, so kept himself somewhat in the shadows of the wharfboat. This afforded him the opportunity to think about what he would do, as well as watch what others in the vicinity were doing.

Soon he became aware from the sounds coming from it that there was a holding pen nearby where most of the livestock were taken when they were led off the boat. Gerald thought that might be a good place for him to stay for a while as he contemplated what he would do in the immediate future. He would not have as good a view of the wharfboat area, but he was also less likely to be seen there. Once again he found himself having to deal with the overpowering odor of so much livestock confined in too small an area. He had almost forgotten the relief he felt when he first got off the boat at being able to breathe fresh air. But, the befouled air was a price he was willing to pay to have the extra time to ponder his future.

Back on board the *Sultana*, Captain Mason was able to move about the boat much more freely, with so many men off the boat. But, he perceived a greater danger. With most of the cargo off the boat, and therefore, most of the ballast, he realized the *Sultana* would be even more top heavy than before. As he came across various crew members, particularly the officers, he cautioned them to watch the soldiers very carefully and impress upon them the need to find their places and stay there without moving about any more than was absolutely necessary. Also, many of the men who were riding topside should transfer to the cargo area. Suddenly, for some reason, he concluded the boat, with so many passengers aboard, was not as safe as he had at first proclaimed.

Meanwhile, Roger and Laureen lingered in the little café about as long as they felt they could safely do so. Each was very reluctant to leave, but the hour was growing late and they knew they must get back to the river before the *Sultana* pulled away from the wharfboat. It was only a few minutes after Laureen sent Gerald on his way that the two of them left the café and followed the route Gerald so recently walked.

They walked very slowly, so that even some of rather inebriated solders, also returning to the boat, overtook and passed them. Watching them, Laureen wondered how they were able to keep to their feet on the damp and slippery cobblestones and with such dim light coming from the street lanterns.

Of course, wherever she walked, her progress was impeded by her extra-long skirts since she had removed her hoop skirt. It was such a relief to be without it on the boat, but on the street, she felt very self-conscious without it and the need to gather so much of her skirts in her hand and lift them a little higher than she would have considered modest, had the circumstances been different.

As they reached the wharfboat, Roger led Laureen to the edge of the cobblestoned area, and into the deep shadows made by the large live oak trees growing near the river, then said, "Well, Dear Laureen, I think we've reached the point where we must say 'Goodbye.' I don't know how late the hotel lobby will be open and I don't want to find I have no room there tonight. But, you can be sure I'll be back this way in no more than two months and we'll see each other again. You will write to me, won't you?"

"Of course, I will. I have your address safely put away on the boat and I'll write to you just as soon as we get settled in at John and Zinnia's place."

"And, I'll write to you just as soon as I get back home."

They stood looking at one another longingly for several moments, then each moved toward the other at the same instant. Roger's arms were around Laureen's waist, holding her tightly, just as her arms were joined around his neck. Their kiss came so naturally. They clung to each other for a minute or more, then each slowly released the other, hating to break away. But, break away they must.

Roger asked, "Would you like for me to walk you back to your stateroom?"

"No," she answered, "I think I'd like to stay here for a little while and think. It's so crowded on the boat, and I need some time to myself."

"Well, after the way all the soldiers have been treating you the last couple of days, almost as though you were a goddess, I don't think you'll be in any danger if I leave you here. No one will bother you. But, I do hate to leave you."

Both of them had let their hands drop down to their sides. Then Roger took her hands in his, brought her fingers to his lips where he kissed them gently, then leaned forward and kissed her cheek. Then he was gone. He walked away, without looking back, as though he did not trust himself to leave her if he did.

Laureen felt like crying, watching his figure fade into the dim light as he put distance between them. These strong feelings she developed for him so quickly had taken her so much by surprise, and she was not entirely sure how to handle them. She was happy to have this little while by herself to try to sort them out.

Gradually the trickle of men going back to the boat became a steady stream. Laureen was so absorbed in her own disquieting thoughts that she did not notice all the activity until someone grabbed her arm, startling her.

She turned quickly to see who had such audacity, as Tolly said, "Heah, Miz Laureen. Tek dis. Quick. An' don' say not'in' to nobody. Ah gits it back from ya later."

Before Laureen could protest, or even ask questions, Tolly had thrust into her hand a large wad of paper money and he was gone. Where Laureen was standing, the light was too dim for her to tell how much money she held. She could tell it was truly money, but she could not see what the denominations were on the bills. Almost instinctively, she dropped her hand to her side and concealed it and the money in the folds of her skirts.

As she stood where she was, trying to understand why Tolly did that, a commotion developed near the area where the men were boarding the boat. "There he is!" shouted one of the soldiers.

"Catch him! Don't let him get away!" shouted another.

As Tolly was identified, several of the soldiers grabbed him, making it impossible for him to escape.

"Now, hand over our money," demanded the soldier who had suspected Tolly of stealing money from the men earlier in the evening at the tavern.

"Wha' money, Mista? Ah ain't got no money. Wha' ya talkin'

'bout?"

"I saw you back there in the tavern. A lot of us had our money stolen and you're the only one who could have taken it. Now, give it back!" demanded the soldier.

"Ah dun' tol' you, Ah ain't got no money. Let me go an' ya kin see fo' ya'sef."

"Do it!" shouted another soldier. "Search him!"

Tolly stood very still as two of the soldiers checked him quite thoroughly, putting their hands in each of his pockets, even feeling inside his shirt and pants.

Finally, one of them said, "It looks like he's telling the truth. There's no money on him."

"I still think he's the one who got our money," grumbled the soldier who had suspected him first. "But, we can't throw him in the river if we can't prove it."

Tolly had almost concluded he got away with taking the money and was about to go back to where Laureen still stood in the shadows, when he overheard one of the soldiers whisper to another, "I don't know what he did with it, but I'm certain he stole our money. So, let's keep an eye on him. I'll bet he doesn't get on the boat right away, so let's stick close to him and see where he goes."

Tolly knew Laureen would get back on the *Sultana*, taking the money with her, so there was no particular hurry in getting it back. He would wait until suspicion was off him, possibly even wait until the Wallace's left the boat at Cairo. He could afford to wait, so he simply waited until most of that group of men who had accosted him boarded the boat, then went on board himself. He made no effort to see what Laureen did or if she had moved from where he left her.

Even though Laureen was standing in the shadows, she saw and heard all that took place. "So, that's what this money is all about," she thought. "He's been stealing again. And, he's using me as his accomplice. First, the necklace and now the money. Well, we'll see about that. I think Tolly has just outsmarted himself!"

Laureen knew at that moment she would not give the money back to Tolly. She did not know which of the men were robbed, because she could not see the faces of the men who accused Tolly, and now they were on board. But, since she knew Tolly had stolen the money, he had no right to it any more than she had. And, she reasoned, she might just as well have it as Tolly.

Laureen stayed where she was for several minutes more, wanting to be certain things pertaining to that money had completely quieted down. At one point she wished she had gone to the boat a little sooner, because some of the officers of the boat had gone out into the city to try to round up the soldiers who went ashore and did not come back as soon as they should have. Some had gotten quite drunk, and as they were being herded back to the boat, they became quite boisterous and rowdy. Rather than let herself be drawn into that kind of environment, she waited until the bunch of men presently being brought aboard the boat found places to settle down for the night.

Finally, she concluded she would not be annoyed by the soldiers, and carefully chose her steps over the rough cobblestones and back on board the *Sultana*.

The men on the boat were settling down, trying to find a comfortable place to spend the night. Several of those who had no blankets chose to sleep as close to the boilers as they dared, grateful for the warmth provided there.

As Laureen moved across the crowded deck, gratified the men

were still treating her with such deference, she knew full well how quickly that would change if they had any idea what she was hiding in the folds of her skirts. She walked slowly, mindful with every step that she must not trip over her skirts, or do anything to reveal what was in her hand. Even though the lighting was very poor, she must not be caught carrying all that money.

Finally, she reached her stateroom, and slipped inside. The little girls were already sleeping, but Florence was still sitting up.

Without even greeting Laureen, she asked worriedly, "Have you seen Gerald? I haven't seen him since this morning, and I don't know if he's even on the boat."

"You mean he's not back yet?" Laureen was surprised. "I saw him, probably no more than an hour ago. He came into the little café where Roger and I were eating. He'd been exploring the city and lost his way. He was looking for directions back to the boat and merely chanced to come into the café where we were. I got him a sandwich, because he said he was hungry, then sent him back here. I supposed he'd be here by now."

"Well, as you can see, he's not. And, I'm getting worried about him."

"Oh, Florence, Gerald's not a little boy any more. He'll be all right."

"No, Laureen, it's not that. Don't you remember even when we were still in Natchez he didn't want to get on the boat? Remember we had to go looking for him?"

"Oh, yes. I guess I had forgotten about that. But, I think it's all right, because he really was looking to find his way back here when he came into the café. My guess is he doesn't want to have to deal with

290

these crowded conditions on the boat any more than he has to and is trying to wait until the last minute before we get under way again to get on board."

Laureen's words seemed to comfort Florence, because she said no more. Laureen looked about the room to decide what she would do now about the money. She would rather not share her secret with Florence, but saw no way to conceal what she intended to do. Still keeping her hand concealed in the folds of her skirt, she reached under the bed where she had stored her sewing box and pulled it out.

Florence watched her, obviously curious, but said nothing. She had learned from long experience in dealing with Laureen, that the fewer questions she asked Laureen about her intentions, the better the two women got along together.

But then, Laureen sat down on the bed and began to take off her dress, letting the money rest on the bed under the width of her skirt. As the dress came off, Florence saw the belt Laureen had sewn around her waist with the bulging pouch just below the waist.

That was too much for her to stifle her curiosity. "Laureen, what in the world are you wearing? I've never seen that before."

"I know you haven't. I didn't intend for you to know about it. Remember when Graham Talbert told you something quite valuable had disappeared and he was questioning the passengers about it?"

"Yes, of course. What does that have to do with you?"

"I have it," said Laureen as she gently pulled it out of the pouch. "It's a diamond necklace. Isn't it the most beautiful thing you've ever seen in your life?" She held it up with both hands for Florence to see.

Florence gasped. "Laureen, you stole it, didn't you? How could you? You have to give it back!"

"No, Florence, I didn't steal it. Tolly did. And, I can't give it back. Mr. Talbert left the boat at Vicksburg. Remember?"

Florence heard only as far as her mention of Tolly. "Tolly!" she cried. "How could Tolly steal it? We left him at Natchez."

"That's what we thought, Florence. But, Tolly didn't go back to Three Willows. He got on the *Sultana* when we did. He's been a stow-away all along."

"When did you find that out?" .

"Soon after we left Natchez. He begged me not to give him away. And, I saw no reason to. He's not a slave any more, he's free to come and go as he pleases. I thought he'd probably get caught and they'd throw him in the river. But, he's still on the boat."

"But, how did he get that necklace. And why did he give it to you? What are you going to do with it?" Florence had regained her equilibrium and the questions were coming fast and furious.

"Slow down, Florence, and I'll tell you all I know. Tolly slipped into Mr. Talbert's room sometime when Mr. Talbert wasn't in there and found the necklace. He said he thought Mr. Talbert had probably stolen it from someone else, so he took it. Then, he got afraid that if he got caught as a stow-away, and they found that necklace on him, they might kill him on the spot. He thought no one would suspect me of having it. He thinks I'm going to give it back to him when we got off the boat."

"And, are you?"

"Absolutely not! Why should I? We don't have any idea who it really belongs to, and I have just as much right to it as Tolly does. Besides, what good would such a valuable piece of jewelry do a darkie?" She laughed as she continued, "He certainly can't wear it!"

"But, Laureen, something about this doesn't seem right. It's stolen."

"I know it's not right, Florence. Nothing about what's been happening to us is right. And, I don't know how to put it right. I just know I have a beautiful diamond necklace I can sell for a lot of money, or I can keep it and maybe someday have a home and clothes I can wear it with. All I know is I'm not going to give it back to Tolly!"

Laureen hesitated for several seconds, then said, "And, that's not all, Florence. He gave me some money tonight. I think he stole that, too."

"Money!" she cried again. "How much money?"

"I don't know. I haven't had a chance to count it yet. But, I know for certain the soldiers suspected him of stealing it from them, and just before they caught him, he passed it on to me. He said he'd get it back later. Here it is." And, she picked the bills up from the bed where she had covered it over with her skirt.

Florence gasped. "Laureen, that looks like a lot. How much is there? Count it quickly!"

"I'm about to do just that," she replied as she began to count the money, all of it in one dollar bills.

As she finished counting, she looked up at her sister-in-law. "Florence, there's forty three dollars here," she said with wonder in her voice.

"What are you going to do with all that?" cried Florence. Then she added softly, "There are so many things this family could do with that much money. We might even go back to Three Willows and repair the burned out wing of the house."

293

"I don't know what I'm going to do with it. But, for right now, I'm going to put it in the pouch I made for the necklace." Laureen quickly dropped the necklace back into the pouch and proceeded to smooth and stack the currency evenly so it would fit in the pouch. By folding the money, it would fit down into the pouch lengthwise. The problem was thatit was not quite deep enough for the flap to fold down properly. She already knew when she put the stack of bills into the pouch, it would need to be sewn shut. That was the reason she had pulled out her sewing box. At first she thought a few stitches would be sufficient to keep it closed. But, now she could see that the little bit of flimsy sewing she first intended to do would not be enough.

So she set to work, needle and thread in hand. Laureen had long been used to making small, strong stitches, and she worked rapidly. Within a very short time, the money was securely sewn into the pouch. She knew there was a much larger bulge in the pouch now, and it would not be as easy to conceal as it might have been if she were still wearing her hoop skirt. But, with so much at stake, she was certain she could figure out some way to prevent anyone from noticing. The weather was cool, and a shawl tucked around her shoulders and held by her arms at her waist should conceal it. She would think of something.

She and Florence had barely finished preparing themselves for bed, when Gerald came back into the room.

CHAPTER 29

"Hello, Mother. Hello, Aunt Laurie," said the boy in a very casual tone as he glanced around the room, being very careful not to let his voice betray his thoughts.

"Gerald! Where have you been?" cried Florence.

"Oh, I looked around Memphis for a while and sort of got lost. Didn't Aunt Laurie tell you she directed me back to the boat?" he asked innocently.

"Yes, she did tell me, but she said that was at least an hour ago, perhaps longer. Why did it take you so long to get back here?"

"Oh, Mother, once I got my bearings again, I saw no reason to hurry. I've been working my way back here, and watching all the activity of getting the soldiers back on the boat. And, something very interesting," he said, hoping to change the subject. "I saw a man who looks just like Tolly. I didn't get a very good look at him, and I know we left Tolly back in Natchez, but that man I saw certainly did look like him."

Florence looked first at Laureen, then at her son. "You probably did see Tolly, Gerald. Laureen has just told me she has known for some time he's been on the boat. He's a stow-away."

"A stow-away! I wonder how he's managed that!" Then, directing his words to his aunt, he asked, "Did he tell you how he did that, Aunt Laureen?"

"No, Gerald, he didn't," replied Laureen. Then she added, "And, I didn't ask. I only talked to him a couple of times. And then only briefly. But, since he's no longer a slave, I saw no reason to turn him in. He's free to come and go as he pleases now. And, since he has chosen to leave Three Willows, we're not in any way responsible for him."

"But, what if he gets caught?"

"That's not our affair, is it? I don't know what they would do to someone under those circumstances. But, since he's colored, it wouldn't surprise me if they would throw him into the river!"

"Oh, no," cried Gerald. "Mother, they wouldn't really do that to him, would they?" Gerald had always had a feeling of respect for the often-times rather sullen Tolly, even though he was only a slave on their plantation.

"Oh, Son, I don't know what they might do. Let's hope it doesn't come to that. Now, keep your voice down so you don't wake your sisters! Your aunt and I were about to retire for the night and I think you should, too."

"Yes, Mother." Gerald saw no reason to argue with his mother. He had made up his mind to leave the *Sultana* that night and was only biding his time so he could secretly gather at least some of his belongings to take with him. He eased himself down onto his pallet and lay quietly while he waited for the regular breathing that would tell him the two women were sleeping.

Florence's mind was in too much turmoil for her to fall asleep quickly that night. She was still trying to assimilate what Laureen's having the diamond necklace and forty three dollars could mean for the family. For quite a long time there had been no money to spare and Laureen had been almost without any money at all of her own. Florence knew that was not an easy thing for Laureen's pride to accept, but she had felt it was necessary, in order to keep the household functioning. But, now she could see there could be a huge price to pay for that kind of economy. She was highly suspicious Laureen was now not inclined to share this newly found wealth.

Florence, surprised by her own thoughts, could not blame her. For the last several years, there had been so little of what they used to have, and both women were so very tired of being poor. What could be more natural, under these circumstances, than for Laureen to want to use her money for herself. And, yet, if she would use it for the good of the whole family, it could go such a long, long way toward restoring Three Willows to its former glory.

At last Florence fell asleep, dreaming of what could be and what she fervently hoped would be in the near future.

Laureen, too, was having difficulty finding sleep that night. She not only was thinking of the necklace and the money, but also about Roger Wainrich. Roger was not an exciting man, but she saw in him a steadfastness that was largely appealing to her. And there could be no doubt of Roger's feelings for her. It appeared he could offer her the kind of stability in life that would see her through any kind of unforeseen problems that might arise.

Yet she could feel an independence born from the necklace and cash money she had never felt before. That was heady stuff. If she sold the necklace, she could set herself up somewhere in a home and live a fashionable life for some time to come.

But then what? Laureen's ever practical mind told her that, eventually, even that amount of money would be spent. Without some source of income, the time would inevitably arrive when she would be poor again. And, then there would be no one to fall back on. Unless she resorted to living off the men she would most certainly meet, moving about in circles of the wealthy and fashionable people.

She had heard of women like that. Some of them did very well for themselves. Some even were able to find husbands of means who were willing to overlook the past lives of their wives.

Laureen tried to picture herself living such a life. Oh, it would be quite exciting and enjoyable for a while. But, could she be truly happy that way? She tried to imagine finding fulfillment in such a life, and finally concluded it might not be possible, at least not for her. She wanted a real home, to be a faithful wife with a faithful husband. She wanted children. That thought brought her back to Roger in a hurry.

Children. With Roger. What would that be like? What kind of a father would he be? For that matter, what kind of a mother would she be? Would his mother interfere too much? Roger made her sound like a wonderful woman, but Laureen knew he could not view his own mother objectively. As Laureen contemplated all those things, soon her thoughts were going in circles and then she was asleep.

Meanwhile, Gerald was awash in his own thoughts. Something he dreamed of for such a long time was about to become a reality. He was ready to leave his mother and his little sisters. How he would miss all of them, but especially his two little sisters.

He was only four years old when Dora was born. Such a sweet little baby. She seemed to adore Gerald from the very first. And Gerald was very possessive of his new little sister. He felt she was his special possession. He petted her, played with her, spoiled her, and as she grew older occasionally fought with her. She looked to him for instruction and protection. And, this relationship only intensified with each year that passed.

Gerald also loved his other little sister, Adelle, but not in the same way he felt about Dora. She was so much younger than the other two. Since Adelle joined the family, Florence focused so much of her attention on the small child, thereby, though unintentionally, leaving Gerald and Dora to sort of fend for themselves, and their devotion to one another deepened dramatically.

So it was a very heart wrenching decision from that standpoint for him leave the family. It especially pained him that he would not be able to say "Goodbye" to Dora. He dared not even attempt to kiss her as she lay sleeping, for fear she might wake and say something, thus waking his mother and his aunt. He knew if he were to get away, it must be done in absolute secrecy. He did not have the strength to resist his mother's pleadings if she were to find out his intentions. And he feared he might never have as good an opportunity to get away as the one within his grasp that night.

There was a place for him to go, a job he could do. The acting company would take him in. He could learn a trade, albeit not the best trade he could choose. But it would support him until he could find something more suitable. And who knows, he might find he liked that one well enough to stay with it. Something drew people to the stage and kept them there. He was willing to find out if it might be for him.

Gerald lay on his pallet for a long time with his jumble of thoughts, waiting for the sounds that would tell him it was all right to get up and leave. He would have to gather his things in total silence and in almost non-existent lighting. But he did not intend to take everything, only those things he thought he would need most. And it should not be too difficult to gather them. He would wrap them in the blanket from his bed and be on his way.

At long last, the deep and regular breathing of both women told him they were asleep. He lay where he was for a little while longer, waiting to make certain they would not hear his stealthy movements in their stateroom. He wondered how much longer the boat would be docked. Time was getting away and he felt the need for speed.

Very quietly he raised himself up from the pallet, and was surprised at how much he could actually see. His eyes had grown accustomed to the dim light and he could move about the room much more easily than he had anticipated. Grateful for that small blessing, he pulled on his socks, but not his boots. He piled a few clothes and other necessities on the blanket, folded it up and then rolled it, picked up his boots, and easing past the others he gently pulled open the door. It squeaked slightly and he waited without breathing to see if the women were disturbed. When they made no sound, he slowly opened it only enough for him to squeeze through it and closed it behind him.

The saloon, as expected, was crowded with soldiers, some sleeping, some still awake and quietly laughing and talking. The lanterns had been dimmed. Even so, there was substantially more light here than in the stateroom Gerald had just left. He picked his way through the soldiers, not finding any opening large enough for him to sit down and put on his boots. He had almost reached the end of the saloon when one of the soldiers spoke to him.

"Hey, Boy, where're you going at this time of night? You look like a boy sneaking around if ever I saw one. You wouldn't be thinking of trying to sneak into some lady's bedroom, would you? Cause, if you are, you can forget about it."

Gerald started. He caught the eye of the young man who he spoken to him. "What're you talking about? I'm not sneaking anywhere. And, I have no interest in some lady's bedroom. I just can't sleep and thought I'd go back out on deck."

"Well, Young'un, if you ain't sneaking, why didn't you put on your boots?"

"The rest of my family is sleeping, and I didn't want to wake them up. The boots can be noisy on a wood floor."

"What's that you got under your arm, then?"

Instinctively, Gerald looked down. He almost panicked. The clothes in the blanket could give him away. But, he had started a bluff and would see it through. He was counting on the dim light not to betray his little white lie. He answered, "I thought it might be a little cold out on deck and I don't want to go back inside right away, so I brought a blanket to wrap around me. You see, this is the first time I've ever ridden on a river boat and we'll probably get to where we're going tomorrow. We're not likely to take another trip for a long time and I want to get the most out of this one while I can. I really don't mean anyone any harm."

A solder sitting next to the one who had been speaking to Gerald spoke up. "Leave the boy alone, Les. He's just a little country boy, like us. When he gets a chance to see a little bit of the world, he wants to take advantage of it. If he was a little older, he might have been a soldier in the war and might not even be here. Let the boy be."

"Yeah, I guess you're right," responded the first soldier. "Here, boy, we'll make a little room for you and you can sit down and put your boots on."

Within a few seconds there was a bare spot on the floor big enough to allow Gerald to sit and draw his boots over his feet. Gerald put the blanket down first and sat on it, thereby not risking the chance that it could come unrolled or perhaps one of the soldiers getting a little curious and unrolling it himself. There was nothing that would break, so he deemed that to be the safest way to keep his secret.

That chore accomplished, Gerald stood with his blanket and continued out of the saloon. He made very slow progress, as everywhere there were soldiers. Many of them detained Gerald along the way. The men were bored and this teenaged boy was fair game for teasing. Gerald did not dare show any impatience, for fear someone might realize what he was doing. So he took the teasing good-naturedly. All the while, time was passing and he was getting more and more worried the *Sultana* could leave the wharfboat at any second.

Slowly, slowly, he made progress toward the deck, which was more brightly lit than the interior rooms of the boat. This would make the gang plank easier to find. And then it happened. He felt the boat moving. He told himself the boat was only riding a wave in the current. He was so close. If the boat were only starting to pull away, he could jump safely onto the wharfboat. Try as he would, he could not speed up his progress to the gangplank. The boat was vibrating, and he could feel a distinctive movement that told him the current had caught the boat.

Finally, he reached his destination. But the boat had, indeed, moved away from the wharfboat. It was only a matter of feet away, though. Gerald stood there, contemplating whether to jump. He knew it was too far for him to jump and land on the wharfboat. But he could swim, and it would not be far to swim. However, if he did that, he would lose the blanket and the things he had stored in it. Was it worth it? Did he really need those things?

And if he decided he did not, then there was the matter of the river itself. He knew the water would be very cold. It was at flood stage, therefore quite swift. Were his swimming skills good enough to compensate for the current? In the dim lights from the wharfboat, he would not be able to see very much. As he stood there trying to decide if the risks of jumping into the water were worth taking, the distance between the *Sultana* and the wharfboat widened. Suddenly the lights on the wharfboat were put out. That did it. If he jumped, then he would be left without a light to guide him.

Reluctantly, Gerald acknowledged defeat. He had missed his goal by mere seconds.

CHAPTER 30

Rather than try to return to his stateroom, Gerald decided to do exactly as he had told the soldier in the saloon. He stayed on the deck, and tried to enjoy his ride on the *Sultana*. The lights from Memphis played on the rippling water like so many silver ribbons dancing in the muted moonlight. As the boat moved out into the river, the ribbons grew longer and thinner. As heartsick as he was, Gerald tried to comfort himself with the knowledge he had at least tried to leave the boat to join the acting troupe. If he had not tried, he told himself, he would always have wondered if he could have made it. Now he knew. It was so hard not to beat himself over those few seconds he was too late. If only he had gotten out of bed even a minute sooner. If only he had not taken the time to sit down and pull on his boots. If only he had moved through the crowd of soldiers even a little faster. If only. If only. He once heard his mother say those were the two saddest words in the English language and now he knew what she meant.

Gradually, he became conscious of the fact that the Sultana was not headed up river as he expected. The lights of Memphis were growing distant, but not in the direction they would if the boat were moving upstream. Instead, the boat was moving across the river, toward the Arkansas shore. For what possible reason, he wondered.

For the next half hour or so, the *Sultana* moved against the current slowly, gently, the pilot being especially careful of the current coming against him sideways. The boat was exceedingly top heavy with so many men on the upper decks and most of the cargo now unloaded. Only a few animals of the cargo remained on board. And, the alligator. In addition to that, with the river at flood stage, there were things floating in the river that could damage, even sink the boat. Extreme caution was in order as he took the boat across the river.

A coaling station at Hopefield, on the Arkansas side of the river and only a little northwest of Memphis, was the immediate destination. It was much better equipped for supplying the boats than was any where in Memphis. The pilot had expressed the thought that he would feel much better about the balance of the boat in the water once the coal could be brought aboard to add some ballast. The boat would need about 1,000 bushels, which would be a considerable weight.

Gerald grew restless, but still did not feel sleepy. He began to wander around the deck. By that time, most of the soldiers were sleeping. As Gerald picked his way among them, he wondered how they were able to get any rest at all. They were so jammed in together and there was not room for them to stretch out into a comfortable position. Suddenly, he felt remorseful of his own unhappiness. He, at least, had the option of going into his stateroom, crawling onto a comfortable pallet and spending the night under shelter where he could be warm. Not so with these men.

The air felt cold and damp and Gerald expected there would be at least showers, if not hard rain, before morning. Those poor men would have no way to get any protection from the cold and rain. Many were already sick, and almost all of them were mal-nourished. Now, for the first time, he thought he understood why his Aunt Laureen had been so concerned for their welfare, even if they were Yankees.

In spite of the coolness of the night, Gerald was not yet ready to return to his stateroom. He thought he might as well make the most of this, in all likelihood, his last night on the river. He decided to check on the alligator. Several of the passengers had left the boat at Memphis and he wondered if the alligator might have belonged to some of those departing passengers and might have been removed. Gingerly, he worked his way toward the stern of the boat, occasionally nudging a sleeping soldier with his foot. Most did not notice the disturbance, and those few who did would merely sigh and change positions. None of them woke up.

As he neared the boiler area, Gerald saw the second engineer approach it. Mr. Wintringer prepared to leave the supervision of the boilers to his midnight replacement. Mr. Wintringer said, "Well, it's all yours for the rest of the night, Sam. Everything seems to be working just fine. All the same, I think you'd better keep a close eye on things. Something about these boilers just doesn't seem right. The patch we got in Vicksburg was not what I hoped for, but it seems to be holding. At least, so far. Maybe I'm being a worry wart."

"I think you're not the only one, then," answered Sam. "Some of the men have overheard the captain expressing his concern for this boat's safety, too."

"What do you mean?"

"Oh, nothing much. It's just that the captain was saying how glad he'll be when we get to Cairo and get all these men are off the boat, that he'll feel much better about everything then."

"So will I, Sam. So will I." Mr. Wintringer looked around once more as if to convince himself that everything was really all right, then said, "Well, good night, Sam. I'll see you in the morning."

"Good night, Sir."

Mr. Wintringer left without seeing Gerald, who had been quietly standing off to one side. He had no desire to disturb the conversation of the two men. By this time Gerald, in spite of his youth, had discovered he could often learn things by being quiet and unobserved, things he would not learn otherwise. Sometimes little gems of information came his way simply because he happened to be in the right place at the right time and did not make his presence known. However, this particular time was not to be one of them. Nothing he overheard on that occasion was useful to him, so he went on his was to see about the alligator.

Sure enough, the alligator was still there. And, a few of the horses were still on the boat. Gerald wondered why they weren't all taken off in Memphis, as he had supposed they were. Oh, well. What did it matter to him if some of them were still on the boat? He decided to go back to the boiler area. It was warmer there, although more crowded. So many of the soldiers were of the same mind, wanting to spend the night in the same area and for the same reason, to keep warm.

In time, the *Sultana* reached the Arkansas side of the river. The boat tied up at the coaling station and the work of loading the needed coal onto the boat was immediately underway. It had taken almost half an hour to cross the river.

Gerald watched in mild fascination as the work progressed. Eventually, he grew a little bored and was again restless. He moved forward toward the bow of the boat, wanting to get away from the coal dust that was beginning to fill the air around the loading activity. He found there was a little more room to move about there. There was a decided difference in the temperature of the air at the bow. Even he would not want to spend a great deal of time there without more clothes on than he had at the moment. He was still reluctant to unroll his blanket and reveal the things wrapped in it, even though nearly all the soldiers were still sleeping.

Then, he thought he could hear a noise coming from out on the river. It was too dark to see, but he moved a little closer along the rail to where he thought the noise was coming from. Gradually, the sounds grew louder and he realized he was hearing oars striking the water. A rowboat was approaching the *Sultana*. Then he could hear men's voices. Gerald watched as the rowboat cleared the bow of the *Sultana* and pulled up against the coaling station.

The man who was rowing the boat sat where he was, while three other men stepped onto the dock. One of them turned back to the oarsman and said, "Thanks, Mister. We thought we'd missed our boat for sure. You're a real life saver."

"Sure thing," answered the man in the row boat. "Next time you're down this way and miss your boat again, just give me a holler."

"Oh, there won't be a 'next time,' Mister. We're heading home and once we get there, we're not likely to be going anywhere again any time soon. But, thanks, anyway."

As the three men went back to where the coal was being loaded and boarded the *Sultana*, the man in the rowboat did an unexpected thing. Gerald was expecting him to turn his little boat around and start back across the river. Instead, he tied it up and got out. From the way the man was looking around, Gerald concluded he was curious to get a better look at the *Sultana*, with all its passengers. After all, there had been a great deal of talk about it in Memphis.

As Gerald watched, he could see a look of disappointment come over the man's face. He concluded the man in the rowboat was unable to see just how crowded the boat was since most of the men were sleeping at that hour and the crowded conditions were not so evident from the level of the water. In time the man must have gotten permission to come aboard because he slowly circled the lower deck then left the boat.

Around 1:00 o'clock in the morning, the coal was loaded and the

Sultana gently pulled away from the dock and back out into the churning water. The pilot worked the boat out into the middle of the river, as it was hard to tell exactly where the main channel was. The flooding water was spilling so far out of its banks and was about four miles wide there. There were several small islands called Hen and Chickens lying only a short distance north of where they were at the moment. They would need to work around those.

The pilot was familiar with their locations. Even though they were only a few miles up river, he was in no hurry to get there. He was more interested in using all the care he could manage in steering the *Sultana* on a safe course up the river. The boat was a little more stable than it had been before taking on the coal, but even that did not offset the weight of the men on the upper decks. The *Sultana* was still very top heavy.

For the next hour or so, the only sounds to be heard aboard the *Sultana* were those of the sleeping men, many of whom could snore with the best of them, as well as the sounds of the water slapping the hull of the boat and the regular pounding of the paddles slapping the water on either side of the boat.

The second engineer, who remained in the boiler area, was extremely conscious of the fragile condition of the boilers. Mr. Wintringer's caution had found its mark in his thinking. He was aware that more hurried repairs were made on the boilers when they were tied up in Memphis. It seemed these boilers were needing more than their share of repairs on this trip. Both on the down river run, and now on the return trip repairs had been necessary. Hopefully, Captain Mason would consider replacing them when they reached St. Louis.

He knew boilers were expensive, but then the loss of a boat would be much more so. It was too risky to have unsafe boilers fueling a boat like the *Sultana*.

It was such a beautiful boat. So many expensive luxuries had been included in the decor to make the paying passengers comfortable and willing to travel on the *Sultana* again. Even the menus for the meals were carefully thought out and prepared.

Sadly, things were much different for all those poor soldiers traveling aboard the *Sultana* that night. They had neither comfort nor food. Not even shelter from the elements. It was began to rain, which caused many of the men to wake up. It was not a heavy rain, but it was so cold. The men were trying to shield themselves as best they could. Those who had blankets were re-arranging them to try to protect as much of their bodies as they could. Those who had no blankets were trying to use their shirts, or whatever they could to try, however futilely, to ward off the showers.

He grew somewhat angry as he watched the wretched condition of those men. He had a strong urge to storm into Captain Mason's cabin, jerk him out of bed, and march him out onto the decks to force him to see the miserable condition the men were in. As he thought about it, though, he concluded it would not make any difference to the captain. After all, the captain knew all this and seemed not to care. Apparently, all the captain cared about was making a sizeable profit on this run and he was oblivious to the suffering this might be causing.

"Well," he thought, "nothing lasts forever. This night and this trip will come to an end and maybe things will get better."

By this time the boat was approaching the islands the pilot remembered. He was not particularly concerned. There was a deep channel running out only a short distance from them. By keeping his progress slow and steady, he would be able to get past them without

310

any real difficulty. The lanterns on the boat threw enough light out on either side, so there was no danger of grounding the boat. Things were looking good. He was grateful he was able to get some sleep earlier when the boat was in Memphis. He wanted to be alert and at his best when he was in close quarters on the river.

Soon, the boat was past the first island. There were several more to go. As he watched the river very carefully, he could see something in the water that could be trouble. Most likely a tree floating down. There was not time enough to change course very far, but he turned the wheel as far as he dared, considering the weight of the men on the upper decks. Too much and the boat would capsize. Too little, and a tree of that size could put a hole in the hull big enough to sink the boat. But, it was enough. The tree passed by the *Sultana*, barely touching its sides.

"That was too close for comfort," said the pilot to no one in particular, breathing a sigh of relief that disaster had been averted. "I hope we don't have too many more of those." The sleeping men spread out before him did not respond.

He continued to strain his eyes into the dim light reflecting on the rushing current. He knew better than to relax his vigil under those conditions. But, as the boat eased its way past more of the islands, he did achieve more of a sense of safety.

However, this moment of false security was extremely short lived.. At that very instant three of the four boilers exploded, sending sound waves of the blast echoing for miles around the countryside! Boiling water and fire erupted, sending hundreds of soldiers and passengers high into the air, and setting the *Sultana* on fire. Hot coals were thrown all around the boat, setting fires wherever they fell. Sleeping men awakened to find themselves flying through the air then hitting the cold and hostile waters of the Mississippi River. Upper decks of the boat, including the pilot house, made of very flimsy wood in order to keep the weight of the boat as light as possible, began to collapse, much like a house of cards falls in no particular order when a lower card is disturbed, each deck in turn collapsing onto the next deck. The massive red hot smoke stacks toppled, amid the penetrating sound of hissing steam, trapping many men under them against their searing heat. The terrified screams of the scalded and dying men only added to the confusion. Many of the passengers who had been thrust airborne were blown into countless bits. Blood mixed with steam fell from the sky like a heavy, deep pink mist, covering everything below. Body parts accumulated in grisly piles on the deck, in some cases completely burying men who found it impossible to extract themselves in time to escape the all consuming flames that overtook them.

The noise of the explosions quickly awakened all the passengers who were not immediately affected by the explosions. This was instantly followed by the screams of men being burned alive or who had been scalded to the point that their skin began to peel completely off them.

As the horror of the moment began to penetrate the minds of those people who had been so suddenly and horribly awakened out of sleep, panic set in. Fire quickly enveloped the whole middle section of the boat. By the way the decks were collapsing on one another, men were, in some cases actually being funneled right into the fire. It was the beginning of the most nightmarish experience any of the people aboard the *Sultana* that night would ever have thrust upon them.

CHAPTER 31

Since the pilot house was directly above the exploding boilers, it was immediately affected. Most of it was blown completely off the boat, much of it in large pieces. With the floor of the pilot house blown out from under him, the pilot fell into the carnage below him, while the man resting next to him was thrown unharmed into the water on a large piece of the decking.

The explosion of the boilers hurled pieces of metal and other debris in all directions, reaching through walls, leaving a circle of dead and wounded. From the air, bodies and body parts began to fall, some into the turgid waters below, but all too many back onto the decks of the burning boat from which they had been ejected.

Around the whole area where the boilers had been, all the sleeping men had completely disappeared. Almost at once, the broken and mangled wooden parts of the boat began to add to the fuel of the fire, some of the boards angling downward from the parts remaining of upper decks, thus taking the flames upward to spread the fire to all levels of the *Sultana*.

The upper decks were already sagging due to the lightweight boards used to construct them and the extraordinary weight from all the hundreds of passengers they were carrying. With the explosion and resulting fire, they quickly gave way, collapsing onto even the cabins of the paying passengers, burning many of them alive. The screams coming from those chambers of fire penetrated to the very bones of those individuals on the decks, powerless to rescue them.

As the flames raged out of control, vast numbers of those soldiers who had survived the initial explosion were faced with a choice of remaining on the boat with its rapidly spreading flames, and the icy cold waters of the Mississippi River. Most of them could not swim. It was apparent they would be burned alive if they stayed with the *Sultana*. Perhaps death was equally certain if they chose the river. Even so, to most of them that 'perhaps' in the water was better than an absolute certainty if they stayed on the boat. As the flames spread, more and more of the passengers on the *Sultana* chose that 'perhaps.' A few had found life preservers, a few more had managed to find scraps of timbers, pieces of railing, even furniture to hang onto. Most had nothing. Still, they jumped, so many of them. Soon the reflection of the flames on the black water showed a solid mass of heads and bodies floundering and bobbing in the fast moving waters.

Screams and prayers were the sounds heard all around the boat. For a short time, anyone jumping from the boat was likely to hit the water on top of someone already struggling there, and knocking him under the choking water. Gradually, that changed. Heads would disappear under the water, reappear, then disappear, never to appear again, until hardly anyone remained. Only those few who could swim were able to last more than a few minutes. Even most of those swimmers were not able to survive for long, however. The water was too cold and the men were too weak from long months of malnutrition and exposure to the elements to deal long with the strong current and the vast distance to either shore.

When the sound of the explosion first sounded throughout the boat, it shook everyone awake. In the cabin where the Lawrence family slept, the confusion at being so abruptly awakened was typical. Little Adelle screamed. Florence and Laureen jumped out of their beds as though they were part of a well rehearsed drill team.

"What happened?" cried Dora, suddenly wide awake.

"I don't know," shrieked Florence.

314

"Let's get out of here. Now!" cried Laureen. Intuition told her there was no time to lose, even though she had no idea what had been the cause of the thunderous tumult she had just heard.

Florence could not clear her thoughts so readily the way Laureen did. It took her a little longer to shake off the sound sleep from which she had been so rudely awakened. As reason returned to her, she thought instantly of her children. She quickly looked around the dimly lit room, and was gratified to see both little girls. But, where was Gerald? He was not there!

"Girls! Wake up! Where's your brother?" She cried.

Adelle began to cry. She was unused to hearing such a shrill tone of voice coming from her mother.

"Florence, get the children and let's go. If Gerald isn't here, there's nothing we can do about it." As she spoke, Laureen grabbed the blanket she had been sleeping under and started to wrap it around her shoulders.

Florence was aghast. "Laureen, you can't go out with no dress on! It's not respectable!" Laureen had been sleeping in her shimmy, as had Florence and the little girls.

"Florence, something bad has happened on this boat for it to make that kind of noise. I'm not waiting around to find my clothes. I'm leaving now and I'll gladly help you with the girls. But, if you aren't ready to come, then I'm going without you."

"Then you'll just have to go without us. We're not leaving this room in our underwear. I can't think anything so terrible has happened that you have to disgrace the family by going out in public in just your shimmy."

Laureen said no more. She opened the door and went out into the saloon, bright light from the fire hitting her full in the face, making it hard for her to see until her eyes adjusted. Even though she did not realize the source of the light was fire, what she could see was a great jumble of men, frantically racing in different directions, desperate to escape the immanent disaster. Panic had overtaken everyone one board. She pulled the blanket tightly around her, afraid she would lose what covering she had as she was jostled by the deluge of people pushing in all directions in total confusion. The stench from the explosion and the ensuing conflagration eating up not only the boat, but everyone and everything in its path, assaulted her nostrils. Since the Lawrence's stateroom was near the bow of the boat, Laureen moved in that direction. Before she could reach the end to emerge on the deck, she could hear the crackling sounds of breaking wood and realized the decks were collapsing. It was only because of the hands of an unknown and unseen benefactor pulling her through the door and onto the open deck that she escaped being crushed in the fall of the deck above.

She screamed. Her instincts were on target, but somehow that brought her no comfort. Florence and the little girls were caught in that collapse! Could some of the screams coming from that shambles be theirs? She could not know. And, she could not contemplate it very long. As she began to get her bearings, she realized the boat was in flames and could not stay afloat very long. It's forward progress had already slowed and was coming to a standstill. The flames coming from the center of the boat were throwing a great deal of light, making it very easy to see what was going on around her. So many men were already in the water and more jumping all the time. It was becoming readily apparent she, herself, could not stay on the boat much longer.

Then, to her added horror, the boat began to turn, so that instead of going upriver, the current was about to steer it back down river. As it did so, the flames changed direction as well. As long as the *Sultana* continued on its run upriver, the flames were basically shooting out to the stern. But, once it turned and faced down river, then it would essentially be going right into the flames. It could not possibly last long under those conditions.

Just then, Captain Mason appeared, moving along the rail, calling for calm.

That was too much for Laureen. She screamed at him, "How can you call for calm amid all this turmoil, Captain? If you hadn't been so greedy, this might not have happened. Do you really think you can save the *Sultana* now? What's wrong with you?"

"No, Miss Lawrence, I can't save the *Sultana*," he answered in a defeated tone of voice. "I'm not that stupid. I only know we still need to be calm and keep our wits about us if we're to salvage anything at all. Even our lives."

"And how do you propose we save our lives? I've only seen one lifeboat on this boat. Has it been launched? And, look at all those men jumping into the water. Do you think they can swim to the bank? It must be at least a mile, perhaps more." Laureen was growing almost hysterical as she screamed at the captain. "And, what about those who've already died in the fire. My whole family is gone! The upper decks have collapsed on them. Do you think your precious calm can save them now?"

"Look, Miss Lawrence, I don't blame you for being bitter. I know I let too many men come aboard the *Sultana*. And, I know I should have had a better job done on repairing the boilers. I wish I could change that, but I can't. Now, since there's nothing to be done about that, we need to get on with the job of trying to save as many lives as

317

we can. I suggest you try to find something to keep you afloat and take your chances in the river." And, he started to move along.

Laureen was livid. How dare that captain try to make light of his role in all this destruction! All around her men were crying out, moaning, trying to comprehend the horrible thing happening to them. Some were injured so badly they were unable to move, let alone try to find a way to stay afloat in the water. Some were trapped under heavy debris, with no help forthcoming for them. How could the captain possibly live with himself after seeing all that his greediness had done. So many lives mangled or lost. It was almost too much for her to comprehend, herself.

Soon, she realized she could not afford the luxury of seething too long about the captain's reprehensible conduct. The flames were spreading rapidly in her direction. She must do something to help herself. She could not swim, so there was no point in jumping into the water, at least not yet. If she must die, she would wait until the last possible moment to do so. But the captain was right about one thing. If she kept her wits about her, she might find a way to save herself.

She had seen some of the men jerking off pieces of planking, even shutters, throwing them into the water, then jumping in afterward where they grabbed hold of the floating pieces and clung to them. Laureen wondered how they could jump into the water where they inevitably sank below the surface, then moments later emerge so close to the floating debris. She contemplated such a course for herself, but concluded that she might not bounce back to the surface, should she try that. She shuddered at the idea of having her head under water. No, she must find another way.

She watched a man working at knocking off part of the rail near her. As soon as he had enough to keep himself afloat, he wrapped his arms around it and jumped. He only barely sank under the water. She wondered if she could do that. But, she was afraid to try. If she lost her balance while trying to loosen a section of the railing, she would go overboard with nothing at all to keep her afloat.

Others had also watched the man taking some of the railing off the edge of the deck and jumping overboard with it. Many of them quickly followed suit until there was no more of it left. The flames were getting closer and closer and time was running out. As men pushed to get away from the flames, they forced those near the edge over the side.

Larueen did not see the captain stop and watch as the sections of railing were frantically dismantled and used as floats. So, when she heard a voice so loud that it carried above the other cries, she turned to see what the special commotion was all about. The answer was instantaneous. One of the soldiers had paused to swear at the captain.

Putting his face only an inch from the captain's and both hands on the captain's shoulders, he yelled at him, "This is all your fault, you greedy, stinking polecat! You knew there were too many men on this boat, and still you put more on. And, now we all going to die. Is this what you wanted? Well, is it?"

The complaining soldier was altogether intent on berating the captain and did not notice they was being inched forward. And, neither did the captain until he felt nothing under his feet. Over the side they both went, screaming until they struck the water and sank.

Laureen shuddered, still contemplating how she could save her own life as she kept her back against the fallen wreckage of the upper decks. She knew the fire was fast approaching where she stood and the momentary protection she felt against the pile of wreckage was about to become nothing more than fuel for that fire. Her heart pounding so hard she could feel the pain, she looked about frantically, hoping to find some alternative to jumping into the river with nothing to keep her afloat.

Just then, she saw a man pulling a charred section of a mattress toward the edge of the deck. The man was injured, both from burns and from metal shrapnel. Blood was pouring from numerous cuts he had sustained. His arm was also broken, but he could not take time to tend to it. Then, as he was about to push the mattress overboard, he fainted and collapsed. Laureen rushed to his side, trying to rouse him. As soon as she touched him, she realized the man had died.

Without further hesitation, she took as firm a hold on the mattress and she possibly could, and pushed it with all her might as she fell across it, clinging desperately to it. Before she even had time to wonder if she could hold onto the mattress when she hit the water, she felt the awful jar of making contact with it. By some strange, unexplainable miracle, she landed on top of the mattress, so holding onto it was not an issue. But, how long would it float, she wondered.

Once it was water logged, would it keep her afloat? She knew she would soon find out. All around her people were disappearing under the water. Some others were able to keep afloat by latching onto various types of debris from the boat. There were many pieces scattered about. As she drifted alongside the burning boat, she could feel the heat of the flames reaching out to her. The warmth was strangely comforting. Suddenly, that became a concern. If she got too close, she could be burned. She was lying across the piece of mattress. She began to paddle furiously with one hand, while holding onto the mattress with the other, to try to put more distance between her and the flames.

Gradually, the distance between her and what was left of the

Sultana grew greater. The light from the flames lessened. As the mattress became waterlogged, it sank below the surface of the water, but did not sink altogether. There was still enough buoyancy to keep her at the surface of the water, although very much in it. But, she was so cold. She had lost the blanket when she jumped. Even though it fell so close to her, she dared not let go of the mattress in order to retrieve it or even lean very far toward it. She wanted to take no chances of upsetting the mattress and risk being dumped completely into the river. It was almost but not quite within her reach. And, then it was gone. She was never quite certain exactly what happened to it. It simply disappeared.

Occasionally she would hear noises in the darkness that told her someone or something was nearby. She would call out, hoping for a response. More often than not, no one answered her, so she never knew what made the sounds. Once, she made contact with four men who were clinging to a log, seeming to drift at about the same speed as she. It was almost more than she could do to talk by that time, as she was shivering so much and her teeth were chattering beyond her control.

But, she could hear them. One of them said, "Did you know that ol' Sammy used his bayonet to kill that 'gator?"

"No," was the response of another one. "Why would he do that?"

"He wanted the crate for himself. And, I guess he got at least part of it. Somebody saw what he was doing and made him give him some of it."

"Well, I'm glad that gator's dead. I don't exactly like the idea of sharing this river with that critter."

Laureen could not hear any more of what they were saying. They drifted away from her. A short time later, behind her, she could hear thrashing in the water. With supreme effort to control her voice, she called out, hoping that whoever or whatever it was would not collide with her. A soldier answered her. "It's all right Ma'am. I'm just holding onto this horse. I hope he knows the way to the bank. 'Cause wherever he goes is where I'm going. I can't guide him, though. I'm hanging onto his tail!"

Laureen was relieved. Silently she wished the soldier well, and hoped that her mattress would also take her to a bank. She did not care which one. She was so cold and wondered if she would be able to continue indefinitely to keep her hold on the mattress.

Then something touched her. She started! It was impossible to see what it was and she was so frightened she almost toppled off her already precarious perch. But, whatever it was did not move, so she somewhat fearfully felt to see what it was. A hand! And it was so cold! This time she spoke, but with great difficulty. "This piece of mattress won't support both of us," she said regretfully. There was no response.

"Look, I want to help you, but I don't see how I can. Please let go," she pleaded. Still, there was no response. Resignedly, Laureen realized she could not turn her back on another human being who needed help, even if it did put her own safety in jeopardy. But what an absurd idea, that of safety. She was hardly safe herself. She grasped the icy hand with both of her own and then, using what little strength she could muster to speak, said, "Give me your other hand and we'll see if this mattress will keep us both afloat.

When there was still no response, Laureen began to get annoyed. "Look, Mister, if you want my help, you have to cooperate!" And she yanked on the hand. When there was no resistance, she almost rolled off the mattress, regaining her balance with awkward difficulty. "What in the world?!!!" she exclaimed. It was then she realized the hand and arm she was trying to help were not attached to a body! She pushed them away with all the strength she could muster, her whole body shuddering with renewed horror.

Her thoughts wandered back to Florence and her children. She felt certain they were killed when the upper decks collapsed onto their cabin. She could only hope they died instantly and did not suffer. Then she thought of Gerald. Where could he have been so late into the night? She remembered hearing someone say the explosion occurred around 2:00 a.m. She knew he was aboard the boat after they left Memphis. In fact, she remembered when he came into the cabin to join the rest of them shortly before the boat got under way. He went to bed at the same time she and Florence did. So he was there! Laureen's mind was not clear enough to remember they had all gone to bed some time before the *Sultana* left Memphis. In her mind, the boat pulled away from that dock about the time they all went to bed.

But when did Gerald leave the cabin and where did he go? She could only hope he was unable to sleep and went out onto the deck somewhere. Perhaps he was one of those who were able to find something to hang onto in the water.

As tired as she was, Laureen positioned herself to take another look at the burning *Sultana*. She had drifted quite some distance ahead of it by then. As she looked, she remembered Roger's saying that riding a river boat was probably a little more dangerous than travel by other means. He almost certainly was not talking about the kind of danger that so recently overtook the *Sultana*, though. Surely, no one could have foreseen that.

As she continued to look at the *Sultana*, the fire seemed to be lessening and then, it was gone altogether. The *Sultana* had burned low and was unable to stay afloat. With much hissing and sizzling, it slipped beneath the waters of the mighty river.

CHAPTER 32

Laureen had no idea how long she drifted in the water. Soon time after the piece of mattress she clung to became waterlogged, she gave up trying to remain upright on it. Instead, she was satisfied to hold on while trying to lie flat on her stomach, letting that remnant support as much of her body as there was room on it to do. She was in a daze from being so cold. Light showers rained down on her several times. Ahead she could hear voices and a light flickered low over the water. Suddenly her mind became more alert. A light on the water. That must mean a boat. But, could anyone see her? The light of the lanterns did not reach very far. Still, it was getting closer. She waited a little longer, then with a supreme effort, she called out weakly, "Help. Help. I'm over here. Help me!"

She heard no response, so she tried again. This time she was able to put a little more strength into her call. "Somebody, please help me. Help me!"

From the rowboat she heard someone say, "Hold the lantern up higher, Andy. I heard something from over there. I think there's somebody in the water."

Laureen, feeling hopeful for the first time since she had drifted past the *Sultana*, called out again. Her voice had a renewed strength. "Here. I'm over here. I **am** in the water. Help me!"

Within a few more seconds, and with much splashing of the oars, the boat pulled alongside her. While one man held the lantern high over the side of the boat, another man's hands reached out to her, grasping her own hands firmly. As he did so, he said in a very calming voice, "Hold on, Ma'am. I'll get you into the boat. Just relax and let me pull you in. We don't want to turn the boat over."

Laureen was more than willing to do exactly as she was told, letting the stranger gently tug her into the boat. As he helped her sit down, he threw a thick fuzzy blanket around her shoulders. "Oh, that feels so good," sighed Laureen weakly.

"I know, Ma'am. When we heard the explosion, we thought we might help at least a few people. We put some blankets and lanterns in the boat and set out to try to help. We'll see if we can find anyone else who might need some help and then take you back to the bank. There'll be lots of help for you there.

Laureen started to express her appreciation for the help they were giving her, but as she spoke, she got no further than "Thank y....." and fainted. She had struggled to help herself longer and beyond any strength she dreamed she had. Now, at last, with someone else was taking charge of her care, she felt free to let go. That was when she fainted.

When she regained consciousness, the boat was almost back at the dock from which it had started. She kept her eyes closed at first, almost afraid to open them. Something was terribly wrong, and she was trying to remember what it was. Where was she and how did she come to be there? She could hear the noise of oars being worked in the water and men's voices speaking softly. Then she realized she was leaning against someone.

She opened her eyes slowly, trying to remember. She looked about her. At first, she saw only the light of the lantern on the boat, but soon realized the boat was full of men. All of them were wrapped in blankets, except for the two men who had helped her into the boat. As her consciousness became fully restored, and she continued to stare at the men, she realized the blankets were all the men wore. It appeared they had no clothes on at all!

She sat up straight. "What's going here?" she demanded.

"It's all right, Ma'am," said the man who held the lantern. "We'll be back at the dock in a couple of minutes and we'll get you some dry clothes."

"Who are all these men, and why aren't they wearing any clothes?" Again Laureen was using a demanding tone of voice.

A glance passed between the man with the lantern and the man working the oars. Even in the dim light, Laureen could see it. "Don't you remember, Ma'am?" asked the one called Andy. "We picked you up out of the river."

"River?" asked Laureen faintly. "What was I doing in the river?"

Again, the questioning look passed between the two men. Gently, the man holding the lantern answered, "You were on the *Sultana*, Ma'am. It burned and sank and you were floating down the river when we found you and helped you into the boat. You fainted. These men around you were other passengers from the boat, also in the river, and we picked them up after we found you. We're going to take you ashore now and get you into some dry clothes."

"Dry clothes!" she exclaimed. "From what I can see, any clothes at all would be in order. Or are my eyes deceiving me? I can't see anything at all covering these men except blankets."

"That's right, Ma'am. They had the misfortune to lose their clothes in the river. But, I think saving their clothes was the least of their worries. They were doing all they could just to save their lives. And, if we hadn't come along when we did, they might not have made it. I'm surprised you were able to keep some of yours on, as swift as this current is. How'd you manage that, anyway?"

That was the first Laureen realized she was wearing only her

327

shimmy and was bare footed. Horrified, she tried to draw her blanket tighter around herself. "Where are my clothes?" she cried.

The man she was leaning against when she regained consciousness answered, "In the river with ours, most likely. Or maybe you left them on the *Sultana*. Either way, you can forget them because they're long gone now."

Laureen struggled to understand what was happening. Questions were pointless because the answers were not making any sense to her.

Since they were so near the dock, she decided to say no more and wait for further developments. It was an easy decision to make as her strength was at such a low ebb. Talking required so much effort.

Many men with many lanterns lined the dock as the rowboat drew alongside it. Hands reached out to steady and tie the boat securely. "Don't try to get out of the boat just yet," called out the one who had been addressed as 'Andy.' Let Jonas and me get out first and then we can help the rest of you."

No one replied. The men in the boat were in a much more weakened state than was Laureen, and some of them were suffering from burns and other injuries, one man quite seriously.

Jonas and Andy were off the boat and on the dock almost as soon as it stopped moving and were reaching for the hands of their passengers. Those least injured were the first ones off the boat, and were directed to a temporary shelter at the edge of the wharfboat where they would be able to receive dry clothes. A local Ladies' Aid Society came together as soon as word spread through the city of the *Sultana*'s misfortune. From all directions women were bringing clothes, blankets, bandaging materials, and food.

As the more seriously injured men were assisted off the boat, suddenly Andy called out, "Can we get a stretcher over here? Right away! We've got a badly burned man here and I don't think he can walk."

Before he could finish speaking, two men were standing next to the boat with a stretcher. Other men reached out to help lift the burned man onto it. Almost in a flash of movement, the stretcher was being hurried down the street by the two strong men, taking the soldier to the hospital.

Meanwhile, Laureen sat where she was on the boat. She was so still, asking for nothing, watching intently all the activity around her. Some of what was happening she understood, but not all. Finally, Jonas and Andy turned their attentions to her. "What is your name, Ma'am?" asked Jonas.

"Why, ah, my name is..." Laureen was thinking hard, trying with all her might to remember. Finally, it came to her. "Wallace. That's what it is. Wallace!"

"Is it Miss or Mrs.?" persisted Jonas.

Again, Laureen was not sure. There were two names that popped into her head. Florence and Laureen. But, which one was hers? She was not certain. She looked at Jonas for a long moment, and realized she needed to give him some kind of answer. "It's Mrs." she said finally. "Mrs. Florence Wallace."

"Do you think you can get out of the boat now, Mrs. Wallace?" His voice was very kind and gentle.

"Yes, I think so," was her answer. "But, I'd appreciate a steadying hand, if you don't mind."

Jonas extended both his hands to her and Laureen accepted them gratefully, as she stepped onto the dock. "I think I need to sit down," she said weakly. "Perhaps I'm not as all right as I thought."

"Do you know anyone in Memphis, some one we could notify who could come and get you?"

Laureen tried to think. Did she know anyone in Memphis? Something in the back of her mind told her she did, but she could not quite bring the thought forward enough to examine it, so she shook her head and said, weakly, "No, no one."

"Then I think we need to find a room for you. There's a big boarding house only about a block away, and if they're not already filled up, you can probably stay there tonight. At least for what little is left of tonight. Maybe after you've had a little rest, things will be clearer to you."

The idea of a warm bed and some sleep sounded wonderful to Laureen. Everything was so confusing. They told her she was drifting down the river before they pulled her into the boat. But, try as she would, she could not remember how she came to be in the river. It made no sense to her. She lived on a plantation. Somewhere. She could not even remember where. And, trying to remember made her head ache.

Meekly, she gained her feet and followed the man, Jonas, to the makeshift shelter where she had seen the men going, stepping very carefully, trying to avoid stepping on the sharp pebbles and other rough bits of debris scattered about the dock. She was not used to being barefooted and her feet were very tender.

As Jonas pushed aside the burlap fabric that served as a door to the shelter, he stuck his head in and asked the woman in charge, "Are all the men covered? There's a woman here who could use some attention. I think she's not hurt much, but she can't remember

330

anything, either. She needs some dry clothes."

"Everything's fine here," was the answer. "Bring her in and we'll see what we can do for her."

Jonas continued, "I think the main thing she needs, other than clothes, is a place to rest. I told her about Sadie's boarding house down the street. Do you think they can take her in?"

"You'd best go on about your business of rescuing people on the river now, Jonas. I'll take care of the woman. Just let me get a look at her."

Jonas put his arm across Laureen's shoulders and drew her to the shelter. He said to her, "This here's Miz' White, and she's going to take good care of you now. Do what she says and you're going to be just fine."

"Off with you, Jonas," chuckled Mrs. White and she took hold of Laureen's arm. "And, what is your name, Dear?"

"Um, it's Wallace. Florence Wallace."

"Jonas said you can't remember much right now. Do you remember where you were going on the *Sultana*? Or where you came from?"

"*Sultana*? I'm not sure," said Laureen very hesitantly.

"Never mind," said Mrs. White. This woman had heard of cases where people sometimes got amnesia, but she had never seen a case of it before. This likely would prove to be quite interesting.

She drew Laureen to a corner of the shelter and stood for a minute, pondering the situation. At last she spoke, "I don't believe we have any women's clothes here at all. I suppose it never occurred to everyone there were women on the boat. Since the vast majority of passengers were men, it seems all the clothes here are for men. The best I can do for you is a shirt and pair of trousers."

Laureen nodded. She was so tired, she could not concern herself with what kind of clothing she wore. All she wanted was to be shown to the boarding house where she could find a bed.

As Mrs. White selected a shirt and pair of trousers she thought would come close to fitting Laureen, she tugged the blanket off Laureen's shoulders. "We'll need to get these wet things off you first." Then, as she looked more closely at Laureen's attire, she noticed the belt and pouch at Laureen's waist. "What's this?" she asked as she looked for a way to unfasten it. Finding none, she added, "I guess we'll have to cut it off."

That brought a response from Laureen. "No! You can't cut it off. Leave it alone!" And she instinctively took several steps backward, away from Mrs. White, both hands clasped across the pouch.

"Child! I'm not going to hurt you! If that thing means so much to you, of course I won't cut if off. But you do need to get out of those wet things. Here, take these clothes and go behind that stack there and change. I don't know if you can get your shimmy off, though, if you don't let me cut that thing off you."

"I can manage," said Laureen. She took the clothes and did as she was told, soon emerging wearing the men's clothing.

"Well, I guess you did manage, after all," said Mrs. White. "Now, you come with me and we'll get you down to Sadie's and see if she has a room you can have."

"How far is it?" asked Laureen. "I don't think I can walk very far," and her voice trailed off.

"You poor dear. Of course, you can't walk very far. I should have known that. You wait here for just a minute and I'll find us a ride."

Mrs. White stepped away from the wharfboat in a hurry and was back almost before Laureen realized she was gone. "There's a horse and wagon back here, and you can sit on the back of the wagon. We'll have you at the boarding house before you know it."

Laureen gratefully accepted the ride, as uncomfortable as it was. There was something vaguely familiar about that ride, but again she could not think what it was.

At the boarding house, Mrs. White left Laureen sitting in the wagon while she went inside and spoke to the landlady. The arrangements were made for Laureen to have a bed on the first floor, since Mrs. White knew it would be especially difficult for Laureen, in her weakened condition, to have to climb stairs.

Mrs. White went back out in the night to retrieve Laureen from the wagon, then helped her up the few steps to the front porch. There the boarding house landlady took charge of her, freeing Mrs. White to go back to the wharfboat and her shelter, ready to help other disaster survivors as they were plucked from the river.

"I'm Sadie," this pleasant-faced middle-aged woman told Laureen. "This is my boarding house. Mrs. White explained to me you were on the *Sultana* when it caught fire. You poor dear. You'll be able to rest here. Just sleep as long as you need to." And, Sadie led her into a room where the covers had already been turned down on the bed. Laureen saw nothing in the small, sparsely furnished room except that bed.

She sank down on it, letting Sadie gently push her head and shoulders onto the soft pillow, then lift her feet and legs onto the clean sheets. Before Sadie could ease the covers over her shoulders, Laureen was fast asleep.

CHAPTER 33

Laureen awoke to a gentle hand slowly stroking her arm. A woman's voice was saying, "Wake up, Mrs. Wallace. You've been sleeping a long time. There's someone here to see you."

"Wha...?" stammered Laureen. "Who are you?" she questioned as she became a little more aware of her surroundings. "Where am I?"

"Don't you remember, Mrs. Wallace? I'm Sadie and you're in my boarding house. You've been sleeping a day and a half, so I thought you might like to see your visitor."

"Visitor?" Laureen's mind was still quite muddled.

Sadie said no more. She motioned to the person waiting in the open doorway to come in.

"Mother!" exclaimed Gerald. "I was so worried." But, as he gained the room and got a better look at Laureen, he cried, "Aunt Laurie! They told me **Mrs.** Wallace was here. What happened? Where are my mother and little sisters?" His voice took on a higher pitch of excitement and fright with each word he spoke.

Laureen peered at Gerald through the fog enveloping her mind and said nothing.

Gerald grew more impatient with each second that ticked by. Sadie had told him Laureen had lost her memory, and barely knew who she was. And, now he had just learned she did not even remember that. "Aunt Laurie," he cried. "Talk to me. Tell me what happened. Where are Mother and the little girls?"

Gradually, the fog began to lift. "Gerald? Is that you, Gerald?" questioned Laureen slowly.

"Yes, Aunt Laurie. It's me, Gerald. You still haven't told me where my mother and sisters are."

"I don't know," Laureen replied, with a long pause between each of the words. "I'm trying to remember," she said, almost as slowly.

"Think! Aunt Laurie, think! You have to know what happened to them." Gerald was growing rather desperate. When Laureen still did not respond, he added, "You were on the *Sultana* with my mother and Dora and Adelle. The boat caught fire and burned, then it sank. How did you get off and are they all right, too?"

"*Sultana*?" Somehow, that sounded familiar. She still said nothing, but little snatches of things were playing around in her memory. She struggled to put them together, to make sense of them. Why was it so hard? What was it she needed to remember?

Finally, Gerald could stand it no longer. He sat down on the bed next to Laureen and put his hands on her shoulders, shaking her vigorously. "You've got to remember, Aunt Laurie. You've got to!"

"Take it easy, Son," cried Sadie who had been standing in the open doorway, taking in all that was going on. "She's had a very bad experience and you have to be patient with her. If she doesn't remember, she can't help that."

Gerald stopped shaking his aunt instantly, aghast at what he had done. "I'm sorry, Aunt Laurie," he said remorsefully. "I didn't mean to do that. It's just that I'm so worried about the others." Then, he added plaintively, "Can't you remember anything?"

Slowly, the fog in Laureen's mind was clearing. The pieces were starting to come together. The *Sultana*! Now she remembered! It had burned. All those people jumping into the river. Even she had jumped, too. And then the boat sank. She remembered seeing all the lights on it disappear. She had been in the water. It was so cold! And then somebody had helped her into a rowboat. That was all she could remember right then.

Gerald was watching her face intently. He seemed to realize Laureen was beginning to get a grasp on the tragedy. He waited for her to speak.

Finally, she did. Very softly, so that he had difficulty hearing what she said.

"I'm so sorry, Gerald. I think the others didn't make it off the boat alive. It all happened so fast. We were sleeping when this awful noise woke us up in the middle of the night. Your mother was trying to get dressed and there wasn't time for that."

"But, how did you have time to get out if they didn't?"

"I had this terrible feeling something dreadful had happened to make that much noise and I didn't wait to get dressed. I ran out of the room as soon as I heard the noise."

"But what about my mother and sisters? Couldn't you help them?" Gerald was almost on the verge of hysteria.

"I tried, Gerald. But your mother insisted on getting dressed. There just wasn't time for that. I told her to forget about getting dressed, but you know how proper she always was. She couldn't imagine letting anyone see her in her shimmy."

As her comprehension grew, Laureen began to wonder about things, too. Suddenly it occurred to her to question how Gerald got off the boat in time. "Where were you, Gerald? You weren't in the room when that happened, I know. How did you make it to safety? And, how did you find me here?" Then, she added as an afterthought, "Not that I know where I am."

Gerald hung his head. He did not want to explain what he had been up to that night. It would be impossible to make his Aunt Laureen understand.

Laureen waited, and when no explanation was forthcoming, she asked again, "Where were you Gerald? I need to know."

"I wasn't on the boat, Aunt Laurie."

"But, you were! I remember seeing you go to bed. We all went to sleep about the time we pulled away from Memphis."

"No, Aunt Laurie. We all went to bed, but the boat didn't leave the dock until sometime later. I waited until you and the others were sleeping, then I got up and was going to leave the boat. But, I was a few seconds too late to get off."

"But, I don't understand. You just said you weren't on the boat."

"That's right. I wasn't. Not when it sank. Do you remember after we left Memphis we went across the river to the Arkansas side and waited there while we took on coal?"

"No, Gerald. I don't remember that at all."

"I suppose not. You probably were still sleeping. But, the *Sultana* was tied up there for an hour or more. Some of the soldiers had lingered in Memphis too long and missed the boat when it left. When they saw it tied up across the river, they got somebody with a rowboat to take them across and got back on it there. I was able to talk the man with the boat to let me ride back across to Memphis with him."

"But, why, Gerald?" cried Laureen. "Why did you leave? That makes no sense."

"Yes, it does, Aunt Laurie. Don't you remember I didn't want to go in the first place. I'd been trying to find a way to leave the boat ever

337

since we left Natchez. I never wanted to go to Missouri."

Laureen was becoming indignant at this rebellious nephew of hers. "And, just what do you think you're going to do if you don't go to Missouri, Young Man?"

"If I hadn't gotten off the boat, Aunt Laurie, I might be dead by now," he answered softly.

That subdued Laureen for the moment. "Yes, I suppose you're right," she replied. "But, what did you do when you got back to Memphis? And, how did you find me?"

"Well, the whole city woke up when the explosion happened. Everybody who was awake heard it. I did. I knew all of you were on the boat, so I took off for the wharfboat. Everybody who had any kind of boat at all, whether river boat or rowboat, went out on the river and tried to help find survivors. I talked somebody into letting me go out in his boat, but we didn't find anyone I knew. We did help some of the survivors, though. We kept bringing in those we found, then going back out to try to find more. By the time it got light enough to see, there weren't very many left to find. Oh, Aunt Laurie, it was just awful, the condition most of those men were in. Some of the ones we found were so badly burned I don't think they will live long." He stopped, his voice cracking with the horrible memory of what he had seen on the river.

Laureen waited for him to continue, and when he did not, she prompted him. "You still haven't told me how you found me."

"Well, finally, we weren't finding any more survivors. Both banks were lined with bodies, but after a while, we decided there weren't any more left alive out there and we came back in. I knew the other boats had brought people in, too. Most of them were being taken to the hospital, so I went there to see if any of my family might be there. When I couldn't find any of you, I started asking everybody I could see if they had head of any women and children who might have survived. Finally, somebody said a Mrs. Wallace was picked up and taken to a place called Sadie's Boarding House. I knew that had to be my mother. And, I knew I had to let her know I was still alive. Then, when I got here, I found you, instead." The disappointment he felt was quite apparent in the way he spoke that last sentence.

"Oh, Gerald, I'm so sorry about your mother and the little girls. I loved them, too, don't forget."

"I know," he agreed softly.

"There's still something you haven't explained. What did you do when you got back to Memphis? Where did you go? Where were you when the boat exploded? There's a piece of the puzzle missing here and I want to know what it is."

"Do you remember the acting troupe that was on the boat? They got off at Memphis, right after we tied up. Remember? You met a few of them."

Laureen thought for a few seconds, then answered, "Yes, I do remember them now. What about them?"

"While the cargo was being unloaded, I went out to explore the city. I chanced to come upon the hotel where they are staying. They were still getting some of their luggage into the hotel and some of them were waiting to claim theirs before going inside. I decided to talk to them about joining up with them. I thought it would be a good chance to see some of the country and earn some money. They agreed to take me on. So, I decided to go back to the boat and get my things. That's when I got lost and wandered into that café where you and Mr.

Wainrich were eating. Remember?"

Laureen thought about that for a moment. She had not remembered Roger up until then. "I got you something to eat and told you how to get back to the *Sultana*," answered Laureen, feeling a little proud of herself for remembering that much.

Gerald continued, "Then, after I left the boat, I went to the actors' hotel."

This was almost too much for Laureen to assimilate. Too much information was being thrown at her too fast. Her head really was starting to ache. She closed her eyes, thinking perhaps she was sleeping and all this was one horribly ugly nightmare. She wanted to wake up and find herself, if not at Three Willows before the War, then at least still on the *Sultana*, and, with her family, on her way to Missouri.

Once more the slightly plump Sadie felt she needed to come to Laureen's rescue. "I think your aunt needs to rest some more, Young Man. She's been through a terrible experience and it's not over yet. I don't think she fully understands exactly what's happened to her, and when she does, it may hit her hard. Do you want to wait here or would you like to come back later after she's had time to sleep some more?"

Gerald pondered that for a moment, then answered, "I think I'll come back later." His emotions were beginning to get the better of him as the impact of what he had learned from his aunt about his mother and sisters was beginning to sink in. He was now an orphan. Only fourteen years old, with no mother or father. No family and no home. It was a lot for him to bear. Before the tears could come, he left the boarding house and sought a place to be alone and give in to his emotions.

Gerald was so caught up in his own grief that he gave no thought

340

to his Aunt Laureen's predicament. She, too, had no family and no home.

But, as Laureen began to get her bearings, she was becoming very much aware of her plight. She was only beginning to realize how much she used to depend on Florence to make decisions, to take the lead. She was so young when her parents died. Her brother, Gerald, was so willing to take care of her and did it so well. Then he married the very competent Florence. Laureen had not thought before how very few actual decisions she was ever called upon to make, and even those were never independent of the rest of the family. She was at a loss to think what she should do now.

Sadie was out of the room, and Laureen tried to sleep. Perhaps if she could, then her head might not hurt so much. She rolled onto her side, and when she did, her arm rested against the pouch at her waist. The necklace! The money! She had forgotten all about those things. She bolted upright in the bed. For the first time, she actually noticed the room where she had slept for so long. The only thing in it besides the bed was a small dresser. There was not even a chair. She stood and looked around for a mirror to see what she looked like, but found none. As she glanced down at the men's trousers she wore, she chuckled to herself, thinking it was just as well she could not see. She thought she would not like what her reflection would show her.

Headache forgotten, Laureen wearily sank back down on the bed. She wanted to assess her situation and try to determine what she must do next. There was no one left to help her, to advise her. It was all up to her. She fingered the pouch containing the necklace and the money. She knew how much money she had there, but she had no idea what the necklace was worth. Perhaps that should be the next step. Try to find out how much money the necklace would bring and try to get it sold.

341

As she turned such thoughts over in her mind, she began to think of Three Willows. Rightfully, it belonged to young Gerald, but he seemed to have forgotten all about the plantation. From the day the Wallaces left Three Willows, Laureen took it for granted that one day Florence would take her children back there to live. But, since that could no longer be, perhaps it should fall to her to revive the plantation. Surely, the necklace would bring enough money to allow her to restore it. Even if there were no more slaves to work it, those darkies had to live somehow. She reasoned that she could hire them at wages low enough to make the plantation profitable once again. It might even work out just as well, doing it that way. After all, if she paid them for their work, then she would not also have the financial burden of providing them with food and clothing. She might even rent out the slave cabins to them for a place to live.

All those thoughts were churning through Laureen's mind, taking a heavy toll on her reduced reserve of strength, without her even realizing it. She had let herself stretch out on the bed once more, her thoughts completely focused on dealing with her future as well as the future of Three Willows.

As her thoughts began to go in circles, with none of them making any sense, Laureen once again fell fast asleep.

CHAPTER 34

Laureen stayed in the tiny boarding house room for almost a week. At times she remembered everything about her experience on the *Sultana*, and at other times she was hard pressed to even remember who she was.

Sadie was very kind and patient with her. This was an empathetic woman, as her own life's experiences had taught her to be. She was struck by the beauty of this young woman who was brought to her like a bedraggled stray cat. No amount of dirt on her face, the wet and tangled hair, or the men's clothing on her could obscure it. As her chores and responsibilities allowed, she studied Laureen's face during those times she was sleeping. She saw to it that Laureen had food as she needed it, as well as cared for her other necessities. Some inner wisdom told her this young woman needed to rest and not have unnecessary worries thrust upon her.

Gerald visited her several times in the next few days, but he always seemed to choose times when Laureen was sleeping. Sadie would not allow him to wake her after that first visit. When Gerald visited, Sadie let him take a chair into Laureen's room and sit at her bedside. But, he never waited long enough to see Laureen awake. He was very much involved with his new job with the actors' group and had very little time to see Laureen. The last day he came, Laureen was asleep again, so he spoke to Sadie, asking her to give Laureen a message from him. He was about to leave, as the group had commitments farther north. They would be in Chicago in a few weeks, and Gerald was eagerly looking forward to seeing that city.

Gerald had been gone only an hour or so when Laureen woke. Before long Sadie came into her room and sat down on the edge of the bed. Gently, she told her what Gerald had said. "So, I truly am alone, now," Laureen said softly to herself.

"What was that?" asked Sadie.

"Oh, nothing," answered Laureen. Then, she pushed herself up against the head of the bed into a sitting position and asked, "Sadie, how can I get some decent clothes? I can't go around dressed in these things I wore here. And, I can't continue to presume on your hospitality. You've been so wonderful to me." Then, as realization came to her, she asked in wonderment, "How long have I been here, anyway?"

"Oh, that doesn't matter," was the reply.

"But, it does. I want to know. Please tell me.

Sadie sat silent for a moment, wondering how much Laureen was ready to hear. She asked, "How much do you remember?"

"I think I remember everything. I was on the *Sultana* with my sister-in-law and her children. We were sleeping when we heard an explosion. I ran out of the room, just ahead of its collapse, but the others didn't make it out in time. The boat was burning, and the people who weren't thrown off the boat in the explosion were jumping off. There was just a mass of people in the water, only in a little while most of them disappeared below the surface. They must have drowned. I jumped in, too, but I had something, a mattress I think, to hold on to. I remember it was so cold and I didn't have any clothes on besides my shimmy. Finally, some people in a boat pulled me out of the water."

She paused there, trying to think what happened next. Nothing else came to her. She said, "I guess that's all I remember."

When Sadie said nothing, Laureen added, "But, I thought you

already knew all that."

"Yes, Child, I did. I just wanted to know how much of it all you remembered. You've been drifting in and out of remembering for several days. You don't remember being brought here, do you?"

"No."

"I thought not. But, you seem different today."

"You mean, like I'm back to my old self?"

"Something like that, I suppose," answered Sadie. "I can't really say what your 'old self' is like since I didn't know you before the boat accident."

Laureen replied, "I feel more like my old self, too.

"Then, I suppose the next question is, What are you going to do, now?"

"I was thinking about that. But you never did answer my question. How long have I been here?

"Almost a week."

"Then I really do need to think about what I must do next. Don't you think the first thing I need to do is get some clothes?"

Sadie smiled. "Yes, I would imagine so. Would you like for me to find a dress maker for you? There's one who lives very close by and she does very good work. She doesn't charge very much, either."

Laureen stared at Sadie. "I don't want to wait for someone to **make** clothes for me. That would take much too long. Is there any place where I might get something that's already made?"

"Well, yes, there is a little shop I could recommend. It's farther into town. Do you want me to get someone to take you there? I think you probably won't want to walk, dressed in men's clothes."

Laureen agreed that would be the better way and an hour or so later found herself inside the shop Sadie recommended. Sadie was correct in saying it was a small shop. Even so, it carried an adequate line of clothing and accessories.

Laureen carefully chose an outfit for herself, starting from the skin out. Before she left the boarding house, she broke some of the stitches in the pouch she wore at her waist, and, when it was time to pay for her purchases, was able to pull enough bills out to pay the woman who assisted her. She begrudged each penny she spent, knowing how far she might need to stretch that money. But, since it was essential for her to have presentable clothes to wear, there was no help for that expense.

At long last, she was once again pleased with her appearance. Before Laureen left the boarding house, Sadie helped her arrange her hair, and now she was dressed in a fashionable gown with proper petticoats underneath, including a hoop skirt. Bonnet, gloves, and even a drawstring bag to carry her handkerchief and other personal items completed her costume. She looked quite the lady of fashion.

In fact, she was so pleased with her appearance, she decided to walk back to the boarding house. That is, if she could find her way. When she left the boarding house earlier, she was so intent on her mission of getting suitable clothing for herself, she neglected to even notice the name of the boarding house, let alone keep track of the route that was taken. Perhaps the wagon was still waiting for her. She rushed outside to the street to check on that possibility, but, in vain. The wagon was gone.

While Laureen stood on the walkway, trying to decide what

should be her next course of action, she was not unmindful of the admiring glances of passers by, especially the men who passed by, tipping their hats as they met her. Also, she was aware of the disapproving looks of the female companions with them.

In time she must have taken on a look of distress, because a gentleman stopped as he approached her and asked, "Are you looking for someone, Miss? Is there anything I can do to help?" This man revealed a shock of gray hair as he removed his hat and held it in his hand, his somewhat wrinkled face and kind eyes gazing at her with no attempt to conceal his admiration.

"Oh, Sir! Thank you. Yes, there is something. I know this sounds a little unusual, but I can't seem to remember where I'm supposed to be going. I'm looking for......" Laureen hesitated. What was she looking for? What was the house called where she was staying? All she knew was that a woman named Sadie had been taking care of her for the last few days.

The gentlemen waited patiently, obviously rather perplexed at the confusion of the young woman who stood before him. When she stared helplessly at him without speaking further, he prodded gently. "I know most of the people around here. I've lived in Memphis most of my life. Perhaps if you'd tell me who it is you're looking for, I might be able to help you."

"Her name is Sadie. I've been staying in her house the last several days. You see, I was on board the *Sultana* before it sank and......"

"Say no more, Miss. You're Miss Wallace, aren't you?"

"Why, yes, but how did you know?"

"I told you I know just about everyone around here. I've known Sadie Benson for as long as she's lived in Memphis. Ever since she was just a little girl when her parents brought her here. When they bought that boarding house she runs now. I'd heard she had a woman staying with her who was picked up out of the river the night the boat sank. So, you're that young lady. And a very pretty one, too, I might add."

Laureen was almost at the point of blushing, when the gentleman spoke again, recognizing the discomfort she was beginning to feel. "I know it's some little distance to walk, but it's a beautiful day and I don't have anything pressing I need to attend to, so if you'll allow me, I'd be delighted to escort you back to Sadie's place."

He extended his arm to Laureen. Laureen looked up at the warm smile on the man's kindly face, and, without hesitation, accepted the proffered arm, saying with more confidence than she felt, "Sadie's place it is, Sir."

The two of them walked quietly at a comfortable pace for several blocks. Finally, the gentlemen spoke. "Do you plan to stay on in Memphis for a while? I understand your home is near Natchez. Are you going back there now, or will you continue on with your journey northward?" He paused a moment before adding one last question. "Where is it you were going on the *Sultana*?"

"I was going to Missouri to live with my sister-in-law's sister and her husband. But, my sister-in-law and her little girls didn't survive the accident. To tell you the truth, Sir, I don't really know what I should do. I know I have to do something, but I don't know what is the best thing for me now."

"Do you have anyone here you could turn to for help and advice?"

"I don't know anyone at all in Memphis. There was a relative of my sister-in-law whom I met on the boat. He got off in Memphis. But, I have no idea where he is, or where he's staying. I think he actually lives somewhere near New Orleans, so you likely wouldn't know him."

"Does he have relatives here?"

"I don't know. But, I think he comes here on business once in a while. He has a plantation. I think he said it is somewhere east of New Orleans."

"And, his name?" persisted the older man.

"Roger Wainrich," answered Laureen quickly.

Her companion's eyes twinkled. "So, Roger Wainrich is more than a mere acquaintance to this young woman," he said to himself. "I'll just have to see what I can do about that."

Laureen realized she had given away more than she intended to do, in responding so quickly. The silence that followed was not lost on her. So, she said nothing more.

As they continued walking, her discomfort eased and she was able to enjoy the attention paid to her as she strolled along on the arm of the distinguished looking gentlemen. She nodded and smiled at each one who acknowledged her presence. She sensed her companion was enjoying the attention as much as she.

Finally, he spoke again. "Do you recognize where you are now?" he asked.

For the first time in several blocks, Laureen actually looked at her surroundings. During most of the walk, she was so preoccupied with the pleasure of the walk and the attention she received and paid no attention to the neighborhood where she was except to be aware there were houses, yards, and trees they were passing.

As some things were becoming familiar to her senses, she

exclaimed, "Why, we're back at Sadie's place, aren't we? Did you say it's actually a boarding house?"

"Yes, My Dear, this is Sadie's Boarding House. You should be all right now. Is there anything more I can do for you?" he asked ever so kindly.

She looked up at him rather saucily, feeling more confident in familiar surroundings, and said, "Short of putting my life back in order, I can't think of a thing."

"Then, I'll bid you 'Good day,' and be on my way." He tipped his hat to her, turned on his heel and walked away.

Laureen picked up the front of her voluminous skirts to start up the stairs, then turned back quickly, saying, "Wait, Sir. You've been so kind to me and I don't even know your name. I really do want to thank you properly."

"That's quite all right, Miss Wallace. My name is James Matthews. That name used to mean something around here, that is, before the war. Perhaps the name will mean something again one day, after we can rebuild what the Yankees destroyed in the war. I'm only afraid that may take a while and I may not live to see things restored to what they once were. In fact, I doubt things will ever be what they once were in the south. But, I can hope. And, I appreciate your wanting to say something to me."

Once again, he turned to go, but turned back and said, "One more thing I'd like to say to you. Whatever you decide to do with your life, don't base it entirely on what seems practical at the moment. You need to give some consideration to your heart and satisfy it, too. Do you understand?"

Laureen hesitated before replying, mulling over what he had just said. "Yes, Sir, I think I do understand. And I thank you for saying it. Perhaps that's what I needed to hear right now."

Then, they parted. Laureen again picked up her skirts to mount the stairs to the boarding house, and when she turned back at the door to look, her companion was out of sight. "It's just as well," she thought. "There's nothing more he can do for me and I have some serious thinking to do."

Sadie was waiting for her as she stepped inside the door, not letting her reach her own room. "Well, just look at you!" she exclaimed. "I knew you'd look different in proper clothes, but this is even better than I expected. It looks like you found everything you needed, and then some," she said with much excitement. "I'm so glad. Who was the gentleman who accompanied you back here?"

"He was just a very kind man who realized I didn't know my way back here and offered to escort me. He said his name is James Matthews. He knows you."

"James Matthews!" she cried. "Of course I know him. He's about the wealthiest man around Memphis. Or at least, he used to be. I don't know about now. He lost a lot in the war, so he may not have so much any more. But I think he's still an important person around here. You were lucky to meet up with him."

"He was very kind to me," answered Laureen. "But, I doubt I'll ever see him again."

"Well, one just never knows, does one?" She fell silent for a few seconds, then exclaimed, "My goodness, I almost forgot. You have a visitor!"

"A visitor?" asked Laureen. "Did my nephew come back? Oh, I'll be so glad to see him again."

Sadie chuckled. "No, it's not your nephew this time. It's........well, see for yourself. Go into the parlor." Sadie opened the door to the parlor and stood aside, waiting for Laureen to go inside, then she closed the door.

As Laureen stepped inside the modestly furnished room with its needlepoint sofa and two cushioned chairs facing a fireplace with a high mantle on the opposite wall, a man rose and turned to face her. "Roger!" cried Laureen, as she recognized him, her face blanching. "Roger! However did you find me?" Laureen's voice was a mixture of laughter and tears.

Roger stepped around the end of the sofa and quickly took Laureen in his arms. She willingly leaned against him, feeling secure for the first time since she heard the explosion on the *Sultana*. "Everything will be all right now," she said to herself, but audible enough for Roger to hear.

"You couldn't be more right," he answered.

CHAPTER 35

Roger and Laureen stood clinging to one another for several minutes. Each one was reluctant to release the other. It was only a week since they had parted, but the time seemed so much longer for both of them. So much had happened during that week.

Finally, Roger gradually released his hold on Laureen and moved his hands to her shoulders, gently pushing her far enough away from him so he could look down at her face. "What's this?" he asked. "Are those tears I see?"

"I can't help it, Roger. I thought I might never see you again. I thought you might just assume I died with the sinking of the Sultana and not try to find me."

"You silly girl," he retorted. "I've been about to move heaven and earth, trying to find out what happened to you. I knew you might not have survived the accident, but I had to know for certain before I could leave Memphis." Once again he pulled her close to himself and held her there.

It was too much for Laureen. For the first time since the accident, she let herself cry. And, cry she did. There seemed to be no end to the torrent. Roger felt quite helpless in the face of such a scene, but remained quiet, keeping his arms around her and waiting for the storm to pass. Finally the tears lessened and he handed her his handkerchief. As Laureen composed herself, he led her to the sofa, then positioned one of the chairs almost directly in front of her and sat down in it.

"Do you feel like talking yet?" he asked her very softly.

"I think so," Laureen sniffed.

"Have you given any thought about what you should do now?"

"What do you mean? What can I do?"

"I mean, are you going on to Missouri? What exactly will you do now?"

"I haven't really given that much thought, Roger. This whole experience has left me so drained. I'm just now getting back enough strength to even think about what I must do next."

"And?" he questioned.

"And I don't know. One thing I do know is that I don't want to go to Missouri. I've never even met Florence's sister and her husband. I don't want to go there and let them assume responsibility for me. No, I suppose the best thing I can do is to go back to Three Willows now."

"But there's nothing there for you to go back to. You told me that on the boat. It will take quite a considerable sum of money to rebuild the burned out wing, and put that place back into operation. You don't have any money. You told me so, yourself." He stared at her for a long moment, then exclaimed. "I knew there was something about you that wasn't quite right. Those clothes you're wearing. Where did you get them? They look new. Did someone buy those things for you?"

"No, Roger. I bought them, myself."

"How? I don't understand. Where did you get the money?"

Laureen looked long and hard at Roger. She remembered she had almost told him about the necklace at one point while they were still on the boat. But the moment passed and she decided it was not a good idea to confide in him, after all. Now, she thought perhaps she should come clean with the whole story.

"Roger, there's something I haven't told you. I almost did when we were on the boat one day, but then we sort of got into a quarrel and I decided against it. I'd like to tell you now and hope you won't think too badly of me."

Roger caught his breath. Just when he was feeling so close to her, wanting to do everything in his power to protect and take care of her, she was making him realize once again how little he knew about her. In spite of himself, he started to fear the worst.

Carefully controlling his voice lest it betray his concerns, he said, "I'm willing to listen to anything you care to tell me, Laureen."

"I guess I'd better start at the beginning..."

"Yes, please do," he interrupted with a tinge of sarcasm in his voice.

"Oh, Roger," she implored, "Please hear me out before you pass judgment on me."

"I'm sorry, Laureen," he said in a slightly more relaxed tone. "Please continue and I'll try not to interrupt any more."

"I told you there were only four slaves, that is, former slaves, left at Three Willows when we left. One of them, a young man named Tolly, drove us to the river the day we boarded the *Sultana*. He was to take the mule and wagon back to Three Willows. Well I don't know what he did with the mule and wagon, but he stowed away on the *Sultana*. I saw him a few times as we went up river. I spoke to him two or three times, and he pleaded with me not to give him away. So, I didn't tell anybody."

Roger was watching Laureen's face intently as she spoke, wanting to ask questions as she revealed such surprising information, but he resisted the urge to do so. Instead, he took hold of one of her hands and stroked it absently, something Laureen found immensely comforting.

She continued, "Do you remember seeing a man on the boat who couldn't talk?"

Roger thought for a moment, then answered, "I don't believe I ever saw him, but I do remember hearing that there was such a man on the boat."

"That man was Tolly. He looks white, but I had told him if he ever opened his mouth to speak, it would be a dead give-away as to who he was. So he pretended not to be able to speak. But, mostly I think he just kept out of sight. Then later, do you remember the 'valuable item' Graham Talbert said was missing? You guessed it might be a diamond necklace. You said he showed one to you and offered to sell it to you."

"Yes, but what does that have to do with anything?"

"I'm coming to that. It was, indeed, a diamond necklace and Tolly stole it. But I have it now."

"How...?" started Roger.

"You said you'd let me finish," Laureen reminded him.

"Yes, you're right," he said. "Go ahead. I'm listening."

"After Tolly stole the necklace, he got afraid he might be caught with it and be thrown into the river, so the next time I ran into him, he passed the necklace on to me and said he'd ask for it back when we docked at Cairo. He said Graham Talbert probably stole the necklace himself and he might as well have it as Mr. Talbert. Before I could argue with him, he was gone, and I had the necklace. I never did see Tolly again until I was ready to get back on the boat here in Memphis after you left me."

"And, you say you have the necklace now?"

"Yes, but there's more. That night when we got to Memphis, you and I went for a walk and to some little café, remember?"

"Yes, I remember. Go on."

"Well, a lot of the men who were on the boat helped unload cargo and after they got paid, went into some of the taverns and inns here. Tolly did, too, and he, uh, 'relieved' some of the men of some of their money."

"Are you saying he stole their money?"

"Yes. I don't know how he did it, but he got quite a bit. And, he almost got caught."

Light was beginning to dawn on Roger. "How do you know all about that, Laureen. Do you have that money, too?"

"Yes, most of it. This afternoon I spent a little of it on the clothes I'm wearing. That's where I was when you came here."

"How much did he give you? And, why? He was already off the boat."

"I was standing off in the shadows after you left, wanting to savor the memories of our evening together. Some of the men were coming back to the boat and then there was Tolly. He saw me and thrust some money into my hand, saying he had helped himself to some of what the men had. He thought they were suspicious of him and if he got caught with it they might kill him. And, from what I saw, I think they would have, too."

Laureen paused, remembering the scene she witnessed that night, and wondering what became of Tolly.

"Go on, Laureen. There must be more to this story."

"Only a little more, Roger. No one suspected me of having the money. Tolly was no where to be seen, so I took the money back to my stateroom. I had no idea how much there was until I got back there and counted it. I had forty three dollars in my hand. And, as I said, I still have most of it. But, there's no way to give it back. Most of those men who had it stolen from them died in the wreck."

"But, how, Laureen? How did you manage to keep it with you in the river?"

"I'm sure you must be wondering about that. When Tolly passed the diamond necklace to me, I made myself a sort of money belt. I made a little pouch and put it on a belt which I sewed shut around my waist. It was very secure. Then, when Tolly gave me those dollar bills, I put them in that little pouch and sewed the pouch shut. I've always been used to sewing strong stitches and it stayed shut."

"But, the current, Laureen. How is it that the current in the river didn't rip it off you? I heard it ripped the clothes off most of the men who were in the water and they pulled the survivors out naked."

"You don't know what happened to me in the river, do you?"

"No. I only heard today you survived and you were here. I didn't learn any details. I wasn't even concerned about that. I was just so happy to learn you were alive. That was all I cared about."

"Oh, Dear Roger. That means so much to me." She smiled at him, looking at his face with adoring eyes, eyes that were melting his feeling of reserve toward her once more. "But, let me finish my story."

"Yes, I want to hear it all."

"There was part of a mattress on the deck. Much of it had burned, but a soldier had rescued a piece of it and I suppose he was going to use it to try to keep himself afloat in the river. The boat was burning and we had to get off it. I was very close to him, and then he collapsed and died. I couldn't help him, so I grabbed the mattress piece and jumped into the water, right on top of it. Pretty soon, it was waterlogged, but it didn't sink. It kept me high enough in the water so I didn't go under. It also protected me from the worst of the current. I stayed with that mattress until some people in a rowboat found me and pulled me to safety. I think you can guess the rest."

"Oh, my poor dearest Laureen. What an ordeal you've been through!" Suddenly Roger no longer cared about the necklace or the money. In his mind's eye he could see Laureen struggling to keep afloat in the swift current of the flooded river and he realized how close he came to losing her. He realized he must do all he could to protect her in the future. He rose from his chair and sat on the sofa beside her, taking both her hands in his.

"Roger, I really think I should go back to Three Willows," Laureen said. "That's where my home is and now I can do something toward making a profitable plantation out of it once again."

"Laureen, forty three dollars won't go very far. And, you just said you've already spent some of it. So, you don't even have that much now."

"But, the necklace, Roger. I know it's worth a great deal. If I can sell it, then I should be able to have enough to do what needs to be done for Three Willows. The only thing is, I don't know how to get it sold. I don't know who buys such things."

"May I see the necklace, Laureen?"

"Why, yes, of course. But, I'm still wearing it. You'll have to wait here. I'll go into my room and remove it and then I'll show it to you."

Laureen left the room, only to return a very short time later with the necklace crumpled in both her hands. She held it in front of him, each hand holding onto one end of it. It sparkled in the afternoon sunlight shining through the large double windows that opened on either side of the fireplace, giving the room the feeling of being much larger than it actually was.

Roger caught his breath. "Laureen, that's absolutely beautiful. I guess I didn't pay enough attention to it when Graham Talbert showed it to me that day on the boat. No wonder you took such pains to keep it with you! Are you absolutely certain you want to sell it?"

"I don't think I have any choice, do you? Three Willows needs money, and I don't have anything else to sell that would bring very much money. Do you think you might be able to help me get it sold?"

Roger took the necklace in his own two hands and was examining it closely. The diamonds were large, and there were many of them, set in a delicate design of platinum which showed them off to excellent advantage. Laureen was right. It was worth a great deal. What a shame to have to sell it.

He sat looking at the necklace for quite a long time. Laureen began to be uncomfortable in the silence that stretched out between them. She wondered if he were having second thoughts regarding her. Did he view her as a common thief, more than willing to take advantage of people when they were off balance? What was he thinking?

Finally, he spoke. "Laureen, I think I know where this can be sold. I think I know someone who would be willing to buy it. Will you trust me with it and let me get the money for you?"

She was not expecting that turn of events. Trust Roger with so valuable a treasure? Now it was her turn to wonder how well she knew him. But, she had to trust him. There was no other way. If he betrayed her, well, then she would just have to think of something else. After all, she did have that little bit of money left.

"Yes, Roger, I trust you," she said. "I'm trusting you with everything I have. That necklace and the cash, that's all I have in the world. Can you sell it for me today? I'd like to get started back to Three Willows."

"You wait here. This shouldn't take very long. And, I'm going to have a very special surprise for you when I get back. You'll like it, I promise." Without waiting for further comment, he rose and left the room and the boarding house.

Laureen loved surprises, that is, good ones. She knew she wanted no more surprises of the kind she experienced on the *Sultana*, though. While Roger was gone, she busied herself with plans to leave Memphis immediately and start her return journey to Three Willows. She thought it would be so good to get back home, but wondered how she would find things when she got there. Things could change a lot in only two weeks. Would Pansy, Willard, and Bessie still be there, or might they have decided to leave the plantation, too. She thought it likely that Pansy and Willard would be there, but Bessie was so young and might have found someone to hire her. Oh, well. No point in trying to cross bridges she might never come to. She would simply deal with whatever the situation was when she got back.

It seemed such a short time had passed before Roger was back. "Look how much I got for you, Laureen," he said as soon as they were again seated in the parlor. He counted out the money for her.

Laureen gasped. She had never seen so much money before. And, all this was hers. It would certainly be enough to put Three Willows back to its former glory and make it a working plantation again. "Oh, Roger. I didn't expect to get this much. Now, I must use it wisely and not waste it. I must find someone to help and advise me. I don't know if I have the ability to do it alone."

"Laureen, I'll help you," said Roger, leaning close to her face and looking directly into her eyes. "I have lots of experience in such matters. Will you let me help you?" He wanted to take that subject much farther, but he knew she was not ready to hear what he really wanted to say to her. He must give her time.

"Do you think you can spread yourself so thin, taking on two farms and so far apart?"

"Yes, I think so. I'll help you find competent help, get you started, and then I'll go on back to my own place. All you need is a good nudge in the right direction, and you'll do quite well on your own."

"Oh, Roger, you're so kind to me." Her eyes were sparkling, the first time he had seen her look like that. Then she remembered something else. "By the way, what was that surprise you said you would have for me when you got back?"

"Oh, I didn't think you'd forget that," he teased. "Come outside with me."

Laureen followed him outside. Waiting in front of the boarding house was a solid buggy behind a very sturdy looking horse. "What's this all about, Roger? I don't understand. How did you find a rig like that? I thought the Yankees took everything."

"No they didn't get them all, just most of them. And I knew where to look. So I'm taking you home, Laureen. First thing tomorrow morning. So be ready as soon as it gets light. We'll be on our way."

"No, Roger. I can't do that. A man and a woman traveling alone together like that. What would people say?" cried Laureen somewhat horrified.

"Laureen, I thought you'd decided long ago you didn't care what people say?"

"It seems I care more than I thought I did."

"Well you don't have to worry. I've thought of that, too. I hired a colored woman to go back to my place and help my mother. After all, my mother's not a young woman any more. This woman will provide a proper chaperone for us so your reputation will hold together just fine for the trip."

Laureen was too overcome with joy to even speak. She looked up at Roger with such adoring eyes. She knew at last she had found independence from her family. This had come in a way she could never in her whole life have anticipated. Certainly in a way she never wanted. Nevertheless, the time had finally come for her to make her own way. This was exactly what she used to tell herself she wanted most of all. Suddenly though, little doubts began to plague her. Could she do it? With no experience in making decisions, how would she handle the myriads of choices certain to present themselves to her? She knew some would be of little importance, but there would be others of major significance. Would she have the wisdom to know the difference? And how to handle them?

"Yes!" she told herself defiantly. Absolutely yes. She would make it. She would get help, get advice from knowledgeable people and apply what she learned. Oh she would make mistakes and she would learn from them. But she would make it. For the first time in her life, she knew she was truly a grown woman and ready to face the world. A world she hoped would be just a little bit better for her having lived in it.

THE END.

www.ingramcontent.com/pod-product-compliance
Lightning Source LLC
Chambersburg PA
CBHW051131120626
46547CB00012B/757